Extended Deterrence and the Prevention of War

Extended Deterrence and the Prevention of War

Paul K. Huth

Yale University Press
New Haven and London

Designed by James J. Johnson
and set in Times Roman type by Keystone Typesetting, Inc.
Printed in the United States of America by BookCrafters, Inc., Ann Arbor, Michigan.

LIBRARY OF CONGRESS CATALOGING-IN-PUBLICATION DATA

Huth, Paul K., 1959–
    Extended deterrence and the prevention of war / Paul K. Huth.
    p. cm.
    Bibliography: p.
    Includes index.
    ISBN 0–300–04167–5 (alk. paper)
    1. Deterrence (Strategy) 2. Military policy. 3. International
relations. I. Title.
U162.6.H88 1989
355'.0217—dc19   88–14206
                                                           CIP

10   9   8   7   6   5   4   3   2   1

To Marina

Contents

List of Figures, Tables, and Maps   ix

Acknowledgments   xi

1
Sources of Deterrence Failure   1

2
Conceptualizing Deterrence   15

3
Hypotheses on Deterrence   28

4
Testing Hypotheses on Deterrence   56

5
Case Studies: The Impact of the Balance of Forces
and Military Preparedness   85

6
Case Studies: The Impact of Diplomacy and Past Behavior   149

7
Implications for Crisis Management and Future Research   199

Index   221

Figures, Tables, and Maps

FIGURES

1. A Typology of Cases of Deterrence   17
2. Stages in the Escalation of Conflict   21
3. Bargaining Strategies and the Outcome of Crisis   31

TABLES

1. Cases of Attempted Extended-Immediate Deterrence,
   1885–1984   24
2a. Probit Analysis of the Determinants of Deterrence Outcome   73
2b. Ability of Probit Analysis to Predict Deterrence Outcome   73
3a. Effect of the Immediate Balance of Forces on
    Outcome of Deterrence   77
3b. Effect of the Short-Term Balance of Forces on
    Outcome of Deterrence   77

MAPS

1. The Middle East   91
2. Central Africa   101
3. The Coastline of China and the Taiwan Straits   110
4. Halder's Plan of Attack   122
5. Hitler's Plan of Attack   123
6. Central Asia   155
7. Northern Europe and the Soviet Union   163

Acknowledgments

I would like to thank Bruce M. Russett for his exceptional support and guidance throughout this research project. Special thanks are due Paul M. Kennedy for sharing with me his extraordinary knowledge of diplomatic and military history and for his support of my efforts to combine historical research with social science methods. The detailed and insightful comments of Robert Jervis and James D. Morrow have greatly improved the entire manuscript and are deeply appreciated. I would also like to thank Russell J. Leng for sharing with me his data set on crisis bargaining.

Archival research was greatly facilitated by the generous support and expert advice of the staff at the following institutions: The Public Record Office at Kew, Richmond, India Office Library and Records, London, and the Navy and Old Army Branch and Modern Military Fields Branch of the National Archives, Washington, D.C. Celeste Wallander, Lorrie Harvey, and Gerald Sorokin provided critical research assistance, and the expert advice of Yoshitaka Nishizawa on problems of data analysis is deeply appreciated. I would also like to thank Marian Neal Ash at Yale University Press for her support of the book and Stacey Mandelbaum for her excellent editing of the manuscript. Finally, I would like to thank the National Science Foundation for its financial support of my research (Grant No. SES–8413022). I assume full responsibility for errors of fact or interpretation.

1

Sources of Deterrence Failure

Escalation, while it conveys resolve, if premature or miscalculated, risks provoking the outcome it was initiated
to forestall. . . . Military passivity, on the other hand, is
decidedly unprovocative but may weaken or even undermine deterrence.

— RICHARD NED LEBOW

The decision to threaten or employ military force as
an instrument of foreign policy is one of the most
critical policy choices that confront the leadership
of a state. Political and military leaders have often believed that their
country's national interests extend beyond their own borders to include
the security of other states. As a result, when such allies have been
threatened with military force by another state, decision makers have
felt it necessary to come to their defense by threatening military retaliation against the potential attacker. This policy of *extended deterrence* is
greatly complicated, however, by two general features of international
relations: first, the difficulty faced by foreign policy leaders in determining the intentions and capabilities of adversaries, and second, the
sensitivity of foreign policy leaders to potential security threats and
challenges to their country's bargaining reputation.

A potential attacker's uncertainty as to the intentions and capabilities of the defender can weaken the credibility of an extended
deterrent threat, while the sensitivity of the potential attacker to mili-

tary threats and challenges to its bargaining reputation can undermine the stability of deterrence. Thus, although the foreign policy leadership of a country may decide that a policy of extended deterrence is in the national interest, deterrence success can be difficult to achieve.

To estimate confidently the intentions and capabilities of opponents is one of the most important yet elusive tasks of intelligence analysts and policymakers. As Richard Betts states, "The role of intelligence is to extract certainty from uncertainty and to facilitate coherent decision in an incoherent environment. To the degree that they reduce uncertainty by extrapolating from evidence riddled with ambiguities, analysts risk oversimplifying reality. . . . To the degree that they do not resolve ambiguities, analysts risk being dismissed by annoyed consumers who see them as not having done their job."[1]

In many situations uncertainty is a result of scant information about the attitudes and beliefs of key decision makers within an opposing state and the nature of policy debates at the highest levels of that government. For example, British policies during the 1930s were influenced by the belief that a group of moderates who could effectively influence Hitler but were opposed by a faction of radicals existed within the Nazi leadership. Many British policymakers therefore mistakenly believed that Hitler was a cautious leader who was susceptible to the influence of extremists.[2] Contemporary U.S.-Soviet relations have also been affected by this problem, because the closed and secretive nature of the decision-making process within the Soviet Union has often made it difficult for U.S. policymakers and analysts to gauge accurately the motivations and likely policy choices of Soviet leaders.[3]

Lacking reliable information about an adversary, policymakers do not know exactly which points and messages need to be emphasized and which need to be clarified when communicating with the adversary. Furthermore, this problem can be compounded by lack of feedback about the impact of previous attempts to change the adversary's

1. Richard K. Betts, *Surprise Attack: Lessons for Defense Planning* (Washington, D.C.: Brookings Institution, 1982), 102.

2. Donald Cameron Watt, "British Intelligence and the Coming of the Second World War in Europe," in *Knowing One's Enemies: Intelligence Assessment before the Two World Wars,* ed. Ernest R. May (Princeton: Princeton University Press, 1984), 249–50.

3. Raymond L. Garthoff, *Detente and Confrontation: American-Soviet Relations from Nixon to Reagan* (Washington, D.C.: Brookings Institution, 1985), chaps. 8, 11, 19, 26.

policies. For example, attempts by the United States to coerce North Vietnam during the Vietnam War were hampered in part by an over-simplified and incomplete picture of the attitudes and internal debates of that country's foreign policy leadership.[4]

Problems in estimating the intentions and capabilities of other states, however, are not always due to lack of information but instead can be related to the inherent difficulties of interpreting information that is available. For example, in many situations the data are inconclusive, and thus intelligence analysts and policymakers present conflicting interpretations and draw different conclusions from the same informa-tion.[5] Ambiguity may also lead analysts and policymakers, inadver-tently or deliberately, to structure and interpret selectively the infor-mation they receive in order to make it consistent with their own preexisting preferences, beliefs, and images of the adversary.[6] One of the best examples of motivated misperception was Stalin's refusal to heed the warnings of imminent attack by Germany in the spring and early summer of 1941, despite the large body of supporting evidence. Stalin believed that through economic concessions and further negotia-tions he could postpone an attack. When faced with intelligence infor-mation indicating that his approach and policies were failing, Stalin downgraded it.[7]

Uncertainty about the intentions and capabilities of adversaries can have an important impact on policy choices and the effectiveness of foreign policy.[8] In the context of extended deterrence, uncertainty is likely to undermine the credibility of a defender's threat. As Thomas Schelling explains, ''The difference between the national homeland

4. Wallace J. Thies, *When Governments Collide: Coercion and Diplomacy in the Vietnam Conflict, 1964–1968* (Berkeley: University of California Press, 1980), 399–406.

5. Richard K. Betts, ''Analysis, War, and Decision: Why Intelligence Failures Are Inevitable,'' *World Politics* 31: 1 (1978):61–89.

6. Robert Jervis, *Perception and Misperception in International Relations* (Prince-ton: Princeton University Press, 1976), 117–202.

7. Barton Whaley, *Codeword-BARBAROSSA* (Cambridge: M.I.T. Press, 1973), 95–129, and John Erickson, ''Threat Identification and Strategic Appraisal by the Soviet Union, 1939–1941,'' in May, ed., *Knowing One's Enemies,* 419–21. It may be rational to discount and selectively interpret information if the source is believed to be biased. See Randell Calvert, ''The Value of Biased Information: A Rational Choice Model of Political Advice,'' *Journal of Politics* 47: 2 (1985):530–55.

8. See, e.g., Ernest R. May, ''Conclusions: Capabilities and Proclivities,'' in May, ed., *Knowing One's Enemies,* 503–42.

and everything 'abroad' is the difference between threats that are inherently credible, even if unspoken, and threats that have to be made credible. To project the shadow of one's military forces over other countries and territories is an act of diplomacy.''[9] The credibility of a deterrent threat depends upon the defender being perceived as possessing (1) military capabilities sufficient to inflict substantial costs on a potential attacker and (2) the will or intention to use those capabilities if necessary.

A potential attacker, however, may find it difficult to estimate what military capabilities of a defender can be extended to the defense of an ally located hundreds, if not thousands, of miles away. Furthermore, if the potential attacker shares a border or is near the ally, then the local imbalance of military capabilities may become the primary reference point for calculating the balance of military power, while the potential strength of the defender, which is more difficult to calculate, is discounted. For example, in 1941 the leadership of Japan decided to wage war against the United States, anticipating a string of quick and decisive victories followed by an American suit for peace terms. In reaching this decision, Japanese policymakers focused their attention on the local balance of military power, which greatly favored Japan, while discounting the long-term military capabilities of the United States.[10]

In situations where the ally is located at some distance from the defender a potential attacker may also question whether the defender can actually deploy adequate military forces in a timely fashion. Thus, even if the potential military strength of the defender is acknowledged, an attacker may still reason that the power of the defender cannot be translated into effective strength quickly enough to prevent the attacker from attaining its immediate goals through the use of military force. For example, Great Britain's attempts at extended deterrence in 1914 and 1939 may have been discounted by German leaders because the possible intervention of the then small British Expeditionary Force was not considered a significant threat to Germany's initial plan of attack.[11]

9. Thomas C. Schelling, *Arms and Influence* (New Haven: Yale University Press, 1966), 36.

10. Michael A. Barnhart, ''Japanese Intelligence before the Second World War,'' in May, ed., *Knowing One's Enemies,* 424–55.

11. The British Expeditionary Force, however, played a critical role in supporting the French against the Germans in the Battle of the Marne in 1914.

Even in situations where the defender shares a border with its ally or potential attacker difficult questions arise regarding the military balance. Will the ally permit the defender to move its troops into its territory on a large scale? Will the defender be willing to initiate an offensive strike against the attacker if this is the only viable option for helping its ally? During the 1938 crisis over Czechoslovakia and in the confrontation with Poland in 1939, Hitler correctly calculated that France would not go on the offensive to aid its allies. He therefore concentrated most of the German army for an offensive in the east, while maintaining weak defensive forces along the Franco-German border.[12]

A potential attacker may question not only the military contribution a defender can make to protecting its ally but even more fundamentally whether the defender is willing to incur the costs of a military confrontation. A potential attacker is likely to consider such questions as: What national interests and issues are at stake that would justify the defender's taking on such a burden? How does the national security of the ally affect the vital interests of the defender? Because these are often difficult questions to answer, a potential attacker may find it hard to believe that the defender's deterrent threat is not a bluff. For example, Hitler in 1939 did not believe that Britain would actually go to war in defense of Poland because, as he stated, "Why should Britain fight? You don't let yourself get killed for any ally."[13] More recently, Gen. Leopoldo Galtieri, head of the Argentine junta at the time of the invasion of the Falklands Islands, discounted the likelihood of a British military response. As Galtieri stated, "Why should a country situated in the heart of Europe care so much for some islands located far away in the Atlantic Ocean . . . islands which do not serve any national interest."[14]

Establishing the credibility of an extended deterrent threat can be a precarious and demanding task, full of uncertainty. Underestimating the defender's motivation and military capacity to respond may lead a

12. Williamson Murray, *The Change in the European Balance of Power, 1938–1939: The Path to Ruin* (Princeton: Princeton University Press, 1984), chaps. 7, 10.

13. As quoted in Ernest R. May, "Conclusions: Capabilities and Proclivities," in May, ed., *Knowing One's Enemies*, 524.

14. As quoted in Robert Jervis, Richard Ned Lebow, and Janice Gross Stein, *Psychology and Deterrence* (Baltimore: Johns Hopkins University Press, 1985), 118.

potential attacker to miscalculate the costs and risks of its own actions. To enhance the credibility of extended deterrence a defender may believe it is crucial to demonstrate resolve and firmness by issuing repeated threats, adopting an uncompromising bargaining position, and undertaking extensive military preparations. But serious risks are associated with this course of action.

Foreign policy leaders are sensitive to potential military threats and challenges to their country's bargaining reputation. Bargaining reputation can be defined as the perceived willingness of a state's political and military leadership to risk armed conflict in pursuit of foreign policy objectives and the likelihood that it will accede to the demands of adversaries under coercive pressure. Glenn Snyder and Paul Diesing, in their comparative study of crisis bargaining, report that in almost all cases policymakers expressed concern about the impact of crisis outcomes on their country's reputation and image.[15] This sensitivity is a reflection of anarchy in the international system.[16] Because there is no central authority with the power to enforce decisions and settle disputes between states, policymakers often believe that their reputations for firmness and resolve are critical in attaining their foreign policy objectives. For example, German Foreign Minister Alfred von Kiderlen argued that if France were permitted to absorb Morocco, "our credit in the world, not only for the moment, but also for all future international actions, suffers an intolerable blow."[17]

Furthermore, statesmen realize that recourse to the use of military force remains the ultimate means for resolving conflicts between states, so they tend to interpret the behavior of their opponents from the perspective of a worst-case analysis. As Michael Howard states, "In general men have fought during the past two hundred years neither because they are aggressive nor because they are acquisitive animals, but because they are reasoning ones: because they discern, or believe that they can discern, dangers before they become immediate, the pos-

15. Glenn H. Snyder and Paul Diesing, *Conflict among Nations* (Princeton: Princeton University Press, 1977), 188–89. See also Raymond Cohen, *Threat Perception in International Crisis* (Madison: University of Wisconsin Press, 1979).

16. For an analysis of the concept of anarchy see Kenneth N. Waltz, *Theory of International Politics* (Reading, Mass.: Addison-Wesley, 1979), 102–28.

17. As quoted in Ima Christina Barlow, *The Agadir Crisis* (Chapel Hill: University of North Carolina Press, 1940), 266.

sibility of threats before they are made."[18] For example, the buildup of German naval forces in the decades before World War I was perceived as a threat by many British political and military leaders. One British official noted, "It is quite ridiculous to believe that we are taken in by the pretense of the necessities of 'defending German commerce' etc. as the reason for a bigger fleet. Commerce is defended in one way and one way only: namely the destruction of the opponent's naval force. There is in reality no difference. . . . We are entitled to form our own conclusion as to the object for which the German navy is built up and we have and will claim every right to act accordingly."[19]

Worst-case analysis is based on the assumption that it is better to err on the side of being overcautious and prepared for the worst than to risk being caught by surprise in a situation that jeopardizes the country's security. The costs of unreciprocated cooperation in security affairs are potentially so high (military defeat, loss of territory, political blackmail) that the potential gains are often discounted.[20]

Military planning and the organization of military forces are heavily influenced by this approach. In the 1950s U.S. military and political analysts were greatly concerned with the possibility of a Soviet surprise attack on a vulnerable U.S. strategic bomber force.[21] To overcome the problem, experts and policymakers developed the concept of the strategic triad as the backbone of the U.S. nuclear deterrent. The idea was to develop and deploy nuclear forces to withstand a devastating first strike and still capable of launching a retaliatory strike

18. Michael Howard, *The Causes of Wars,* 2d ed. (Cambridge: Harvard University Press, 1984), 15.

19. As quoted in Paul M. Kennedy, *The Rise of the Anglo-German Antagonism, 1860–1914* (London: Allen and Unwin, 1980), 421. For an excellent study of the impact of worst-case analysis on German naval planning, see Ivo Nikolai Lambi, *The Navy and German Power Politics, 1862–1914* (Boston: Allen and Unwin, 1984).

20. Charles Lipson, "International Cooperation in Economic and Security Affairs," *World Politics* 37: 1 (1984):1–23, and Robert Jervis, "Cooperation under the Security Dilemma," *World Politics* 30: 2 (1978):167–214. See also George H. Quester, *Offense and Defense in the International System* (New York: John Wiley and Sons, 1977), and Jack S. Levy, "The Offensive/Defensive Balance of Military Technology: A Theoretical and Historical Analysis," *International Studies Quarterly* 28: 4 (1984):219–38.

21. Robert H. Johnson, "Periods of Peril: The Window of Vulnerability and Other Myths," *Foreign Affairs* 61:4 (1983):950–70, and Lawrence Freedman, *The Evolution of Nuclear Strategy* (New York: St. Martin's, 1981), 158–63.

that would inflict unacceptable damage on the Soviet Union.[22] Since the mid-1970s there has been a good deal of concern in the United States about the increased vulnerability of land-based strategic forces to a Soviet first strike and the need to close the "window of vulnerability."[23]

This conservative bias in military planning and analysis is reinforced by the tendency of foreign policy leaders to view the actions of an adversary as part of a coherent and well-thought-out plan of action and strategy.[24] Consequently, decision makers are quick to perceive and pay a great deal of attention to potential military threats and to view the actions of other states as a test of their country's bargaining reputation.

During the Moroccan crisis of 1911 a number of British policymakers were deeply suspicious of German intentions. In Sir Eyre Crowe's words, "We begin to see the light. Germany is playing for the highest stakes. If her demands are acceded to . . . it will mean the subjection of France. . . . This is a trial of strength."[25] British policymakers viewed German naval maneuvers during the crisis as a potentially serious threat. As Sir Arthur Nicolson noted in a dispatch to Sir Edward Grey, the foreign secretary, "Please do not think me demented—but Ottley has drawn my attention, once directly and once through Crowe, to the fact that the German High Sea Fleet, cruiser squadron and torpedo flotilla are all concentrated near and about

22. Alain C. Ethoven and K. Wayne Smith, *How Much Is Enough? Shaping the Defense Program, 1961–1968* (New York: Harper and Row, 1971).

23. Paul Nitze, "Deterring Our Deterrent," *Foreign Policy* 25 (1976–1977):195–210; Robert Jervis, *The Illogic of American Nuclear Strategy* (Ithaca: Cornell University Press, 1984), 126–46; Robert P. Berman and John C. Baker, *Soviet Strategic Forces: Requirements and Responses* (Washington, D.C.: Brookings Institution, 1982), 113–40; and David Holloway, *The Soviet Union and the Arms Race* (New Haven: Yale University Press, 1983), 29–62. More recently the vulnerability of the U.S. command and control system for strategic forces has become an issue of increasing concern. See John D. Steinbruner, "Nuclear Decapitation," *Foreign Policy* 45 (1981–82):16–28, and Bruce G. Blair, *Strategic Command and Control: Redefining the Nuclear Threat* (Washington, D.C.: Brookings Institution, 1985).

24. This seems particularly true in assessing the actions of such a long-standing rival as the Soviet Union. See Garthoff, *Detente and Confrontation,* and Jervis, *Perception and Misperception,* 319–29.

25. G. P. Gooch and Harold Temperley, eds., *British Documents on the Origins of the War, 1898–1914* (London: Her Majesty's Stationary Office, 1932), 7: no. 392.

the Norwegian coasts—and in a good position for a 'bolt from the blue.' "[26]

In the fall of 1950 Chinese policymakers perceived the advance of U.S. armed forces across the thirty-eighth parallel and into North Korea as a serious threat to China's security, despite statements by U.S. officials, such as the president and secretary of state, disclaiming any aggressive intentions toward China. China thereupon intervened militarily in order to prevent the collapse of North Korea.[27] During the Berlin crisis of 1961 Dean Acheson submitted a report to President John F. Kennedy analyzing the basic issues at stake in the conflict. Arthur Schlesinger summarizes the report as follows: "Acheson's basic thesis . . . was that West Berlin was not a problem but a pretext. Khrushchev's demarche had nothing to do with Berlin, Germany or Europe. His object, as Acheson saw it, was not to rectify a local situation but to test the general American will to resist; his hope was that by making us back down on a sacred commitment, he could shatter our world power and influence."[28]

In a situation of attempted deterrence, the sensitivity of a potential attacker to military threats and challenges to its reputation make it difficult for a defender to undertake actions that demonstrate resolve while avoiding provocation. For example, in a crisis situation military preparations by a defender may be perceived as preparations for a potential attack and may thereby create incentives for a preemptive strike by the state that is supposed to be deterred. The distinction between an offensive and a defensive posture is often difficult to discern, and therefore policymakers assuming the worst may perceive the defender's military preparations as a potential offensive threat. This possibility may also arise from the psychological biases of the adversary, which produce distorted perceptions and exaggeration of provocation. In this situation the actual scope and type of the defender's military actions are not as important as the predisposition of the adversary to interpret those actions as threatening.[29]

26. Ibid., no. 636.
27. Allen S. Whiting, *China Crosses the Yalu: The Decision to Enter the Korean War* (Stanford: Stanford University Press, 1980), and Alexander George and Richard Smoke, *Deterrence in American Foreign Policy: Theory and Practice* (New York: Columbia University Press, 1974), 184–231.
28. As quoted in Snyder and Diesing, *Conflict among Nations,* 300.
29. Jervis, "Cooperation under the Security Dilemma," 186–200.

In the Middle East crisis of 1967, the initial buildup of Egyptian military forces along the Israeli border was intended to deter a potential attack by Israel against Syria. But Israeli leaders quickly perceived the potential for an offensive strike by Egypt and mobilized their own forces to strike first if necessary. As Moshe Dayan stated at a cabinet meeting at the height of the crisis, ''Our best chance of victory was to strike first . . . it would be fatal for us to allow them to launch their attack.''[30] In the European theater, the dispersal and positioning of North Atlantic Treaty Organization (NATO) tactical nuclear weapons in a crisis may increase the chances of a Soviet preemptive strike.[31]

Military preparations, verbal threats and warnings, and the adoption of a firm negotiating position by the defender may also be perceived as a challenge to the bargaining reputation of the potential attacker. The willingness of the potential attacker to back down from its threat to use force when confronted with a determined opponent may therefore be counterbalanced by the attacker's determination to avoid the appearance of weakness and of retreating under pressure. The French refusal to cede the French Congo in the Moroccan crisis of 1911 led Foreign Minister Kiderlen of Germany to argue to his chancellor that ''when our prestige in foreign lands is lowered we must fight.''[32] Janice Gross Stein found that a consistent factor that pushed Egypt in the direction of using force in 1973, despite an inferior military position, was the belief that a continuing lack of progress in negotiations with Israel would seriously undermine Egypt's international reputation, in particular its position of leadership in the Arab world.[33]

Both the defender and the potential attacker may become committed to their own positions and expect a concession from the other side to break the deadlock. In 1898 Great Britain and France almost went to war when the French refused to withdraw from Fashoda without receiving compensation, while Britain maintained that French withdrawal was to be unconditional and therefore refused negotiations.

30. As quoted in Michael Brecher, *Decisions in Crisis: Israel, 1967 and 1973* (Berkeley: University of California Press, 1980), 167.

31. Paul Bracken, *The Command and Control of Nuclear Forces* (New Haven: Yale University Press, 1983), 129–78, and Stephen M. Meyer, *Soviet Theater Nuclear Forces: Parts I and II,* Adelphi Papers 187 and 188 (London: International Institute for Strategic Studies, 1984).

32. As quoted in Barlow, *Agadir Crisis,* 327.

33. Jervis, Lebow, and Stein, *Psychology and Deterrence,* 34–59.

The French position was recorded by the British ambassador following a meeting with the French foreign minister: "It is impossible for the French Government to give up Fashoda, their right to occupy which Her Majesty's Government do not even choose to discuss. Neither this nor any other Ministry could submit to what would be the humiliation of France. . . . He could not think it is wished in England to go to war over such a question, but France would, however, unwilling, accept war rather than submit."[34]

The combination of a potential attacker's uncertainty about the intentions and capabilities of the defender and sensitivity to threats and challenges suggests that policymakers who are attempting to deter an adversary should try to determine whether the underlying political and military conditions favor or do not favor deterrence success and what specific diplomatic and military actions can enhance or reduce the likelihood of success. A successful policy of deterrence can of course prevent the outbreak of war and may even lead to the resolution of the conflict through negotiations. An unsuccessful policy not only can fail to deter the use of military force but may even provoke armed conflict or make it more likely in the future.

Divergent Objectives and Deterrence Success

The delicate task for policymakers is to deter an adversary who is likely initially to doubt their commitment while remaining sensitive to the potential threat and challenge posed by their actions. Policymakers should therefore try to devise a deterrent posture that is simultaneously credible and stable.

A stable deterrent does not lead the potential attacker to fear an offensive strike by the defender and avoids challenging a potential attacker's bargaining reputation to such an extent that backing down from the threat to use force becomes more difficult. A stable deterrent posture must maintain a fine balance between demonstrating firmness and readiness to use force on the one hand and provoking the attacker and creating a spiral of escalating hostility on the other.[35]

34. Gooch and Temperley, eds., *British Documents*, 1:200.

35. Jervis presents an excellent analysis of this problem and formulates a number of propositions to explain when deterrent threats and actions will prevent or provoke an attack (*Perception and Misperception*, 58–113).

Achieving an effective balance between credibility and stability in diplomatic and military actions has been difficult for policymakers to realize in practice. Policymakers may emphasize the need for moderation and flexibility in diplomacy and military preparations in hope of a negotiated settlement and in fear of provoking the adversary. Or they may adopt a firm diplomatic stance and build up military forces to optimal strength to meet the tactical requirements of operational plans in the event of war, responding to the perceived need to demonstrate resolve to protect their vital interests and to be prepared for armed conflict if deterrence fails.[36]

When confronted with evidence concerning the hostile intentions of a potential attacker, defenders of the status quo have often reacted cautiously in an attempt to avoid actions that might escalate a tense situation. For fear of provoking the military junta, Great Britain failed to issue any verbal warnings or undertake military preparations as a deterrent signal to Argentina in March 1982 despite evidence of an Argentine intention to attack.[37] Preceding the outbreak of the 1973 Arab-Israeli War, some of the Israeli leadership concluded that Egypt and the Arab countries had not been intent on attacking Israel in 1967 and that therefore the Israeli preemptive strike had not been necessary. As a result, in the 1973 crisis when Egypt and Syria began extensive military preparations, the Israeli leadership decided not to mobilize immediately in an attempt to avoid intensifying the crisis through a spiral of military escalation. Thus when Egypt and Syria did attack, Israeli defenses were not fully prepared, and substantial losses were suffered at the outset of the war.[38] Richard Betts has found that defenders of the status quo have often been the victims of surprise attack through failure to react quickly and effectively in response to warnings of attack.[39] The danger is that the failure to act may signal to a potential attacker the defender's intention not to intervene or an inability to respond effectively to an attack. An uncompromising diplomatic stance

36. Alexander George, "Crisis Management: The Interaction of Political and Military Considerations," *Survival* 26: 5 (1984):223–34.

37. Jervis, Lebow, and Stein, *Psychology and Deterrence*, 89–124.

38. Ibid., chap. 4. I should like to thank Robert Jervis for suggesting this example.

39. Betts, *Surprise Attack*, 27–86.

and extensive military preparations, however, can create a situation in which the pace of military events exceeds the time required for the diplomatic stalemate to be broken and a negotiated settlement agreed upon.

The difficulty in striking a balance between credibility and stability lies in the defender's inability to know confidently what factors are critical in a potential attacker's calculus of loss and gain. Consider the important but by no means exhaustive list of following questions:

1. How does the attacker evaluate the military balance? Is an approximate balance of forces between attacker and defender a robust deterrent? Does superiority significantly enhance deterrence success? Do the likely outcomes of a short versus a long war carry equal weight in the calculations of the potential attacker?

2. Should offers to compromise be combined with coercive pressure, or will such flexibility signal to the potential attacker a lack of resolve and thereby undercut deterrent threats?

3. How important are estimates of the costs of inaction for a potential attacker in determining the success or failure of deterrence?

4. What impact does the defender's past behavior have on deterrence outcomes? How important are reputations for weakness or firmness in comparison to the diplomatic and military actions of the defender in influencing the potential attacker's assessment of the defender's intentions?

In this book I will analyze historical cases of attempted extended deterrence. My objective is to formulate and then empirically test a set of hypotheses on the political and military conditions under which deterrence is likely to succeed or fail. My theoretical focus will be an analysis of how the balance of military capabilities, alternative strategies of bargaining, past behavior, and issues at stake relate to the credibility and/or stability of the defender's deterrent posture and actions.

I view the combination of statistical analysis of a large number of cases and the more detailed examination of individual cases as potentially the most productive method for deriving generalizations about political behavior. The two approaches are essential to the development and verification of theories in social science research.[40] I use these two approaches in an interactive process of model specification and empirical testing. A number of basic concepts and insights derived from the work of scholars who rely on the case-study method serve as the building blocks for the formulation of hypotheses for statistical analysis. Probit analysis is utilized to test these hypotheses on the universe of fifty-eight cases of attempted extended deterrence during the past century. Comparative case studies are then used to evaluate critically and illustrate the generalizations suggested by the statistical analysis.

40. On the use of case studies in social science research see Bruce M. Russett, *Power and Community in World Politics* (San Francisco: W. H. Freeman, 1974), chap. 2; Alexander George, "Case Studies and Theory Development: The Method of Structured, Focused Comparison," in *Diplomacy: New Approaches in History, Theory, and Policy,* ed. Paul Gorden Lauren (New York: Free Press, 1979); and Harry Eckstein, "Case Study and Theory in Political Science," in *Handbook of Political Science,* vol. 7, ed. Fred I. Greenstein and Nelson W. Polsby (Reading, Mass.: Addison-Wesley, 1975).

2

Conceptualizing Deterrence

The concept of deterrence has been defined and conceptualized in a number of ways by scholars and policymakers.[1] To clarify the meaning of this term, and my use of it in this book, three central concepts need to be defined:

1. Deterrence: Drawing on the work of Michael Howard,[2] I define *deterrence* as a policy that seeks to persuade an adversary, through the threat of military retaliation, that the costs of using military force to resolve political conflict will outweigh the benefits.[3] A policy of deterrence, then, seeks to prevent an adversary from using military force to achieve foreign policy objectives through the threat of a counterattack. The deterrer's threat of retaliation may be based on the military capability to repulse an attack and thereby deny the attacker its battlefield objectives and/or prevent the loss of one's own territory (or that of an ally), or the capability to inflict heavy military losses on the adversary in an armed conflict of attrition. The relative deterrent value of a "denial" versus "punishment"[4] military capability is addressed in

1. Patrick M. Morgan, *Deterrence: A Conceptual Analysis* (Beverly Hills: Sage Publications, 1977), 17–46.

2. Michael Howard, "Reassurance and Deterrence: Western Defense in the 1980s," *Foreign Affairs* 61: 2 (1982–83):315.

3. The costs of using military force include: battlefield casualties, destruction and depletion of arms and equipment, possible occupation and damage to national territory, the opportunity cost of diverting economic resources and national expenditures to wartime production, and the potential loss of domestic political support if defeated in armed conflict.

4. The distinction between denial and punishment is drawn from Glenn H. Snyder, *Deterrence and Defense: Toward a Theory of National Security* (Princeton: Princeton University Press, 1961), 14–16.

chapter 3, where I develop hypotheses on the balance of military forces for empirical testing.

2. Extended Deterrence: The term *extended deterrence* refers to a situation in which policymakers (I use the term defender) threaten military retaliation against another state (the potential attacker) in an attempt to prevent that state from using military force against an ally (or protégé) of the defender. The objective of extended deterrence is to protect and defend allies from attack rather than to prevent a direct attack on one's own territory and borders.

3. Extended-Immediate Deterrence: Based on the work of Patrick Morgan, I define *extended-immediate deterrence* as a policy in which (a) A potential attacker is actively considering the use of military force against a protégé of the defender; (b) Policymakers in the defender state are aware of this threat; and (c) Recognizing that an attack is possible, policymakers of the defender state, either explicitly or by the movement of military forces, threaten the use of retaliatory force in an attempt to prevent the use of military force by the potential attacker.[5]

A case of extended-immediate deterrence is therefore a confrontation between adversaries in which the threat of armed conflict is possible if neither the potential attacker nor defender retreats. The concept of international crisis defined as "a sequence of interactions between the governments of two or more sovereign states in severe conflict, short of actual war, but involving the perception of a dangerously high probability of war"[6] nicely captures the dangers of an extended-immediate deterrence confrontation. Cases of attempted extended-immediate deterrence form a subset of all potential cases of attempted deterrence in international relations (fig. 1, cell 3). In figure 1 a simple classification scheme places cases of attempted deterrence into one of four possible categories.

In contrast to extended-immediate deterrence, extended-general deterrence (fig. 1, cell 4) refers to political and military competition between a potential attacker and defender in which the possibility of an armed conflict over another state is present but the potential attacker is neither actively considering the use of force nor engaging in a confrontation that threatens war. Competition and rivalry in a situation of

5. Morgan, *Deterrence*, 38.
6. Glenn H. Snyder and Paul Diesing, *Conflict among Nations*, (Princeton: Princeton University Press, 1977), 6.

FIGURE 1. A Typology of Cases of Deterrence

Threat Posed by Attacker

		Actual	*Potential*
Target of Attack	*Defender*	**2** Direct-Immediate Deterrence (Outbreak of Russo-Finnish War, 1940)	**1** Direct-General Deterrence (Sino-Soviet border dispute since 1970)
	Protégé of Defender	**3** Extended-Immediate Deterrence (U.S.-Chinese crisis over North Korea, 1950)	**4** Extended-General Deterrence (U.S. forces stationed in South Korea since 1953)

extended-general deterrence are manifested in the development of arms races, the formation of opposing alliance systems, the provision of economic and military aid to regional powers, and broad declarations and policy statements of a country's foreign policy leadership regarding national security interests.[7]

In a situation of general deterrence (fig. 1, cells 1 and 4), a defender allocates resources and deploys military forces for the contingency of an armed attack by an adversary even though there is no imminent or short-term threat of an attack. United States armed forces are stationed overseas in a number of countries to back up the U.S. commitment to defend those countries if attacked. Examples include U.S. forces stationed in South Korea as a deterrent to a potential North Korean attack and U.S. forces deployed in Western Europe as a deterrent to a possible Soviet attack. A situation of direct-general deterrence is represented by

7. Morgan, *Deterrence*, 40–43.

the buildup of Soviet conventional and nuclear forces since the early 1970s along its border in the Far East as a deterrent to the perceived military threat of China.[8]

In cases of direct-immediate deterrence (fig. 1, cell 2), a country threatened with imminent attack must defend itself using its own military forces in the absence of military support from other states. In autumn 1939 the Soviet Union demanded territorial concessions and threatened Finland with military force unless it complied. The Finnish government rejected the demands and warned the Soviet Union that it would use military force to defend its borders.[9] In the summer and fall of 1962 the long-standing border dispute between China and India escalated to a direct military confrontation in which China attempted to deter India from using military force in the disputed border areas.[10]

I will examine cases of extended-immediate deterrence in this book for four reasons. First, failures of extended-immediate deterrence have led to the outbreak of some of the most destructive and important international conflicts of the twentieth century. Research on extended-immediate deterrence can therefore make an important contribution to the development of general theories of international conflict and the causes of war by providing insights into the origins of the major wars of the past century. The outbreak of the Russo-Japanese War in 1904 was the result of a confrontation between Russia and Japan over the future of Korea and Manchuria, whereas both World War I and World War II resulted from the breakdown of extended deterrence among the Great Powers of Europe.[11]

In the postwar era, failures of extended-immediate deterrence have also had a great impact on U.S. foreign policy and involvement in international conflict. In October 1950 the United States failed to heed the warnings of China and invaded North Korea in an attempt to reunify Korea. The U.S. decision to cross the thirty-eighth parallel led to the

8. Harry Gelman, *The Soviet Far East Buildup and Soviet Risk-Taking against China,* R–2943–AF (Santa Monica, Calif.: Rand Corporation, 1982).

9. Max Jakobson, *The Diplomacy of the Winter War: An Account of the Russo-Finnish Conflict, 1939–1940* (Cambridge: Harvard University Press, 1961), and Vaino A. Tanner, *The Winter War: Finland Against Russia, 1939–1940* (Stanford: Stanford University Press, 1957).

10. Allen S. Whiting, *The Chinese Calculus of Deterrence: India and Indochina* (Ann Arbor: University of Michigan Press, 1975), 42–106.

11. I present case studies of the outbreak of these wars in chapters 5 and 6.

military intervention of China in support of North Korea and a disastrous military reversal and retreat for U.S. forces in North Korea.[12] The escalation of U.S. involvement in the Vietnam War from 1964 to 1965 was closely linked to the U.S. failure to deter North Vietnam from entering into combat against South Vietnamese and U.S. forces in support of the Viet Cong.[13]

Second, one of the most likely sources of future confrontation between the two superpowers lies in the involvement and escalation of the United States and the Soviet Union in a regional conflict in support of local allies. The study of past cases of extended-immediate deterrence may improve our understanding of the limits and possibilities of effective crisis management in such a confrontation. The Middle East may be the best example of a region where local rivalries and long-standing disputes threaten to entangle the two superpowers in an extended-immediate deterrence confrontation. A potentially dangerous confrontation between the United States and the Soviet Union developed during the 1973 Arab-Israeli War when the Soviets threatened unilateral intervention to prevent Israeli encirclement of the Egyptian Third Army Corps. The United States strongly opposed any such intervention and placed its military forces on a worldwide alert to signal its concern and to prepare for a possible confrontation with Soviet forces. Soviet forces were not dispatched, and Israel, under U.S. diplomatic pressure, curtailed its operations against the Egyptian Third Army.[14]

Third, the study of extended-immediate deterrence can be integrated with research on the larger question of international crisis behavior. In particular, I will attempt to develop and test propositions from research on crisis bargaining behavior and coercive diplomacy.

Fourth, and most important, the study of extended-immediate de-

12. I present a case study of the U.S. decision to cross the thirty-eighth parallel in chapter 5.

13. Wallace J. Thies, *When Governments Collide: Coercion and Diplomacy in the Vietnam Conflict, 1964–1968* (Berkeley: University of California Press, 1980), 71–142.

14. Barry M. Blechman and Douglas M. Hart, "The Political Utility of Nuclear Weapons: The 1973 Middle East Crisis," *International Security* 7: 1 (1982):132–56; Raymond L. Garthoff, *Detente and Confrontation: American-Soviet Relations from Nixon to Reagan* (Washington, D.C.: Brookings Institution, 1985), 374–85; and Richard K. Betts, *Nuclear Blackmail and Nuclear Balance* (Washington, D.C.: Brookings Institution, 1987), 123–29.

terrence provides the opportunity to test hypotheses on the effectiveness of deterrence under demanding circumstances. The potential attacker is motivated strongly enough to challenge the status quo with the threat of force and is likely to question the commitment of the defender to the protégé. Under such circumstances the attempt to identify the political and military conditions that promote successful deterrence is a challenging one with potentially high payoffs—theoretically as well as for policy. Can generalizations about deterrence success be formulated and empirically confirmed in situations where success is not easily achieved? Although failures of general deterrence give rise to extended-immediate deterrence confrontations, the consequences of deterrence failure are more severe in immediate deterrence. The failure of general deterrence leads to an international crisis, but the defender's policy of immediate deterrence is the final opportunity to prevent an international dispute from escalating to large-scale armed conflict.

In the concluding chapter I will consider the extent to which my theoretical approach as well as the empirical results can be applied to cases of direct deterrence. At this point, I will simply note that there are similarities between the two classes of deterrence cases but also differences that make it problematic to generalize without qualification from extended to direct deterrence.

Deterrence and Conflict Escalation

The failure of extended deterrence and the outbreak of war can be broken down into specific stages in a process of conflict escalation (fig. 2). Not all conflicts pass through each stage, but each conflict is likely to pass through one or more of these stages in the process of escalating to war. In the first stage a potential attacker challenges the status quo by threatening to use force to advance its foreign policy objectives. At this point a latent or potential conflict of interest between a defender and potential attacker becomes a direct and open confrontation.

Syrian support for Palestinian Liberation Organization (PLO) forces within Jordan became a direct conflict between the Syrian and Jordanian governments when Syria threatened military intervention in support of the PLO in September 1970. Although Israel had not become directly involved in this inter-Arab conflict, Syria and other Arab countries knew that Israel wished to prevent the collapse of the Hussein

FIGURE 2. Stages in the Escalation of Conflict

Attacker's Move:	Defender's Response:	State of Relations
No action taken	General deterrence	Status Quo
↓	↓	↓
Challenge		
↓	Immediate deterrence	International crisis
Acute confrontation	↓	↓
↓		
Large-scale use of force	Compulsory termination of armed conflict	War

regime in Jordan for fear that a more radical, militant regime would replace it. The Syrian threat of military intervention was thus a direct challenge to Israel's security interests in Jordan.[15] Extended-general deterrence had then failed because Israel's policy of tacit support for Hussein against the PLO had not prevented Syria from threatening direct intervention.

Israeli policymakers responded to threats of Syrian intervention with extended-immediate deterrence. They countered that they were watching the situation closely and were prepared to take any steps necessary to protect Israel's security interests. The failure of general deterrence and the development of immediate deterrence represents the transition from the status quo to an international crisis in relations between defender and potential attacker. The potential attacker thus faces a threat of military retaliation if it uses force.

Conflict escalation became acute when both Syria and Israel mobilized forces.[16] By 20 September 1970, Syrian armored brigades had crossed the Jordanian border to engage in combat with Jordanian armed forces. Israel, in response, began large-scale concentration of armed forces in the Golan Heights and partial mobilization of reserves. On the verge of a direct armed confrontation with Israel, Syria withdrew its

15. I present a case study of Syrian intervention in the Jordanian Civil War in chapter 5.

16. Charles A. McClelland, ''The Acute International Crisis,'' *World Politics* 14: 1 (1961):182–204.

forces from Jordan on 23 September before its military involvement reached large-scale confrontation with Israeli forces.

Limited armed conflict between potential attacker and protégé threatens the outbreak of war and the failure of immediate deterrence. Deterrence continues to operate as the potential attacker weighs the risks of further escalation and the commitment of military force in pursuit of foreign policy objectives. Once the potential attacker has committed itself to the use of force and engages in large-scale, continuous combat with the protégé or defender, immediate deterrence has failed and further efforts at coercion will require the defender to compel the attacker to de-escalate the armed conflict and terminate the war.

Extended deterrence may fail therefore at one, if not two, different stages—general then immediate deterrence. The failure of extended-immediate deterrence represents the transition from an international crisis to the outbreak of armed conflict between attacker and defender. Not all confrontations pass through these two stages of deterrence. In the case of Argentina's invasion of the Falklands Islands, for example, the failure of extended-general deterrence led directly to the outbreak of war because Great Britain did not respond to the imminent threat of an Argentine invasion with any deterrent threats; that is, they did not attempt extended-immediate deterrence. The Thatcher government responded only after Argentina had invaded the islands, and then its task was to compel Argentina to withdraw its forces from the islands.[17]

Conversely, in some cases of conflict escalation the confrontation between a potential attacker and defender first emerges at the stage of immediate deterrence, as when a defender intervenes in support of a country in which it had not previously been seen as having a direct security interest. Before the outbreak of the Korean War in June 1950 the Truman administration had explicitly announced its intention to refrain from direct involvement in the bitter conflict between the newly formed communist government on the Chinese mainland and the nationalist forces of Chiang Kai-shek, which had retreated to the offshore island of Taiwan. After Chinese communist forces had been preparing to invade Taiwan for several months, President Truman announced on 26 June that the U.S. Seventh Fleet was to be sent to the Taiwan Straits

---

17. Robert Jervis, Richard Ned Lebow, and Janice Gross Stein, *Psychology and Deterrence* (Baltimore: Johns Hopkins University Press, 1985), 89–124.

to prevent an armed confrontation between communist and nationalist forces. United States policymakers were concerned that occupation of Taiwan by Chinese communist forces might pose a potential threat to U.S. forces in South Korea. The United States therefore reversed its past policy of nonintervention and confronted Chinese communist forces with the threat of military retaliation if they attempted to invade Taiwan.[18]

I focus only on those conflicts between a potential attacker and defender in which there is an open and direct confrontation. The fundamental question is: Will the confrontation between the potential attacker and defender be resolved short of armed conflict or will it escalate to the outbreak of war?

Cases of Extended Deterrence

I have identified what I believe to be the universe of historical cases of attempted extended-immediate deterrence from 1885 to 1984 (see table 1). The following criteria were used in identifying cases of extended-immediate deterrence:

1. The initial threat of force by the potential attacker had to be explicit and the target of the threat clearly identifiable. Military and political actions by the potential attacker that constituted a threat to use force included:
   a. Statement of intent to use force: A verbal threat to use force against the protégé.
   b. Buildup of military forces for potential use: The reinforcement and movement of forces to positions behind the border or off the coast of the protégé.
   c. Preparation of military forces for imminent use: The concentration and alerting of forces on the border or off the coast of the protégé.

---

18. Although the leadership of China recognized that an amphibious attack on Taiwan would be a difficult military operation, policy statements, the buildup and training of troops for an amphibious operation, and the concentration of naval transport opposite Taiwan indicated that the PRC leadership was determined to attack Taiwan and to end the civil war. See Allen S. Whiting, *China Crosses the Yalu: The Decision to Enter the Korean War* (Stanford: Stanford University Press, 1980), 20–22, 47–65.

TABLE 1. Cases of Attempted Extended-Immediate Deterrence, 1885–1984

Case	Year	Potential Attacker	Protégé	Defender	Outcome
1	1885	Russia	Afghanistan	Britain/India	Success
2	1885–86	Bulgaria	Serbia	Austria-Hungary	Success
3	1886	Greece	Turkey	Britain	Success
4	1894	Japan	Korea	China	Failure
5	1897	Greece	Crete	Britain/Turkey	Success
6	1898	France	Egyptian Sudan	Britain	Success
7	1902–03	Germany	Venezuela	United States	Success
8	1903–04	Japan	Korea	Russia	Failure
9	1903–04	Colombia	Panama	United States	Success
10	1905–06	France	Morocco	Germany	Failure
11	1905–06	Germany	France	Britain	Success
12	1906	Turkey	Egypt	Britain	Success
13	1908–09	Serbia/Russia	Austria-Hungary	Germany	Success
14	1911	Italy	Tripoli	Turkey	Failure
15	1911	France	Morocco	Germany	Failure
16	1911	Germany	France	Britain	Success
17	1912–13	Serbia/Russia	Austria-Hungary	Germany	Success
18	1913	Rumania	Bulgaria	Russia	Success
19	1913	Bulgaria	Greece	Serbia	Failure
20	1913	Serbia	Albania	Austria-Hungary	Success
21	1914	Austria/Germany	Serbia	Russia	Failure
22	1914	Russia/Serbia	Austria-Hungary	Germany	Failure
23	1914	Germany	France	Britain/Russia	Failure
24	1914	Germany	Belgium	Britain	Failure
25	1921	Panama	Costa Rica	United States	Success
26	1922	Turkey	Greece	Britain	Success
27	1935	Italy	Ethiopia	Britain	Failure
28	1935–36	Japan	Outer Mongolia	Soviet Union	Success
29	1937	Soviet Union	Manchukuo	Japan	Success
30	1938	Soviet Union	Manchukuo	Japan	Failure
31	1938	Germany	Czechoslovakia	Britain/France	Failure
32	1938–39	Italy	Tunisia	France/Britain	Success
33	1939	Germany	Poland	Britain/France	Failure
34	1940–41	Soviet Union	Finland	Germany	Success
35	1946	Soviet Union	Iran	United States	Success
36	1946	Soviet Union	Turkey	United States	Success
37	1948	Soviet Union	West Berlin	U.S./Britain	Success
38	1950	China	Taiwan	United States	Success
39	1950	United States	North Korea	China	Failure
40	1954–55	China	Quemoy-Matsu Islands	United States	Success
41	1957	Turkey	Syria	Soviet Union	Success
42	1961	Iraq	Kuwait	Britain	Success
43	1961	North Vietnam	Laos	United States	Success
44	1961	India	Goa	Portugal	Failure
45	1961–62	Indonesia	West Irian	Netherlands	Failure

TABLE 1. *Continued*

Case	Year	Potential Attacker	Protégé	Defender	Outcome
46	1964–65	Indonesia	Malaysia	Britain	Failure
47	1964–65	North Vietnam	South Vietnam	United States	Failure
48	1964–65	United States	North Vietnam	China	Success
49	1967	Israel	Syria	Egypt	Failure
50	1967	Turkey	Cyprus	Greece	Failure
51	1970	Syria	Jordan	Israel	Success
52	1971	India	Pakistani Kashmir	China	Success
53	1974	Turkey	Cyprus	Greece	Failure
54	1975	Morocco	Western Sahara	Spain	Failure
55	1975	Guatemala	Belize	Britain	Success
56	1977	Guatemala	Belize	Britain	Success
57	1979	China	Vietnam	Soviet Union	Failure
58	1983	Libya	Chad	France	Success

2. The threat of military retaliation by the defender had to be clearly directed at and perceived by the potential attacker. Military and political actions that indicated a threat of possible retaliation included:

   a. Statement of intent to use force: A verbal threat to use force against the potential attacker.

   b. Show of military force: Exercises held near the border or off the coast of the potential attacker or protégé.

   c. Buildup of military forces for potential use: The reinforcement and movement of forces to positions behind the border or off the coast of the potential attacker or protégé.

   d. Preparation of military forces for imminent use: The concentration and alerting of forces on the border or off the coast of the potential attacker or protégé.

I have identified fifty-eight cases of attempted extended-immediate deterrence.[19] Thirty-four cases occurred before the end of World War II whereas twenty-four cases occurred after 1945. The confrontations

19. The cases listed in table 1 represent an extended, revised version of an early data set that was used in a previous study: Paul Huth and Bruce Russett, ''What Makes Deterrence Work? Cases From 1900 to 1980,'' *World Politics* 36: 4 (1984):496–526. The revised and original list differ in two ways: 1) the new list covers 1885–1984 as compared with 1900–80; 2) based on further research, reading of new sources, and the advice of diplomatic historians and experts, I have added a number of new cases and have

centered in geographic regions ranging from the Far East and Indochina
to Western Europe and northern Africa. In most cases both the potential
attacker and defender were Great Powers; in a small number of cases
both adversaries were regional powers. In some confrontations I have
identified multiple cases of attempted deterrence. For example, I have
divided the outbreak of World War I into four cases.[20]

Twenty-four cases were coded as failed deterrence, and thirty-four
cases were coded as successful deterrence. Successful deterrence is
defined as those cases in which the potential attacker refrains from
using military force or engages in small-scale combat with the protégé
(fewer than 200 fatalities among the regular armed forces of both sides
combined) and fails to force the defender to capitulate to its demands
under the threat of force. Identifying cases of successful deterrence can
be difficult when detailed information on the calculations and intentions of the potential attacker is lacking. In such cases I closely sur-
veyed secondary sources and consulted with country experts and diplomatic historians to determine if a threat to use force was present and if

---

deleted or consolidated other cases. The net impact of these changes has been to increase
the total from fifty-four to fifty-eight. Previously identified cases were deleted because
information from new sources indicated either that the defender's intervention occurred
after the hostilities had escalated to large-scale armed conflict (constituting attempted
compellence, not attempted deterrence) or that there was disagreement about whether a
threat of attack actually existed.

20. The sources used to identify and select cases of attempted deterrence were
William J. Langer, *The Diplomacy of Imperialism*, 2 vols. (New York: A. A. Knopf,
1935); William J. Langer, *An Encyclopedia of World History*, 5th ed., rev. (Boston:
Houghton Mifflin, 1972); Ernest C. Helmreich, *The Diplomacy of the Balkan Wars,
1912–1913*, (Cambridge: Harvard University Press, 1938); Snyder and Diesing, *Conflict
among Nations*, 531–70; David Walder, *The Chanak Affair* (London: Hutchinson,
1969); *Survey of International Affairs, 1923–1963* (London: Oxford University Press,
1923–77); *Keesing's Contemporary Archives, 1933–1984* (London: Keesing's, 1933–
84); Martin Blumenson, "The Soviet Power Play at Changkufeng," *World Politics* 12: 2
(1960):249–63; H. Peter Krosby, *Finland, Germany and the Soviet Union, 1940–1941:
The Petsamo Dispute* (Madison: University of Wisconsin Press, 1968); Bruce R.
Kuniholm, *The Origins of the Cold War in the Near East: Great Power Conflict and
Diplomacy in Iran, Turkey, and Greece* (Princeton: Princeton University Press, 1980);
Robert Butterworth, *Managing Interstate Conflict* (Pittsburgh: University Center for
International Studies, 1976); Alexander George and Richard Smoke, *Deterrence in
American Foreign Policy: Theory and Practice* (New York: Columbia University Press,
1974); Whiting, *China Crosses the Yalu;* Whiting, *Chinese Calculus of Deterrence,*
170–95; Daniel Dishon, ed., *Middle East Record, 1969–1970*, vol. 5 (Jerusalem: Israel

the defender's threat of retaliation played a crucial role in the potential attacker's decision to retreat.[21] A definitive answer was simply not possible in some cases, but having followed the procedure described above I am reasonably confident of the coding decisions made.

The failure of deterrence is defined as those cases in which the potential attacker commits its armed forces on a large scale and in sustained combat against the defender and protégé (totaling more than 200 fatalities) or forces the defender to accede to its demands under the threat of war. The Syrian intervention and withdrawal from Jordan (case 51) was coded as a case of successful deterrence since total fatalities among regular armed forces were between 100 and 200 and Syria failed to achieve its objectives. In five additional cases listed in table 1—cases 5, 7, 28, 44, 58—the attacker and protégé engaged in armed conflict resulting in fewer than 100 fatalities. In all of these cases the attacker failed to achieve its primary objectives and de-escalated its military involvement following the defender's threat of intervention. The critical distinction between extended deterrence success and failure is whether the potential attacker decides to commit itself to the sustained use of military force to achieve its foreign policy objectives against the defender and protégé. Thus, the limited use of force by the attacker is not a failure of immediate deterrence if the threats of the defender cause the attacker to step back from the escalation necessary to achieve its goals. Whether any force is used is not the dividing line between the success or failure of immediate deterrence since the critical question for the attacker is whether to take whatever steps are necessary militarily to achieve its goals or to try to settle for some form of a negotiated agreement.

Universities Press, 1977); Stephen S. Kaplan, *Diplomacy of Power: Soviet Armed Forces as a Political Instrument* (Washington, D.C.: Brookings Institution, 1981); Barry M. Blechman and Stephen S. Kaplan, *Force without War: U.S. Armed Forces as a Political Instrument* (Washington, D.C.: Brookings Institution, 1978); and the Correlates of War Project data set—"Militarized Disputes, 1816–1976"—made available through the Interuniversity Consortium for Political and Social Research at the University of Michigan, Ann Arbor.

21. I would like to thank Paul Kennedy, Allen Whiting, Richard L. Merritt, H. Bradford Westerfield, and Naomi Joy Weinberger for their advice on a number of cases.

3

Hypotheses on Deterrence

> Whatever may be the underlying causes of international
> conflict . . . wars begin with conscious and reasoned de-
> cisions based on the calculation . . . that they [states]
> can achieve more by going to war than by remaining at
> peace.
>
> —MICHAEL HOWARD

The success or failure of extended-immediate deterrence depends on whether the potential attacker
challenges the defender's threat to use force to
protect the protégé. To formulate and test hypotheses on deterrence I
have made several assumptions about how a potential attacker decides
whether to challenge the defender's threat and what variables are
critical in that decision.[1]

First, a potential attacker chooses between reliance on military
threats and/or the use of military force and reliance on negotiations and
a diplomatic solution to resolve the conflict with the defender and
protégé. The attacker either presses ahead with the use of force against

1. A number of studies have examined deterrence from the perspective of the
potential attacker. See Bruce Russett, ''Pearl Harbor: Deterrence Theory and Decision
Theory,'' *Journal of Peace Research* 4: 2 (1967):89–105; Alexander George and
Richard Smoke, *Deterrence in American Foreign Policy: Theory and Practice* (New
York: Columbia University Press, 1974), 519–33; Richard Ned Lebow, *Between Peace
and War: The Nature of International Crisis* (Baltimore: Johns Hopkins University
Press, 1981), 82–97, 273–81; and Robert Jervis, Richard Ned Lebow, and Janice Gross
Stein, *Psychology and Deterrence* (Baltimore: Johns Hopkins University Press, 1985),
chaps. 3, 8, 9.

the protégé or backs off and seeks a nonmilitary solution through negotiations. In game-theoretic terms, these alternatives define the underlying structure of the confrontation for the potential attacker—the choice between the coercive strategy of standing firm and the accommodative strategy of cooperation and limited concessions to the defender's bargaining position.[2]

A number of variants exist for each of these two courses of action, but the fundamental choice for the potential attacker remains between a policy of military coercion and a policy of compromise. A potential attacker may attempt to combine or separately pursue each of these two policies at different stages of the confrontation with the defender and protégé, but once the intentions of the defender become clear, the potential attacker must make a fundamental decision about which policy to rely on. If military threats and negotiations have not induced the protégé and defender to make sufficient concessions, the potential attacker must then choose between either further coercive pressure and the use of force or accommodation to the firm position of the defender and the best possible diplomatic settlement.

By the summer of 1903 the leadership of Japan had decided that the competition with Russia for influence in Korea and the Far East had to be settled definitively. The Japanese leadership initiated negotiations with Russia in an attempt to settle the dispute over Korea, reserving the option of military force to resolve the conflict if negotiations failed. When negotiations with Russia reached a stalemate by the end of 1903, Japan began extensive military preparations in anticipation of a possible armed confrontation. In early February 1904 Japan broke off negotiations with Russia, concluding that they were futile, launched a surprise attack against Russian naval forces at Port Arthur, and declared war on Russia shortly thereafter.[3]

In contrast in the Iranian confrontation of 1946, the Soviet Union initiated a dispute with Iran by coupling extensive demands on the Iranian government with active military preparations and threats of

2. Glenn H. Snyder and Paul Diesing, *Conflict among Nations* (Princeton: Princeton University Press, 1977), 40–41. See also James Morrow, "A Spatial Model of International Conflict," *American Political Science Review* 80: 4 (1986):1131–50, and Bruce Bueno de Mesquita and David Lalman, "Reason and War," *American Political Science Review* 80: 4 (1986):1113–29.

3. See chapter 6 for a case study of the outbreak of the Russo-Japanese War.

force. The intervention of the United States in support of Iran, however, played a crucial role in convincing the Soviets to reverse their policy of military and diplomatic pressure and to turn to negotiations. The Soviets withdrew their forces from Iran and accepted a settlement in which their initial demands were considerably reduced.[4]

The second assumption is that, in deciding between a military and a diplomatic solution to the conflict, a potential attacker considers the dangers or costs associated with each course of action. These potential dangers act as constraints on the acceptability of each alternative by identifying conditions that a policy should not violate if it is to be adopted. Snyder and Diesing, for example, have identified a number of common constraints that influence the policy choices of leaders in international crises: (1) avoid alienating allies; (2) avoid provoking opponents; and (3) avoid spoiling the negotiating atmosphere.[5] For example Germany and France were determined to support their allies, Austria-Hungary and Russia, in the 1914 crisis, and Chamberlain was determined to avoid provoking Hitler in the 1938 Czechoslovakian crisis for fear that negotiations would then be impossible.

A simple classification of crisis outcomes illustrates the risks associated with the potential attacker's policy choices (see fig. 3). Military pressure and refusal to make concessions may force the defender to back down from its deterrent threats and capitulate to the attacker's demands. But a coercive strategy also risks escalation of the crisis to war if the defender adopts an equally firm position and refuses to back down. Conversely, an accommodative strategy by the potential attacker may be reciprocated by the defender, in which case the crisis can be de-escalated through mutual compromise. But accommodation, may also be exploited by the defender to force the potential attacker into accepting a diplomatic defeat. The risks of a coercive strategy center on the potential costs of escalation and armed conflict: What if

4. Iranian policy at the United Nations and in direct negotiations with the Soviet Union also induced the Soviets to withdraw, but without active U.S. support Iranian resistance would probably have been insufficient. See Bruce R. Kuniholm, *The Origins of the Cold War in the Near East: Great Power Conflict and Diplomacy in Iran, Turkey, and Greece* (Princeton: Princeton University Press, 1980), 304–42; and Mark Hamilton Lytle, *The Origins of the Iranian-American Alliance, 1941–1953* (New York: Holmes and Meier, 1987), 138–73.

5. Snyder and Diesing, *Conflict among Nations*, 366–68.

FIGURE 3. Bargaining Strategies and the Outcome of Crisis

	Potential Attacker's Strategy	
	Accommodation	*Coercion*
Accommodation	De-escalation of crisis	Capitulation of defender to demands of attacker
Coercion	Forced acceptance by attacker of Diplomatic Defeat	Escalation of crisis to war

Defender's Strategy

the defender refuses to yield and meets force with force? The primary constraint on a policy of coercion for the potential attacker is that military force be utilized only when the costs of military victory are unlikely to be high; that is, don't escalate unless one is in a strong military position. The risks of accommodation center on the potential costs of compromising and accepting a diplomatic solution to the crisis: What if the defender perceives accommodation as a sign of weakness that encourages it to stand firm and apply further pressure? The primary constraint for a potential attacker regarding a policy of accommodation is that its bargaining reputation be protected in reaching a settlement; that is, don't be bullied into an agreement. The stringency with which a potential attacker applies each of these constraints can vary from case to case,[6] but the general principle of considering these potential costs plays a crucial role in determining which policy is adopted.

A third assumption regarding the potential attacker's decision-making process is that it includes the search for new information on the intentions and capabilities of the defender from the defender's diplomatic and military actions. As noted in chapter 1, uncertainty in estimating the intentions and capabilities of opponents is inherent to inter-

6. When the potential attacker perceives a threat of preemption by the defender the costs of escalation and initiating force are likely to be far less constraining than when it perceives no threat of preemption. An example would be the Israeli air strike against Egypt at the outset of the 1967 War.

national relations. A potential attacker's uncertainty in a situation of extended-immediate deterrence can weaken the credibility of a defender's deterrent threat. Or uncertainty may contribute to a potential attacker's desire to obtain more information on the intentions and capabilities of the defender before deciding whether to initiate force. The desire to clarify the defender's intentions is especially important in crises where the potential attacker's initial threat is a probe designed to test the resolve of the defender in support of the protégé.

In addition, the military and diplomatic responses of the defender to the initiatives of the potential attacker may be an important source of feedback for the potential attacker that leads to a reassessment of the intentions and capabilities of the defender. With this new information, the attacker reevaluates the dangers of using military force or accommodating the defender. In his study of the origins of brinkmanship crises, Richard Ned Lebow found that policymakers initiated confrontations on the expectation that the adversary would back down under pressure.[7] As Snyder and Diesing state in their study on the impact of crisis bargaining on patterns of information processing, "What is adjusted is the estimate of the opponent's specific aims, interests, degree of resolve, and capabilities in the particular conflict."[8] The final decision of the potential attacker is thus assumed to be based on a relatively careful consideration of the costs and benefits of both war and peace.[9]

The final assumption is that the potential attacker's decision to initiate the confrontation is likely to be motivated by a combination of offensive and defensive aims. Defensive motives establish the minimum or more limited goals to be pursued, whereas offensive motives establish the maximum or more ambitious aims of the potential attacker. It may be possible to distinguish between these two opposing motives analytically, but in practice the two are likely to be inseparable in the calculations of the potential attacker. Richard Ned Lebow, who

7. Lebow, *Between Peace and War*, 57–58.

8. The underlying image of the adversary is much more resistant to change (Snyder and Diesing, *Conflict among Nations*, 336).

9. For a general study of the applicability of the rational decision-making model to post-World War II U.S. decision-making in crises, see Greg M. Herek, Irving L. Janis, and Paul Huth, "Decision-Making During International Crises: Is Quality of Process Related to Outcome?" *Journal of Conflict Resolution* 31: 2 (1987):203–26.

has criticized deterrence theory for assuming that the potential attacker is motivated solely by aggressive and offensive aims and who has instead emphasized that defensive reactions and perceptions of vulnerability are important in understanding challenges to deterrence, acknowledges this. Policymakers seek not only to counter threats to their security but also to restructure the status quo to their advantage. As Lebow explains, "Brinkmanship is thus more than a defensive reaction to threatening developments in the international environment. It is an attempt to secure a significant, perhaps even decisive hedge against such developments in the future."[10]

The Syrian intervention in Jordan was in part a reaction to King Hussein's decision to impose control over the PLO within Jordan. Intervention in support of the PLO, however, also provided Syria with an opportunity to help overthrow a regime that it had opposed for years and to establish a new, more militant regime with which it would have close ties and influence. In the Russo-Japanese confrontation, Japanese policymakers sought Russian recognition of Japan's predominant political and economic influence in Korea as a minimum goal and a virtual protectorate over Korea and the expulsion of the Russian military, economic, and political presence in Manchuria and Korea as a maximum goal. The important implication of this assumption is that in most international crises conflict may be resolved through diplomacy and negotiations because the potential attacker is not likely to be motivated solely by far-reaching and aggressive aims.[11]

The Calculus of Deterrence

An effective deterrent threat is credible and stable. As noted in chapter 1, a credible deterrent depends upon whether the defender appears to possess both the military capabilities to inflict substantial costs on an attacker and the will to use those capabilities if necessary. A stable deterrent avoids both increasing the potential attacker's fears of a preemptive strike and engaging the bargaining reputation of the poten-

10. Lebow, *Between Peace and War*, 66.

11. Snyder and Diesing's distinction between soft- and hard-line policymakers in decision-making helps to explain why both offensive and defensive motives influence and shape the potential attacker's objectives (Snyder and Diesing, *Conflict among Nations*, 297–309).

tial attacker to such an extent that negotiations become deadlocked in stalemate.

Four sets of variables are critical in determining the credibility and stability of the defender's deterrent threat and influence whether the potential attacker decides to challenge deterrence. These variables form the basis for developing hypotheses on the conditions under which deterrence is likely to succeed or fail. The four sets of factors can be divided into two broader categories: the structural features of a deterrence policy and the behavioral features of a deterrence policy.

The structural features of a deterrence policy include the balance of military capabilities between the potential attacker and the defender and protégé as well as the value of the protégé to the defender. These two structural features define the underlying military strength and interests at stake for the defender and have a crucial impact on the credibility of the defender's deterrent threat. What is the relative capacity of the defender to mobilize and deploy its armed forces in the early stages of an armed confrontation or its capacity to sustain its military strength in a prolonged war? What are the relatively stable and enduring ties between defender and protégé that are important enough to justify the defender using military force to protect the protégé if attacked?

. The behavioral features of a deterrence policy include the actions of the defender in previous international confrontations, the adoption of specific diplomatic strategies by the defender in the current case of attempted deterrence, and the movement and positioning of military forces by the defender in the current case of attempted deterrence. The behavioral features of a deterrence policy refer to both the past and current actions of the defender. The past behavior of the defender in interstate disputes may have an important impact on the credibility of the current deterrence attempt. Has the defender stood firm in defense of allies, or has it backed down under pressure in previous confrontations? The actions of the defender in the current confrontation influence both the credibility and stability of deterrence. Military preparations by the defender not only signal resolve and commitment to an ally; they can also be perceived as a threat and can provoke the potential attacker. The flexibility of the defender in negotiations can signal not only how determined the defender is to protect the protégé's interests but also whether the potential attacker can make concessions without serious damage to its bargaining reputation.

I have formulated hypotheses on the underlying structural conditions and the past behavior of the defender that contribute to the success of extended-immediate deterrence. I have also identified the short-term diplomatic and military actions of the defender that both enhance the credibility of deterrence and avoid provoking the potential attacker.

The military balance. In a situation of extended-immediate deterrence, the potential attacker wants to know how the defender can augment the military capabilities of the protégé and how this will affect the costs of using military force. Deterrence is likely to succeed when the potential attacker believes that the probability of military success is relatively low and that the costs of using military force to achieve its objectives are high. A potential attacker is likely to consider three options[12] for using military force: limited aims strategy, rapid offensive attack strategy, and attrition strategy.

The objective of a limited aims strategy is to seize control of and occupy a specific area of disputed or strategic territory held by an opponent. To achieve this goal an attacker may defeat the armed forces of the opponent in a well-protected border region or may seize territory that is poorly defended. The key to success for the attacker in seizing the territory is to achieve military surprise.[13] The attacker is then in a position to either overwhelm the opponent's underprepared forces or to occupy territory before the opponent can build up local forces. The attacker wishes to minimize direct contact with the military strength of the adversary and to use force where local superiority has been achieved.

Having seized the opponent's territory, the attacker assumes a

12. John J. Mearsheimer, *Conventional Deterrence* (Ithaca: Cornell University Press, 1983), 23–66, and Alexander George, David K. Hall, and William R. Simons, *The Limits of Coercive Diplomacy: Laos-Cuba-Vietnam* (Boston: Little, Brown, 1971), 15–21.

13. Strategic surprise occurs when a defender fails to react to intelligence information indicating a threat of attack and is militarily unprepared to counter the attack when it is launched. Tactical surprise occurs when a defender receives warning of an attack but has insufficient time to mobilize fully and position forces for optimal defense against the impending attack.

defensive posture and prepares for a potential counterattack, shifting the burden of escalation to the opponent. As John Mearsheimer explains, "The victim, should he choose to strike back, would have to attack an alerted and prepared defense. In essence, the attacker-turned-defender is saying to the victim: you can reestablish the status quo ante only by starting a war of attrition."[14] The attacker anticipates that the opponent will not start a war of attrition and will instead be forced to seek a political settlement or accept the change in the status quo. In 1973, Egypt occupied a narrow strip of territory on the east bank of the Suez Canal and formed defensive positions to repulse an Israeli counterattack in a carefully planned assault named Operation Shark. Egyptian leaders expected Israel to accept a stalemate reluctantly and believed that this limited military victory would have important political repercussions in the Arab-Israeli conflict.[15] A limited aims strategy often seeks quick but narrowly defined military objectives at low cost.

The second military strategy available to a potential attacker is rapid offensive attack. The principal objective of this strategy is the defeat and destruction of the opponent's armed forces. In contrast with the limited aims strategy, the goal is not to minimize armed combat and to seize disputed or strategic territory but to defeat the opponent's armed forces in a series of large-scale battles and to paralyze its fighting capacity. Although territory is occupied by the attacker in a rapid offensive attack, this results from the retreat and disorganization of the adversary's defeated forces and is not the primary objective of the attacker.

The attacker assumes that rapid destruction of the adversary's armed strength will force the adversary to accept defeat before it can mobilize the economy and the civilian population for war and before allies can effectively intervene in support. Thus, as with the limited arms strategy, the attacker seeks a quick military victory in order to avoid a larger and more costly war. In 1938 Hitler assumed that German armed forces could achieve such a rapid and decisive defeat of Czech forces that Britain and France would not be able to intervene before the military situation was completely hopeless.[16] When it at-

14. Mearsheimer, *Conventional Deterrence*, 53.

15. Ibid., 155–62; and Jervis, Lebow, and Stein, *Psychology and Deterrence*, 34–59.

16. I present a case study of the 1938 Czech Crisis in chapter 5.

tacked the United States in 1941, Japan gambled that it could inflict a string of such decisive defeats on U.S. armed forces in the early stages of a war that the United States would capitulate rather than continue fighting.[17] The attacker may, however, anticipate that outside powers will be able to intervene in defense of the target of attack and conclude that the armed conflict cannot be kept isolated. The attacker may nevertheless believe that it can defeat the combined forces of its adversaries without becoming engaged in a protracted war. German policymakers went to war in 1914 on the expectation, based on the Schlieffen Plan, that the armies of France and Russia could each be rapidly defeated by precisely planned major offensives against each country.[18]

The third military option available to a potential attacker is the strategy of attrition. The objective of a strategy of attrition is similar to that of the rapid offensive attack—decisive defeat of the adversary's armed forces. The principal difference between the two strategies, however, is in the time required to achieve military victory. With a strategy of attrition the attacker anticipates not a series of rapid and decisive victories but instead a protracted conflict in which the goal is to wear down the opponent until it can no longer fight. The attacker recognizes that armed conflict cannot be localized and that military victory will be costly. The strategy of attrition is analogous to the advance of a steamroller that slowly but surely presses ahead against all forms of resistance and eventually overwhelms all obstacles in its path. Rapid offensive attack in contrast seeks knockout of the adversary in the early stages of the armed conflict.

The probability of success and the costs to a potential attacker with each of these military strategies can depend on such variables as

---

17. Nobutaka Ike, ed. and trans., *Japan's Decision for War: Records of the 1941 Policy Conferences* (Stanford: Stanford University Press, 1967); Robert J. C. Butow, *Tojo and the Coming of the War* (Stanford: Stanford University Press, 1961); Bruce Russett, "Pearl Harbor: Deterrence Theory and Decision Theory," *Journal of Peace Research* 4: 2 (1967):89–105; and Michael A. Barnhart, "Japanese Intelligence before the Second World War: 'Best Case Analysis,' " in *Knowing One's Enemies: Intelligence Assessment before the Two World Wars,* ed. Ernest R. May (Princeton: Princeton University Press, 1985), 440–45.

18. L. C. F. Turner, "The Significance of the Schlieffen Plan," in *The War Plans of the Great Powers, 1880–1914,* ed. Paul M. Kennedy (London: Allen and Unwin, 1979), and Jack Snyder, *The Ideology of the Offensive: Military Decision Making and the Disasters of 1914* (Ithaca: Cornell University Press, 1984), 107–56.

terrain, force-to-space ratios, quality of armaments, and mobility of forces. One factor that is critical to a plan of attack is the balance of military forces between the attacker and the defender and protégé.[19] Consider a situation in which the potential attacker debates using a limited aims strategy to achieve its objectives. The potential attacker wishes to use its superior military position in a specific area of attack and to act before the opposition can deploy an effective defense. The best defense against a limited aims strategy is having sufficient, well-prepared forces at the point of likely attack, with reinforcements in position for quick backup support if necessary.

In a rapid offensive attack, the outcome of an armed confrontation between local units of the attacker and defender in a specific border area is not very important. The crucial question is what the outcome of major armed battles will be. The goal of the attacker is to defeat the adversary in the initial battle and to build on that advantage with a series of rapid attacks that complete the destruction of the adversary's main forces.

The critical impact of the balance of forces depends on the relative capacity of the attacker and defender to mobilize and deploy their standing armed forces on the battlefield. If the potential attacker can mobilize superior forces in the short term, then it is likely to achieve a decisive victory over the opponent by a rapid offensive attack. The capacity of the defender to prevent a decisive defeat and to establish a stalemate on the battlefield enhances the likelihood of successful deterrence.

The balance of forces is critical in determining the success of deterrence in a war of attrition. The attacker wishes to inflict heavy military losses on the opponent and exhaust its military strength. Success depends on the capacity of each side to sustain large armies on the battlefront for an extended time. To accomplish this, a country must be able to absorb heavy casualties and to constantly replace the equipment and arms lost on the battlefield. In Mearsheimer's words, "Success in a war of attrition largely depends on the size of the opposing forces. . . .

19. For an excellent analysis of the conventional balance of forces between NATO and the Warsaw Pact that incorporates a number of different dimensions of military capabilities see Barry R. Posen, "Measuring the European Conventional Balance: Coping with Complexity in Threat Assessment," *International Security* 9: 3 (1984–85):47–88.

The side with the greater manpower and a larger material base will ultimately prevail.''[20] For the manpower and material resource base to prove decisive, domestic political support for the war must be maintained and the state must possess the administrative capacity to mobilize the population and economy for war.

For all three military strategies of the potential attacker, increases in the balance of forces in favor of the defender reduce the likelihood of success and increase the costs of using force for the attacker. A favorable immediate balance of forces should thwart an attacker's limited aims strategy or rapid offensive attack strategy that is designed to defeat the protégé before the defender can intervene, whereas a favorable short-term balance of forces should deny the attacker a victory in a rapid offensive attack that is designed to defeat both the defender and protégé. Finally, a favorable long-term balance of forces should reduce the chances of victory for the attacker in a war of attrition. In all three cases, deterrence should succeed.

A potential attacker is unlikely to initiate a war of attrition deliberately. A critical constraint on the use of military force for a potential attacker is minimizing the costs of military victory. Victory in a war of attrition, even if likely, is not an attractive military option because of the high costs involved.

A number of recent studies have argued persuasively that military organizations are biased toward doctrines and strategies that call for the rapid and decisive use of military force.[21] The desire by the military to increase the autonomy and the resource base of the armed services contributes to this bias. Offensive doctrines require larger military forces, which justify increased and high levels of defense spending. Carefully designed and more complex offensive doctrines also reduce the opportunity for civilian intervention in operational planning. In his study of the influence of the military on U.S. decisions in crises since

20. Mearsheimer, *Conventional Deterrence*, 34.
21. Jack L. Snyder, "Civil-Military Relations and the Cult of the Offensive, 1914 and 1984," *International Security* 9: 1 (1984):118–22; Stephen Van Evera, *Causes of War* (Ph.D. diss., University of California, Berkeley, 1984), chap. 7; and Barry R. Posen, *The Sources of Military Doctrine: France, Britain, and Germany between the World Wars* (Ithaca: Cornell University Press, 1984), 47–50. See also Jack S. Levy, "Organizational Routines and the Causes of War," *International Studies Quarterly* 30: 2 (1986):193–222.

1945, Betts argues that military advice has generally counseled against the use of force unless the United States was in a strong military position to defeat the adversary quickly and decisively.[22] Contemporary Soviet doctrine for conventional war in Europe seeks a quick and decisive military victory by means of a blitzkrieg offensive against NATO forces.[23] Political leaders have a strong interest in avoiding costly armed conflicts and sanctioning the use of force when a rapid and decisive victory is anticipated. In a prolonged war, heavy battlefield casualties and substantial economic burdens on the population may lead to a loss of elite or broad domestic political support. Arthur Stein has reported that popular support for U.S. participation in World War II, the Korean War, and the Vietnam War declined steadily over time.[24] For Russia, the Russo-Japanese War in 1904–05 produced a severe political crisis and World War I led to the collapse of the czarist regime and a revolution. In his study of historical cases of conventional deterrence, Mearsheimer found that military leaders were often under considerable pressure from political leaders to devise plans of attack that projected a quick victory.[25]

If policymakers believe that a quick and decisive attack will be successful, then deterrence is likely to fail. Conversely, if policymakers estimate that military force cannot be applied successfully in a quick and low-cost manner, then deterrence is likely to prevail. Calculations regarding the outcome of a protracted conflict have less impact on deterrence outcomes because policymakers generally do not initiate the use of force with the intention of engaging in a lengthy armed conflict. Aggressors have often mistakenly assumed that they could rapidly defeat their adversaries.[26] Consider German calculations

22. Richard K. Betts, *Soldiers, Statesmen, and Cold War Crises* (Cambridge: Harvard University Press, 1977), 3–15.

23. Mearsheimer, *Conventional Deterrence,* 165–88; Michael MccGwire, *Military Objectives in Soviet Foreign Policy* (Washington, D.C.: Brookings Institution, 1987), 67–89; and Philip A. Peterson and John G. Hines, "The Conventional Offensive in Soviet Theater Strategy," *Orbis* 27: 3 (1983):695–739.

24. Arthur Stein, *The Nation at War* (Baltimore: Johns Hopkins University Press, 1980). See also John Mueller, *War, Presidents, and Public Opinion* (New York: Wiley, 1973), and Timothy Cotton, "War and American Democracy," *Journal of Conflict Resolution* 30: 4 (1986):616–35.

25. Mearsheimer, *Conventional Deterrence,* chaps. 4, 5, 8.

26. This is particularly true of wars between Great Powers. The long-term balance of forces is often critical to understanding which side will prevail in the protracted

that war with France and Russia in 1914 would last a few months at most, Hitler's belief that the Soviet Union could be defeated in 1941 in a similar period of time, or Iraqi expectations of a quick victory over Iran in 1980. The important point is that the initial decision of whether to wage war is generally based on a potential attacker's estimate of the chances of military victory at the outset to early stages of armed conflict.

Hypothesis 1.1: The probability of deterrence success increases as the balance of military forces between attacker and defender shifts to the advantage of the defender. The immediate and short-term balance of military forces will have a greater impact on deterrence outcomes than will the long-term balance of military forces.[27]

The possession of nuclear weapons by a small number of states since 1945 has introduced another component of the military balance. A good deal of controversy exists concerning the deterrent value of nuclear weapons in international relations.[28] It can be argued that the destructive power of nuclear weapons is so great that adversaries will be extremely cautious in challenging a nuclear power for fear of provoking a nuclear response. Thus even if the threat of nuclear retaliation is uncertain, the potential costs to an adversary are so great that the possession of nuclear weapons may be a powerful deterrent. As Michael Howard states, "When we discuss the question of nuclear credibility we are doing so on a quite unique scale of magnitude—or, if

---

conflict. See Paul M. Kennedy, *The Rise and Fall of the Great Powers: Economic Change and Military Conflict from 1500 to 2000* (New York: Random House, 1987); and Paul M. Kennedy, "The First World War and the International Power System," *International Security* 9:1(1984):7–40.

27. This is a refinement of the concept of the local balance of forces presented in Paul Huth and Bruce Russett, "What Makes Deterrence Work? Cases from 1900 to 1980," *World Politics* 36: 4 (1984):509–10.

28. Robert Jervis, *The Illogic of American Nuclear Strategy* (Ithaca: Cornell University Press, 1984), chap. 5; and Richard K. Betts, *Nuclear Blackmail and Nuclear Balance* (Washington, D.C.: Brookings Institution, 1987). Barry M. Blechman and Stephen S. Kaplan, *Force without War: U.S. Armed Forces as a Political Instrument* (Washington, D.C.: Brookings Institution, 1978), 127–29, report that the balance of strategic power was not strongly correlated with favorable outcomes for the United States in confrontations with the Soviet Union.

such a word exists, minitude. A microscopic degree of credibility, as of some hideously powerful poison, may be all that is needed to work effectively.''[29]

The credibility of nuclear retaliation will vary depending on the political-military situation. To defend oneself against conventional attack and to prevent a nuclear attack on one's own territory, the threat of nuclear retaliation is likely to be credible.[30] In this study, of the fifteen cases in which the defender possessed nuclear weapons, the potential attacker was a nonnuclear power in fourteen cases (the only exception is the 1979 case in which the People's Republic of China (PRC) was the potential attacker and the Soviet Union was the defender of Vietnam). When the potential target is a nonnuclear power, the deterrent value of nuclear weapons will be minimal for two reasons. First, nuclear use would be likely to increase the incentives for horizontal nuclear proliferation, which the existing nuclear powers have consistently opposed. Second, the potential for collateral damage to civilians, whether the weapons were used tactically on the territory of the protégé or were targeted directly at attacker territory, might provoke strong criticism internationally and domestically. Explicit nuclear threats conveyed by the movement and alerting of nuclear forces may have a greater deterrent value despite the political and military costs described above, but there are only two such cases in this study: the Berlin blockade confrontation of 1948 and the Quemoy-Matsu crisis of 1955. As a result, I have not attempted to test the proposition.[31]

Hypothesis 1.2: The possession of nuclear weapons and the latent threat of nuclear use by the defender will not increase the probability of extended deterrence success when the potential attacker is a non-nuclear power.

29. Michael Howard, *The Causes of Wars,* 2nd ed. (Cambridge: Harvard University Press, 1984), 95–96. See also John J. Mearsheimer, ''Nuclear Weapons and Deterrence in Europe,'' *International Security* 9: 3 (1984–85):22.

30. The credibility of NATO's threat of first use of nuclear weapons depends not so much on a deliberate decision to initiate nuclear war but, more importantly, the potential for the breakdown of centralized political control stemming from problems of command and control in the European theater. See Paul Bracken, *The Command and Control of Nuclear Forces* (New Haven: Yale University Press, 1983), 129–78, and Daniel Charles, *Nuclear Planning in NATO: Pitfalls of First Use* (Cambridge: Ballinger, 1987).

31. For a detailed examination of explicit nuclear threats in the postwar period, see Betts, *Nuclear Blackmail and Nuclear Balance.*

The value of the protégé. The willingness of the defender to incur the costs of using military force to protect its protégé depends on the economic and political-military value of the protégé. If a potential attacker does not believe that a defender has important interests at stake in the protection of its ally, then the potential attacker is likely to question the credibility of its deterrent threat. As Alexander George and Richard Smoke argue, "Sophisticated opponents will judge credibility on the basis of a more fundamental analysis of the defender's interests. . . . the opponent is likely to pay more attention to strategic, political, economic, and ideological factors determining the nature and magnitude of those interests than to rhetorical and other signaling devices the defending power may employ to enhance credibility."[32]

The value of the protégé to the defender is determined in part by the economic and political-military ties linking the defender to the protégé. The stronger those links, the more important they are to the defender to protect. One way in which a defender can demonstrate its interest in the security of another state is to form a military alliance, pledging that it will come to the aid of that state if attacked. The terms of an alliance treaty may not specify the conditions under which a country will intervene or the exact form of aid to be provided. A defense pact, however, specifies the conditions under which a commitment to aid an ally exists and the extent of military assistance to be provided.

Alliance commitments are credible because states value their reputations for honoring agreements and for being willing to use force in support of allies. A failure to honor an alliance commitment may not only undermine the credibility of a country's remaining commitments; it may also make it difficult for that country to cultivate allies in the future. As Sir Edward Grey argued in 1906, the failure of Great Britain to support France fully in the confrontation with Germany over Morocco would have far-reaching consequences: "The United States would despise us, Russia would not think it worth while to make a friendly arrangement with us about Asia, Japan would prepare to re-insure herself elsewhere, we should be left without a friend and without the power of making a friend."[33]

Empirical evidence supports the conclusion that policymakers value their country's reputation for honoring alliances. Bruce Bueno de

32. George and Smoke, *Deterrence in American Foreign Policy,* 560-61.
33. As quoted in Bernadotte E. Schmitt, *The Coming of the War, 1914,* vol. 1 (New York: Howard Fertig, 1966), 37.

Mesquita reports that, in the period from 1816–1965, 76 percent of allied nations that were attacked received armed support from one or more allies, whereas only 17 percent of nonallied states received such aid.[34] Bruce Russett and I report that the probability of a defender extending armed support to a protégé that is attacked increased by more than 40 percent when the defender and protégé shared an alliance.[35]

Hypothesis 2.1: The probability of deterrence success will increase if the defender and protégé are linked by a military alliance.

Less direct military ties between defender and protégé can also persuade a potential attacker that the defender has important interests at stake in protecting its protégé. Arms transfers from defender to protégé often either reflect close political ties or provide the basis for developing closer relations. The dependence of regional powers on arms transfers from a Great Power provides indirect evidence of a Great Power's sphere of influence in a region and of those states with which it is most closely aligned. Arms transfer ties do not represent a formal commitment between states, but they often evolve into tacit alliances in which the provider of arms is perceived by other states as the protector of its local client.[36] A Great Power's prestige becomes intertwined with the security of its client. Furthermore, a defender may view years of arms

34. Bruce Bueno de Mesquita, *The War Trap* (New Haven: Yale University Press, 1981), 113.

35. Paul Huth and Bruce Russett, "Deterrence Failure and Escalation to War," *International Studies Quarterly,* 32: 1 (1988):40–42. The evidence concerning the deterrent value of alliances is ambiguous. Randolph M. Siverson and Michael R. Tennefoss, "Power, Alliance, and the Escalation of International Conflict, 1815–1965," *American Political Science Review* 78: 4 (1984):1057–69; and H. K. Tillema and J. R. Van Wingen, "Law and Power in Military Intervention by Major States after WWII," *International Studies Quarterly* 26: 2 (1982):220–50, report that alliance ties are associated with deterrence success. But Jack Levy, "Alliance Formation and War Behavior: An Analysis of the Great Powers, 1495–1975," *Journal of Conflict Resolution* 25: 4 (1981):581–614; Bruce M. Russett, "The Calculus of Deterrence," *Journal of Conflict Resolution* 7: 1 (1963):97–109; and Paul Huth and Bruce Russett, "What Makes Deterrence Work?" found no association between alliances and successful deterrence.

36. Huth and Russett report that arms transfers from defender to protégé were associated with a greater likelihood of successful extended deterrence ("What Makes Deterrence Work?").

transfers as an investment that should be protected.[37] Senator Richard Russell argued along these lines when explaining why the United States could not withdraw from South Vietnam, "It was a mistake to get involved there in the first place; I have never been able to see any strategic, political, or economic advantage to be gained by our involvement. . . . Whether or not the initial decision was a mistake is now moot. The United States does have a commitment in South Vietnam. The flag is there. U.S. honor and prestige are there."[38]

In the Middle East Soviet influence has been tied to the Soviet role as the principal arms supplier for a number of Arab states, such as Egypt, Syria, Iraq, and more recently Libya.[39] Soviet-Egyptian relations have closely followed trends in arms transfer linkages between the two countries. Before the mid-fifties, relations between the two countries were not particularly close. The emergence of the Soviet Union as the principal source of military arms for Egypt from the mid-fifties to the early seventies led in part to such close ties between the two countries that the Soviets intervened in the War of Attrition to protect Egypt from strategic bombing raids by the Israeli air force in 1970 and threatened military intervention to protect an Egyptian army threatened with encirclement in 1973. Since 1973 Egypt's decision to establish closer political and military ties with the United States has resulted in the virtual termination of military arms transfer ties between the Soviet Union and Egypt and the movement of Egypt away from the Soviet sphere of influence in the Middle East.

Hypothesis 2.2: The probability of deterrence success increases as the dependence of the protégé on military arms transfers from the defender increases.

Economic considerations can also determine how vital the protégé is to the security of the defender. Extensive foreign trade between

37. Leslie H. Gelb and Richard K. Betts, *The Irony of Vietnam: The System Worked* (Washington, D.C.: Brookings Institution, 1979), 192, 213, 216.

38. Ibid., 216.

39. U.S. Central Intelligence Agency, *Communist Aid Activities in Non-Communist Less Developed Countries, 1954–1979* (Washington, D.C.: Government Printing Office, 1980), and U.S. Arms Control and Disarmament Agency, *World Military Expenditures and Arms Transfers* (Washington, D.C.: Government Printing Office, 1965–85).

defender and protégé provides evidence of both the economic interests linking the two countries and the potential costs if the protégé is forced by the attacker to cut its ties with the defender. Exports from the defender to the protégé increase domestic employment and contribute to a favorable balance of payments. Imports from the protégé may provide raw materials and essential commodities for military or commercial production by the defender. The economic costs of a disruption or threatened loss of foreign trade with the protégé may provide strong incentives for a defender to use force if necessary to protect the protégé—incentives that enhance the credibility of the defender's deterrent threat.[40]

Hypothesis 2.3: The probability of deterrence success increases with higher levels of foreign trade between defender and protégé.

The value of the protégé may also influence the outcome of deterrence by shaping the potential attacker's assessment of the issues at stake. The potential attacker will ask what are the prospective gains and concessions to be attained by coercing the protégé and whether they justify the risks and potential costs of armed conflict. The more substantial the gains for the potential attacker, the stronger the incentive to risk armed conflict in the dispute with the protégé and defender and therefore the more difficult to achieve successful deterrence. One way to assess the issues at stake is to determine the strategic and military importance of the protégé to the potential attacker. If the protégé shares a border with the potential attacker, then dominance of the protégé is important to establishing a friendly buffer state against external threats or as a territorial basis for projecting military power beyond the potential attacker's own borders. Control over the foreign policy of a neighboring state can advance both defensive and offensive goals for the potential attacker.

40. Both Russett, "The Calculus of Deterrence," and Huth and Russett, "What Makes Deterrence Work?" found that foreign trade between defender and protégé was associated with successful extended deterrence. Direct foreign investment by the defender in the protégé's economy would theoretically increase the economic interests at stake and therefore the credibility of deterrence. Data on foreign investment are sketchy and unavailable for many cases prior to World War II.

Hypothesis 3.1: The probability of deterrence success decreases if the potential attacker is contiguous with the protégé.

The strategic importance of the protégé is also reflected in its size. Because a large population provides one of the bases for the military strength of a country, the foreign and defense policies of a protégé with a large population have important national security implications for the potential attacker. The potential attacker would at least like to prevent the protégé from developing close military ties with states that are considered adversaries. Preferably, the potential attacker would pursue policies that lead to close cooperative military ties with the protégé and thus enhance its relative military position in the future.

Hypothesis 3.2: The larger the population of the protégé, the lower the probability that deterrence will succeed.

The final way to assess the issues at stake is to examine the strategic value of economic ties between protégé and potential attacker. The critical question for the potential attacker is whether the protégé is a source of raw materials that are important to military production. If the protégé is a source of such raw materials and the potential attacker must import one or more of those raw materials, then substantial military gains are associated with strong economic ties to the protégé. Less compelling than the direct strategic importance of economic ties with the protégé would be a situation in which the protégé was a source of vital raw materials but the potential attacker was self-sufficient. In such a situation, denying adversaries the military advantages of economic ties with the protégé would be of indirect strategic value.

Hypothesis 3.3: If the protégé is a source of strategic raw materials that the potential attacker must import, then the probability of deterrence success will decrease.

Bargaining behavior. The potential attacker's uncertainty about both the defender's intentions and sensitivity to challenges illustrates the importance of the defender's bargaining behavior. An effective bargaining strategy by the defender reduces the potential attacker's uncertainty and thereby enhances credibility, whereas ineffective strategies reduce credibility and may provoke the potential attacker. The optimal bargaining strategy enhances the defender's credibility and avoids provocation of the potential attacker.

Two principal dimensions comprise the bargaining process between the potential attacker and defender: (1) diplomacy and negotiations and (2) military preparations and the movement of forces.[41] The diplomatic dimension of the bargaining process consists of the communication of policy positions by each state and the exchange of competing proposals for the terms of a negotiated settlement. Diplomacy and negotiations can provide crucial feedback for a potential attacker on both the salience of the interests at stake for the defender and the defender's determination to support its protégé. The flexibility of the defender in the negotiations can determine for the attacker the costs of cooperation. That is, can the potential attacker back down from its threat and accept the terms of a diplomatic solution without feeling that its bargaining reputation has been compromised? Will the terms of an agreement that reestablishes the status quo be too costly for the potential attacker to submit to, or will such terms be acceptable?

The military dimension of bargaining consists of the movement and positioning of military forces by the defender. Military preparations by the defender can signal the defender's resolve and capacity to use military force in support of its protégé and can thus influence the potential attacker's estimate of the costs of challenging the defender's deterrent threat.

The military and diplomatic bargaining behavior of the defender can range on a three-point scale of cooperation and coercion from accommodation and caution to reciprocity to intransigence and maximum preparedness. How effective is each bargaining strategy in balancing the requirements of deterrence credibility and stability?

Military preparations by the defender can enhance the credibility of deterrence by demonstrating the defender's intention to use force if necessary as well as its capacity to intervene in a timely and effective manner. At the same time, the military preparations could provoke the potential attacker and heighten fears of a preemptive strike or perceptions of deliberate intimidation. The timing and extent of military

---

41. Snyder and Diesing, *Conflict among Nations*, 183–281.

escalation by each state is critical to the strategic interaction. Three general policies of military escalation are available to the defender:[42] (1) *Policy of strength*—the defender responds to the military actions of the potential attacker with greater than equal levels of military preparedness; (2) *Policy of tit for tat*—the defender responds to military actions of the potential attacker with equal levels of military preparedness; and (3) *Policy of caution*—the defender responds to military actions of the potential attacker with less than equal levels of military preparedness.

Henry Kissinger argues that a policy of strength is more effective than a policy of caution or tit for tat:

> In my view what seems "balanced" and "safe" in a crisis is often the most risky. Gradual escalation tempts the opponent to match every move; what is intended as a show of moderation may be interpreted as irresolution. . . . A leader must choose carefully and thoughtfully the issues over which to face confrontation. . . . Once he is committed, however, his obligation is to end the confrontation rapidly. For this he must convey implacability. He must be prepared to escalate rapidly and brutally.[43]

A policy of caution by the defender minimizes the risks of provocation and thereby enhances deterrence stability. Military unpreparedness, however, may undermine the defender's credibility. The critical problem with a policy of caution is that it is tailored for a potential attacker that is motivated only by a sense of vulnerability and limited defensive goals. Such a policy fails to recognize that the potential attacker is also likely to consider more ambitious goals to alter the status quo to its advantage.

Defenders of the status quo often believe that a strong military response to the threats of an adversary will escalate a crisis, whereas moderation will contribute to resolution of the conflict. A cautious policy of military escalation in crises, however, can be counterproduc-

---

42. This categorization draws on the work of ibid., 209–43; Russell J. Leng and Hugh G. Wheeler, "Influence Strategies, Success, and War," *Journal of Conflict Resolution* 23: 4 (1979):655–84; and Noel Kaplowitz, "Psychological Dimensions of International Relations: The Reciprocal Effects of Conflict Strategies," *International Studies Quarterly* 28: 4 (1984):373–406.

43. Henry Kissinger, *White House Years* (Boston: Little, Brown, 1979), 621.

tive either by signaling the defender's lack of resolve or placing the defender in a weak military position to repulse an attack if it actually occurs. The decision by the British government not to respond to indications of an Argentine threat to invade the Falklands Islands for fear of provoking the junta only reinforced the Argentine belief that Britain would not intervene militarily if the islands were seized.[44] The decision by Israeli policymakers in the fall of 1973 to avoid military actions that might provoke Egypt resulted in Israeli unpreparedness when Egypt attacked and losses in the initial stages of the war.[45] Betts reports that states that have delayed mobilization to avoid provocation of the adversary are often the victim of surprise attack.[46]

A policy of military strength puts the defender in a favorable position to intervene if deterrence fails. But it may also increase the likelihood that deterrence will fail by causing the attacker to either fear a preemptive strike or become determined to avoid concessions under pressure. Such a policy is optimal if the potential attacker is motivated solely by offensive aims, but it may provoke a potential attacker with more limited defensive objectives and self-perceptions of vulnerability.

A policy of tit for tat in military escalation by the defender may most effectively balance deterrence stability and credibility. Reciprocity—responding in kind to the military preparations of the potential attacker—enhances credibility by signaling the defender's resolve to accept the risks of escalation. Deterrence stability is preserved because the level of military escalation by the defender does not exceed that of the potential attacker, avoids placing the potential attacker's forces in an acutely vulnerable position, and reduces the political costs of retreating for the potential attacker. A tit-for-tat policy of military escalation is effective primarily in situations in which the security dilemma exists but not in cases in which there are psychological biases that lead a potential attacker to exaggerate and misperceive provocation. In the latter case a policy of caution would probably be more effective because any substantial level of escalation by the defender might be perceived as threatening given the potential attacker's psychological

44. Jervis, Lebow and Stein, *Psychology and Deterrence,* 89–124.

45. Ibid., 60–88, and Michael Brecher, *Decisions in Crisis: Israel, 1967 and 1973* (Berkeley: University of California Press, 1980), 171–229.

46. Richard K. Betts, *Surprise Attack: Lessons for Defense Planning* (Washington, D.C.: Brookings Institution, 1982).

predispositions. Presumably, the credibility of the defender's actions is not seriously questioned in such cases.

Experimental evidence, as reported by social psychologists, and the work of such game theorists as Robert Axelrod support the argument that a policy of tit for tat is generally an effective strategy for eliciting cooperation from an adversary.[47] In a number of studies on crisis bargaining, Russell Leng reports that a policy of reciprocity was an effective strategy for conflict resolution between states.[48]

Hypothesis 4.1: The adoption of a policy of tit for tat in military escalation by the defender will increase the probability of deterrence success as compared with alternative policies of military escalation.

The defender must also balance deterrence stability and credibility in a diplomatic strategy. An effective diplomatic strategy demonstrates the defender's commitment to the security of the protégé and reduces the political costs of backing down for the potential attacker. Three general diplomatic strategies are available to a defender:[49] (1) *Bullying strategy*—the defender adopts a firm and unyielding position and does not reciprocate accommodative initiatives taken by the potential attacker; (2) *Firm-but-flexible strategy*—the defender adopts a mixed policy of standing firm in response to the repeated demands of the potential attacker while offering compromise based on reciprocal ac-

47. Martin Patchen, "Strategies for Eliciting Cooperation from an Adversary: Applications to Relations between Nations," *Journal of Conflict Resolution* 31: 1 (1987):164–85, and Robert Axelrod, *The Evolution of Cooperation* (New York: Basic Books, 1984).

48. Russell J. Leng, "Reagan and the Russians: Crisis Bargaining Beliefs and the Historical Record," *American Political Science Review* 78: 2 (1984):338–55; Charles Gochman and Russell J. Leng, "Realpolitik and the Road to War: An Analysis of Attributes and Behavior," *International Studies Quarterly* 27: 1 (1983):97–120; Russell J. Leng and Charles S. Gochman, "Dangerous Disputes: A Study of Conflict Behavior and War," *American Journal of Political Science* 26: 4 (1982):654–87; and Russell J. Leng and Hugh G. Wheeler, "Influence Strategies, Success, and War," *Journal of Conflict Resolution* 23: 4 (1979):655–84.

49. This categorization of diplomatic strategies draws on the work of Snyder and Diesing, *Conflict among Nations,* 243–51; Kaplowitz, "Psychological Dimensions of International Relations"; Leng and Wheeler, "Influence Strategies, Success, and War"; and Robert O. Keohane, "Reciprocity in International Relations," *International Organization* 40: 1 (1986):4.

commodation; and (3) *Conciliatory strategy*—the defender adopts a policy of concessions and accommodation despite a lack of reciprocation by the potential attacker.

An intransigent diplomatic stance clearly signals the defender's intention to support the protégé and risk armed conflict if negotiations break down. The defender's refusal to reciprocate concessions, however, is likely to increase the potential attacker's estimate of the costs of backing down and accepting the status quo. Loss of political influence and stature are the potential short-term domestic costs of inaction for the policymakers of the potential attacker. The potential long-term foreign policy consequences include a loss of influence over the policies of allies and adversaries due to perceptions that the potential attacker was averse to risk and susceptible to diplomatic and military coercion.[50] A bullying diplomatic strategy shares the weakness of a policy of strength in military escalation: defender credibility is maximized at the expense of deterrence stability.

Conciliation in negotiations by the defender avoids the problems associated with a bullying strategy and strengthens deterrence stability. Conciliation is an effective strategy of conflict resolution, however, only if the potential attacker is motivated solely by limited defensive goals. In such a case unilateral concessions by the defender may resolve the issues in conflict without signaling a lack of determination to support the protégé. But if the potential attacker also desires substantial gains, then unilateral concessions may encourage it to push for greater concessions. The credibility of the defender's commitment to the protégé is thus weakened, and the potential attacker may attempt further coercion.

The most effective diplomatic approach for the defender is, then, a mixed strategy in which opposition to the demands of the potential attacker is coupled with diplomatic initiatives to break negotiating deadlocks through reciprocal compromise. Opposition to the demands of the potential attacker demonstrates determination to support the protégé, whereas conditional offers of compromise signal to the potential attacker the possibility of reaching an agreement that protects its

50. It should be emphasized that whether allies and adversaries draw conclusions from the behavior of other states in specific cases is an empirical question. Policymakers are, however, generally concerned that other states will draw conclusions from behavior and decisions in particular cases.

political position and bargaining reputation. If the potential attacker has decided to back down from its initial threat, the defender's offer of conditional compromise may provide the means to de-escalate.[51] Another advantage of a firm-but-flexible strategy is that it enables the defender and potential attacker to identify possible trade-offs based on differences in each state's priorities.[52] It should be emphasized that the defender does not sacrifice the vital interests of the protégé while exploring trade-offs in negotiations with the potential attacker. The defender's offer of reciprocal compromise may overcome what Axelrod terms the "echo effect," in which the initial defection of the adversary triggers an unending process of reciprocal defection unless the adversary initiates a cooperative move. A firm-but-flexible strategy is more cooperative than a strict tit-for-tat policy.[53] Schelling captures the essential problem of devising a diplomatic strategy for the defender and the reason that a firm-but-flexible strategy is potentially very effective: "Equally important [for the defender] is to help to decouple an adversary's prestige and reputation from a dispute; if we cannot afford to back down we must hope that he can, and if necessary, help him."[54]

Hypothesis 4.2: The adoption of a firm-but-flexible diplomatic strategy by the defender will increase the probability of deterrence success as compared with alternative diplomatic strategies.

51. Robert Jervis, *Perception and Misperception in International Politics* (Princeton: Princeton University Press, 1976), 101 also argues that policies that reduce the costs of retreating for the adversary will enhance the likelihood of deterrence success.

52. James D. Morrow, "A Spatial Model of International Conflict," and T. Clifton Morgan, "A Spatial Model of Crisis Bargaining," *International Studies Quarterly* 20: 4 (1984):407–26. See also Robert Fisher, "Fractionating Conflict," in *International Conflict and Behavioral Science,* ed. Roger Fisher (New York: Basic Books, 1964), 91–109.

53. Axelrod, *Evolution of Cooperation,* 186–87. See also Per Molander, "The Optimal Level of Generosity in a Selfish, Uncertain Environment," *Journal of Conflict Resolution* 29: 4 (1985):611–18, and Edward Saraydar, "Modeling the Role of Conflict and Conciliation in Bargaining," *Journal of Conflict Resolution* 28: 3 (1984):420–50.

54. Thomas Schelling, *Arms and Influence* (New Haven: Yale University Press, 1966), 125. A similar argument has been used to help explain why economic sanctions often fail to achieve compliance—the public nature of most sanctions make it difficult for the target to reverse policy without a loss of face. See James Lindsay, "Trade Sanctions as Policy Instruments," *International Studies Quarterly* 30: 2 (1986):160; and David A. Baldwin, *Economic Statecraft* (Princeton: Princeton University Press, 1985), 142.

Past behavior. Uncertainty about the reactions of an adversary and the risks of escalation make an international crisis dangerous and unpredictable. The uncertainty of a crisis also allows states to manipulate the risks of escalation to deter or compel adversaries.[55] A critical variable, which may then influence the outcome of deterrence, is a potential attacker's perception of the risk-taking propensities of its adversary.

A potential attacker can gauge the risk-taking propensities of a defender by considering its behavior in previous international confrontations. Such behavior may suggest its actions in a current dispute and may color the credibility of its current deterrent threat. Many studies of deterrence theory assume that a state's commitments are interdependent. As Schelling states, "Few parts of the world are intrinsically worth the risk of serious war by themselves. . . . but defending them or running risks to protect them may preserve one's commitments to action in other parts of the world and at later times. 'Face' is merely the interdependence of a country's commitments: it is a country's reputation for action, the expectation other countries have about its behavior."[56] Thus even if the defender lacks vital interests in the immediate conflict, it may still credibly threaten intervention to strengthen its general bargaining reputation and its commitments to more important states.

If the deterrent threat is to be perceived as credible, the defender must convince a potential attacker that the outcome of the immediate conflict is closely connected with the protection of vital interests. American policymakers in the postwar period have tried to protect the United States's reputation of being willing to risk war in support of containment.[57] Secretary of State John Foster Dulles argued that the Chinese threat to occupy the offshore islands of Quemoy and Matsu in September 1958 challenged U.S. interests: "You cannot isolate it and say that the only problem involved here is Quemoy and Matsu. What is involved, and what is under threat, is the entire position of the United States and that of its free-world allies in the Western Pacific, extending

55. Schelling, *Arms and Influence,* 92–125.

56. Ibid., 124.

57. Robert H. Johnson, "Exaggerating America's Stakes in Third World Conflicts," *International Security* 10: 3 (1985–86):32–68, and Patrick Morgan, "Saving Face for the Sake of Deterrence," in Jervis, Lebow, and Stein, *Psychology and Deterrence,* 125–52.

from Japan, Korea, Okinawa, Formosa, the Philippines, on down to Southeast Asia.''[58]

The work of Robert Jervis suggests that historical events affect policymakers most when they or their country is directly involved. Jervis argues that personal experience can be a powerful determinant of a policymaker's image of an opponent.[59] The past behavior of the defender can thus be divided into two sets of cases: cases of attempted extended deterrence in which the identity of the potential attacker varied from case to case and those conflicts in which the defender confronted the same potential attacker as in the current case of extended-immediate deterrence.

Hypothesis 5.1: The past behavior of the defender in confrontations in which the current attacker was directly involved will have a greater impact on deterrence outcomes than in cases in which the current attacker was not directly involved.

A record of firm-but-flexible bargaining by the defender increases the probability of future deterrence success. A record of making concessions under coercion and being unwilling to risk armed conflict weakens the defender's future credibility, whereas a record of intransigence and bullying will have already imposed domestic and international costs on the potential attacker and left it determined to protect its bargaining reputation and avoid another retreat before the defender.[60]

Hypothesis 5.2: Firm-but-flexible bargaining by the defender in past confrontations between defender and potential attacker enhances the deterrent actions of the defender in the next confrontation between the two states. If the defender, however, has adopted a bullying or conciliatory strategy in the past, then the probability of deterrence failure in the next confrontation increases.

58. U.S. Department of State, *American Foreign Policy Current Documents 1958* (Washington, D.C.: Government Printing Office, 1962), 1153.

59. Robert Jervis, *Perception and Misperception,* 239–70.

60. See Russell J. Leng, ''When Will They Ever Learn? Coercive Bargaining in Recurrent Crises,'' *Journal of Conflict Resolution* 27: 3 (1983):379–419. Hypotheses 5.1 and 5.2 represent refinements of Huth and Russett, ''What Makes Deterrence Work?'' in which we analyzed the past behavior of the defender only for past cases of attempted extended deterrence.

4

Testing Hypotheses
On Deterrence

T he hypotheses formulated for empirical testing represent both complementary and competing explanations for the outcome of extended-immediate deterrence. Hypotheses on the military balance and the bargaining strategies, for example, supplement each other by examining both the defender's capabilities to inflict costs on the potential attacker in an armed confrontation and indicators of the defender's determination to use force if needed to protect the protégé. To examine either the military balance or bargaining strategies exclusively would result in too narrow an analysis of the factors influencing deterrence outcomes.

At the same time, the relative weight given to variables by the potential attacker in its calculus of deterrence enables me to test the hypotheses as competing explanations of deterrence outcomes. The credibility of the defender's deterrent threat is influenced, for example, by the potential attacker's estimate of the defender's intent to use force. A number of variables can influence that estimate—the bargaining behavior of the defender, the strength of economic and military ties between defender and protégé, and the past behavior of the defender. The critical question, then, is which variables the potential attacker consistently considers in gauging the defender's intentions. Is the defender's reputation for firmness or weakness a more important determinant than the specific interests at stake, or are the diplomatic and military actions of the defender even more critical in signaling intentions?

To identify the political and military conditions under which deterrence is likely to succeed or fail, I have tested the relative explanatory power of the hypotheses formulated in chapter 3 on the historical cases of attempted extended-immediate deterrence from 1885 to 1984 using probit analysis. I begin by defining the theoretical and operational criteria for the measurement of variables and subsequently report the empirical results of the probit analysis on the fifty-eight historical cases of attempted extended-immediate deterrence.

Measurement of Variables

The military balance. To test the impact of the balance of military forces on deterrence outcomes, I have constructed three measures of the military balance: the immediate balance of military forces, the short-term balance of military forces, and the long-term balance of military forces. Each of these measures corresponds to the balance of military forces that predominantly determines the outcome of the three principal military strategies available to a potential attacker: limited aims, rapid offensive attack, and attrition, respectively.[1]

The immediate balance of forces can critically influence the outcome of a limited aims strategy by the potential attacker. To seize a disputed or strategic area of the adversary's territory, the potential attacker wishes to occupy the territory before the adversary has had a chance to deploy local forces. By attaining local superiority in forces, the potential attacker seeks to defeat the adversary in a quick and low-cost military operation over a few days or weeks at most. The critical factor determining the success or failure of this strategy for the potential attacker is whether it can mobilize superior local forces at the outset of armed confrontation. In 1898 a small contingent of French troops advanced to Fashoda to claim the territory before British forces could arrive and oppose their plans. The French plans, however, were frustrated when a much larger British force soon landed at Fashoda. The immediate balance of local ground forces shifted decisively, as a result,

1. I have used operational indicators of the balance of military capabilities based on comparisons of manpower of the potential attacker and the defender and protégé, because limited data were available. Although a multi-dimensional indicator of military capabilities would have better measured the effectiveness in combat of each state, high-level political leaders are unlikely to have considered sophisticated indicators of military capabilities in actual historical cases. The best indicator, from a decision-making perspective, might very well fall somewhere between a simple measure of troop strength and a measure that combined manpower, armaments and firepower, terrain, and logistics capabilities.

against France.[2] In contrast, in 1938 the Soviet Union settled a dispute with Japan along the Manchukuo-Soviet border by moving forces into the disputed territory (the area of Changkufeng) and reinforcing with superior local forces to defeat a counterattack by Japanese and Manchukuo forces.[3]

When the potential attacker seeks to defeat the armed forces of the protégé before the defender can intervene militarily—rapid offensive attack—the immediate balance of forces is also critical. The potential attacker's time frame for victory can usually be measured in weeks. The critical measure of military strength is, as was the case with the limited aims strategy, the balance of forces that can be deployed at the outset of an armed confrontation. In the Czechoslovakian crisis of 1938, the immediate balance of forces involved the forces mobilized by Germany for an attack by the end of September and those forces mobilized by Czechoslovakia to defend itself. French and British ground forces were not in a position at that time to intervene directly in support of their ally, Czechoslovakia. In early October 1950 as U.S. troops prepared to cross the thirty-eighth parallel and invade North Korea, the immediate balance of forces strongly favored the United States. Chinese forces, concentrated on the Manchurian-North Korean border, were not in a position to contest the crossing by U.S. forces. Only after U.S. forces had invaded North Korea did Chinese forces move into North Korea to defend their protégé.[4]

The immediate balance of forces is defined as those land forces of the potential attacker in a position to initiate an attack and those land forces of the defender and protégé in a position to repulse such an attack. For purposes of statistical analysis, the balance of forces is expressed as the ratio of defender and protégé forces to potential attacker forces. To be in a position to engage in combat, the opposing forces must either be concentrated and prepared for action at the point

2. William L. Langer, *The Diplomacy of Imperialism*, vol. 2 (New York: A. A. Knopf, 1935), 537–80, and G. N. Sanderson, *England, Europe and the Upper Nile, 1882–1899: A Study in the Partition of Africa* (Edinburgh: University of Edinburgh Press, 1965), 332–62.

3. Martin Blumenson, "The Soviet Power Play At Changkufeng," *World Politics* 12: 2 (1960):249–63, and Alvin Coox, *The Anatomy of a Small War* (Westport, Conn.: Greenwood Press, 1977).

4. See the case studies in chapter 5 on the Czech crisis and the U.S. decision to invade North Korea.

of likely attack or be capable of mobilization for immediate combat from forward positions to the point of attack. The immediate balance of forces is measured at the final stage of each case of attempted deterrence—when the potential attacker either initiates the large-scale use of force and deterrence fails or when the potential attacker decides to step back from the threat of force and pursue a diplomatic settlement, in which case deterrence succeeds. When the potential attacker considers a limited aims strategy, the immediate balance of military strength involves those troops that are actually deployed on or near the disputed territory (in 1898 those forces in position at Fashoda and in 1938 those forces in position at Changkufeng). When the potential attacker considers a rapid offensive attack, the immediate balance of forces centers on the forces of the defender and protégé that are prepared and in position to engage the armed forces of the potential attacker if it initiates the use of force (in the Czech crisis, the mobilized forces of Czechoslovakia opposed the German army; in 1950 the remaining forces of the retreating North Korean army opposed the advancing forces of the United States). To collect data on the immediate balance of forces for each case of attempted deterrence I have consulted diverse primary and secondary sources for the location and size of opposing land forces. Where sources differed in estimates of a country's armed strength, the mean value was taken as the final measure.

The short-term balance of forces is critical to the outcome of rapid offensive attack when the potential attacker's objective is to defeat the armed forces of both the protégé and defender. The potential attacker calculates that the defender will be able to intervene before the protégé is completely defeated and therefore includes the costs of defeating the defender's armed forces in calculations for a relatively rapid military victory. In 1914 Austro-Hungarian and German leaders concluded, by late July, that an attack on Serbia would lead to the intervention of Russia in defense of Serbia, which in turn would lead to the intervention of France in support of Russia. A military victory for Austria-Hungary and Germany therefore would have had to entail the defeat of not only the Serbian army but the armies of Russia and France as well.[5]

The time frame for victory in a rapid offensive attack in which the attacker seeks to defeat both the protégé and defender is no more than a

---

5. Luigi Albertini, *The Origins of the War of 1914,* vol. 3, trans. and ed. Isabella M. Massey (London: Oxford University Press, 1957), chaps. 1–5.

few months. Because the opposing sides have the time to fully mobilize their standing armed forces, the immediate balance of forces is not as critical as the balance of forces that can be deployed on the battlefield in the short term.

The short-term balance of forces is defined as the capacity of the attacker and the defender and protégé to augment the immediate balance of forces by mobilizing ground and airforce manpower as well as the first class of trained reserves (expressed as the ratio of defender and protégé forces to potential attacker forces). The short-term balance of forces measures the potentially effective strength of the opposing sides in the first few months of war, in which the armed strength of a country depends largely on the mobilization potential of standing peacetime forces.[6] I have adjusted the short-term balance of forces to reflect the effects of distance. If the defender and attacker share a border or share one with the protégé, then no adjustment for distance was made. Otherwise the measure of the short-term balance of forces was adjusted for the distance between the attacker's and defender's principle point of embarkation and the point of debarkation on the territory of the protégé.[7]

The long-term balance of forces is critical in determining the outcome of a war of attrition between defender and attacker. Military

6. The short-term balance of forces corresponds to the existing local balance of forces in Paul Huth and Bruce Russett, "What Makes Deterrence Work? Cases from 1900 to 1980," *World Politics* 36: 4 (1984):509–10. Sources used to calculate the short-term balance of forces included: *The Statesman's Yearbook: Statistical and Historical Annual of the State of the World, 1885–1961* (London: Macmillan, 1886–1962); Bernadotte E. Schmitt and Harold C. Vedeler, *The World in the Crucible, 1914–1919* (New York: Harper and Row, 1985); Norman Stone, *The Eastern Front, 1914–1917* (New York: Charles Scribner's Sons, 1975), 37–91; Ernest May, ed., *Knowing One's Enemies: Intelligence Assessment before the Two World Wars* (Princeton: Princeton University Press, 1984), chaps. 3–6; John Erickson, *The Soviet High Command: A Military-Political History 1918–1941* (London: St. Martin's Press, 1962), 763–68; Williamson Murray, *The Change in the European Balance of Power, 1938–1939: The Path to Ruin* (Princeton: Princeton University Press, 1984), 217–63, 310–54; Matthew Cooper, *The German Army 1933–1945: Its Political and Military Failure* (New York: Stein and Day, 1978), 159–76; B. H. Liddell Hart, *History of the Second World War* (New York: Paragon Books, 1979), 17–19; Thomas W. Wolfe, *Soviet Power and Europe, 1945–1970* (Baltimore: Johns Hopkins University Press, 1970); and *The Military Balance, 1961–1984* (London: International Institute for Strategic Studies, 1961–1984).

7. The function for this adjustment is from Bruce Bueno de Mesquita, *The War Trap* (New Haven: Yale University Press, 1981), 105.

victory is achieved through the gradual exhaustion of the opponent's fighting strength in a series of prolonged battles. The time frame for attaining this objective is measured in months, if not years, required to defeat the adversary. Following the Japanese attack on Pearl Harbor in December 1941, U.S. policymakers recognized that a lengthy military campaign was required to overcome initial losses and ultimately defeat the Japanese. Similarly, following the German attack on the Soviet Union in summer 1941, Stalin realized that the only way to achieve victory was to engage Germany in a war of attrition.[8]

The long-term balance of forces is defined as the capacity of the defender and protégé and the potential attacker to build up their existing armed forces (army, air, and naval manpower) and to maintain an increased level of fighting strength by mobilizing the economy and civilian population for war. Industrial development in such basic industries as coal, steel, chemicals, and manufacturing are essential if a country is to support its armed forces on the battlefront for months or years. A large population provides the basis for the simultaneous maintenance of a large army on the battlefront and a work force for wartime production at home.

Calculations of the long-term military capabilities of the defender and protégé and the attacker are based on each state's existing level of armed strength, its industrial strength, and its population size.[9] To measure the long-term military capabilities of the defender and potential attacker, I have adopted the composite national capabilities index as developed by the Correlates of War Project. Each state's existing military capabilities (percentage share of world military personnel and military expenditures) were multiplied by the sum of that state's indus-

8. Samuel Eliot Morison, *History of United States Naval Operations in World War II*, vol. 3 (Boston: Little, Brown, 1968), 218–22, and John Erickson, *The Road to Stalingrad: Stalin's War with Germany* (London: Weidenfeld and Nicolson, 1975).

9. The operational measure of the long-term balance of forces does not include an indicator of each state's capacity to mobilize efficiently the economy and the population for protracted war. A. F. K. Organski and Jacek Kugler, *The War Ledger* (Chicago: University of Chicago Press, 1980), chap. 2, develop an indicator of political mobilization capacity, but the data required is not available over the time period of cases tested in this study. The resultant measurement error overestimates the capabilities of the defender and protégé by assuming that all available economic and manpower resources will be mobilized for war and enhances the deterrent strength of the long-term balance of forces indicator.

trial and demographic resources (percentage share of world steel production, industrial fuel consumption, urban, and total population). The ratio of defender's and protégé's capabilities to potential attacker's capabilities was then calculated.[10] As with the short-term balance of forces, the long-term capabilities of the defender and potential attacker were adjusted to reflect the impact of distance if appropriate.[11]

The final component of the military balance to consider is the impact of nuclear weapons. To test whether the latent threat of nuclear use (that is, possession of nuclear weapons) by the defender contributed to the success of extended deterrence, I have constructed the following variable: if the defender possessed the operational capability to strike the territory of the potential attacker with nuclear weapons, a value of 1 was recorded, whereas a value of 0 was given to the remaining cases, in which no such capability existed.

The value of the protégé. I hypothesized that the more important the interests of the defender at stake, the more credible is the defender's threat to use force. One way to estimate the national interests at stake for the defender is to examine the strength of economic and military ties between defender and protégé: the greater the level of economic and military ties between the two states, the greater the national interests at risk for the defender.

I have considered three types of ties between defender and protégé. First, I hypothesized that the existence of a military alliance increases the probability of deterrence success. A military alliance is defined as either a bilateral or multilateral written agreement between defender and protégé. Both defense pacts and ententes are considered alliance

10. The measurement of the long-term balance of forces is a refinement of the potential local balance of forces variable in Huth and Russett, ''What Makes Deterrence Work?,'' in which an additive function was utilized. On the composite national capabilities index, see J. David Singer, Stuart Bremer, and John Stucky, ''Capability Distribution, Uncertainty, and Major Power War, 1820–1965,'' in *Peace, War, and Numbers,* ed. Bruce M. Russett (Beverly Hills: Sage Publications, 1972), 19–48. Data for the calculation of the long-term balance of forces were obtained from the Correlates of War Project data set—''National Capabilities, 1816–1980''—made available through the Interuniversity Consortium for Political and Social Research at the University of Michigan, Ann Arbor.

11. Bueno de Mesquita, *War Trap,* 105.

commitments in my analysis.[12] In ten cases in this study the protégé is a colony of the defender. A formal military alliance did not exist between defender and protégé in these cases. I assume, however, that a colonial relationship was recognized by other states as entailing an implicit obligation on the part of the metropole to defend its colony and have therefore treated this relationship as an alliance commitment. For purposes of statistical analysis, the existence of an alliance between defender and protégé is given a value of 1, whereas the absence of an alliance is given a value of 0.

The second type of ties examined was the extent of arms transfers from defender to protégé. I hypothesized that as the dependence of the protégé on arms transfers from the defender increases so will the probability of deterrence success. To measure the extent to which the defender had developed a close supplier relationship with the protégé, I calculated the share of arms imported by the protégé from the defender as a percentage of total arms imported by the protégé. This figure was calculated as the average over the three to five years, depending on the availability of data, prior to each case of attempted deterrence. Because precise data was lacking in some cases, I used a ten-point scale to represent the percentage share imported by the protégé from the defender: $0-10\% = 1$, $11-20\% = 2$ . . . , $91-100\% = 10$.[13]

12. I would have preferred to construct separate measures for defense pacts and ententes, but the small number of ententes made this impractical for statistical analysis. The sources used to identify alliances were Bruce M. Russett, "An Empirical Typology of International Military Alliances," *Midwest Journal of Political Science* 15 (1971): 262–80; J. David Singer and Melvin Small, "Formal Alliances, 1815–1939," *Journal of Peace Research* 3: 1 (1966):1–32; and *Military Balance, 1961–1984.*

13. This is the same measure presented in Huth and Russett, "What Makes Deterrence Work?" except that a four-point scale was used in the earlier study. Sources used to calculate arms transfer shares included: *Statesman's Yearbook, 1886–1939;* Reginald Rankin, *The Inner History of the Balkan War* (London: Constable, 1914), 551–60; Robert Harkavy, *The Arms Trade and International Systems* (Cambridge: Ballinger, 1975); John L. Sutton and Geoffrey Kemp, *Arms to Developing Countries, 1945–1965,* Adelphi Paper 28 (London: International Institute for Strategic Studies, 1966); U.S. Central Intelligence Agency, *Communist Aid Activities in Non-Communist Less Developed Countries, 1954–1979* (Washington, D.C.: Government Printing Office, 1980); U.S. Arms Control and Disarmament Agency, *World Military Expenditures and Arms Transfers, 1963–1986* (Washington, D.C.: Government Printing Office, 1975–87); *Military Balance 1965–1984; SIPRI Yearbook of World Armaments and Disarmament,*

The third type of ties examined was the level of economic interaction between defender and protégé. I hypothesized that the more the defender trades with the protégé, the more likely deterrence is to succeed. The economic importance of the protégé to the defender is measured as the protégé's percentage share of the defender's total merchandise exports and imports. The percentage share is calculated as the average level over a three-year period prior to each case of attempted deterrence.[14]

I also hypothesized that the value of the protégé to the potential attacker influences deterrence outcomes. The greater the strategic importance of the protégé, the stronger the incentives for the potential attacker to use force to achieve its objectives in the confrontation with the protégé and defender. Three measures of strategic importance will be used: (1) Territorial proximity—if the potential attacker and protégé share a border, a value of 1 will be recorded whereas a value of 0 will be coded for the remaining cases; (2) Population size—data on the total population of the protégé for each case was collected.[15] (3) Source of

---

1968–1971 (New York: Humanities Press, 1970–72); *World Armaments and Disarmament: SIPRI Yearbook, 1972–1985* (New York: Humanities Press, 1973; Cambridge, Mass.: M.I.T. Press, 1974–78; and London: Taylor & Francis Ltd., 1979–86); and Military Archives, Modern Military Field Branch, Basic Intelligence Directives, Record Group 165, Files 6510, 9510 (Turkey, 1943–46; Iran, 1943–46; Finland, 1938–40) and Files 6505, 6510, 9510 (Poland, 1936–39), National Archives.

14. I would have preferred to test separately the impact of exports and imports, but the high correlation between the two renders this impractical for statistical analysis. The sources used to calculate trade shares included: *Statesman's Yearbook, 1885–1940;* H. R. Mitchell, *European Historical Statistics, 1750–1970* (New York: Columbia University Press, 1975); *Memorandum on Balance of Payments and Foreign Trade Balances, 1910–1923* vol. 2 (Geneva: League of Nations, 1924); *International Trade Statistics, 1933–1938* (Geneva: League of Nations, 1934–39); U.S. Bureau of the Census, *Statistical Abstract of the United States, 1946–1950* (Washington, D.C.: Government Printing Office, 1946–50); *Yearbook of International Trade Statistics, 1950–1984* (New York: United Nations, 1951–86); Alexander Eckstein, Walter Galenson, and Ta-Chung Liu, eds., *Economic Trends in Communist China* (Chicago: Aldine, 1969), 671–738; and U.S. Central Intelligence Agency, *Communist China's Balance of Payments* (Washington, D.C.: Government Printing Office, 1966).

15. The sources used to determine total population were the Correlates of War Project data set—"National Capabilities, 1816–1980," and the *Statesman's Yearbook, 1885–1984.*

vital raw materials—a list of raw materials essential to military production was drawn up for three time periods, pre–World War I, the interwar period, and post-1945. If the potential attacker imported one or more of the strategic raw materials and the protégé was mining and/or engaging in the production of those imported raw materials, then a value of 1 was recorded for that case whereas a value of 0 was coded for the remaining cases. The list of strategic raw materials for each period was as follows:[16] (1) Pre–World War I—coal, iron ore, petroleum, copper, nickel, lead, sulfur; (2) Interwar Period—coal, iron ore, petroleum, copper, nickel, lead, sulfur, cotton, rubber, bauxite, manganese, chromium; (3) Post-1945—iron ore, petroleum, copper, nickel, lead, sulfur, bauxite, manganese, chromium, titanium, cobalt.

Bargaining behavior of the defender. I previously identified three diplomatic strategies for the defender—a bullying strategy, a firm-but-flexible strategy, and a conciliatory strategy—and hypothesized that a firm-but-flexible strategy was the most effective in promoting deterrence success. A critical difference between the bullying and firm-but-flexible strategies is that in the latter case the defender does more than react negatively to the demands of the potential attacker: it also initiates proposals for possible compromise. In a bullying strategy, the defender adopts a firm position and awaits for the potential attacker to make the critical concessions.

In the Fashoda conflict, the British adopted a bullying strategy as they insisted on their right to retain exclusive control over the Nile basin. The French pressed initially for the right to territorial gains, but the British rejected the French position. The French then responded by reducing their claims and called for a commercial outlet in the area in return for the withdrawal of their forces. The British again refused, maintaining that withdrawal was to be nonconditional. Finally, the French proposed a conference to discuss the issue of a commercial

16. The sources used to construct this indicator were U.S. Bureau of Mines, *Minerals Yearbook, 1932–1983* (Washington, D.C.: Government Printing Office, 1933–84); *Statesman's Yearbook, 1885–1983; International Trade Statistics; Yearbook of International Trade Statistics, 1950–1984;* and B. H. Liddell Hart, *History of the Second World War* (London: Cassell, 1970), 23.

outlet. The British agreed only to consider the possibility of an outlet in a future conference, insisting on the withdrawal of French forces. French efforts to establish a sphere of influence in the Nile basin were completely rejected by the British.[17]

In the Anglo-Russian confrontation over Afghanistan in 1885, Great Britain adopted a firm-but-flexible strategy, proposing mutual compromise while rebuffing the one-sided proposals of the Russian government. At the outset of the confrontation, the British government proposed a compromise on the delimitation of the Afghan border in which the Russians would incorporate the territory in and around Panjdeh in return for acceptance of Afghan claims to strategically important areas along its border. Russia initially agreed to the trade-off but then attempted to press Britain into further concessions that the British consistently opposed.[18] The critical difference between a firm-but-flexible and a conciliatory strategy is that in the latter case the defender is willing to make concessions despite a lack of reciprocation by the potential attacker. During the Czech crisis of 1938 Chamberlain agreed not only to Hitler's demand that the Sudetenland be incorporated into the German Reich but also to the demand that unless the territory were transferred immediately, Germany would take it by force.

To determine which strategy applied to the diplomatic behavior of the defender, I compiled a detailed chronological summary of the bargaining process for each case of attempted deterrence, consulting many primary and secondary sources to develop a thorough record of the negotiating positions of defender and potential attacker. After a complete summary for each case was completed, the diplomatic exchanges between defender and potential attacker were divided into a series of sequential interactions. The demands and position of the potential attacker at time t were coupled with the defender's response at $t+1$, the demands of the potential attacker at $t+2$ were coupled with the response of the defender at $t+3$ . . . , until the end of the dispute. I then examined the diplomatic response of the defender for each round

17. Langer, *Diplomacy of Imperialism,* 537–80, and Sanderson, *England, Europe and the Upper Nile,* 532–62.

18. See the case study in chapter 6 of the Anglo-Russian confrontation over Afghanistan.

of interaction in the context of earlier responses to determine which diplomatic strategy the defender had adopted.[19]

In the statistical analysis I treated the diplomatic strategy of the defender as a dummy variable. A value of 1 was used for all cases in which a firm-but-flexible diplomatic strategy was adopted by the defender; a value of 0 (the excluded category) was used for the remaining cases, in which an alternative strategy was adopted or there was no ongoing process of negotiations between defender and potential attacker.

I previously identified three general strategies of military escalation—policy of strength, policy of tit for tat, and policy of caution—and hypothesized that a policy of tit for tat by the defender was the most effective deterrent. To determine which strategy the defender adopted, I compiled a detailed record of the military actions of the defender and potential attacker during the confrontation. As with coding the diplomatic strategies of the defender, the record of military actions was divided into a series of moves and countermoves. I then examined each round of military escalation and the previous pattern of responses to determine a strategy of military escalation.[20]

The military actions of defender and potential attacker were categorized according to the following scale of escalation.[21] (1) Symbolic show of force or display of military presence: Naval visits to ports of protégé, the dispatch of a warship to coast of protégé, naval reconnaissance off coast of protégé; (2) Demonstration of military capabilities: Naval exercises or war games held near the coast of the protégé or adversary, land exercises or war games held near the border of protégé or adversary; (3) Buildup of military forces: Reinforcements of ground

19. The coding rules of Leng and Wheeler, "Influence Strategies, Success, and War," *Journal of Conflict Resolution* 23: 4 (1979):657–63, have been adopted. The intercoder reliability score on a random sample of twenty cases was r = 0.91.

20. The intercoder reliability score on a random sample of twenty cases was r = 0.88.

21. The following sources were consulted in constructing this scale of military escalation: Barry M. Blechman and Stephen S. Kaplan, *Force without War: U.S. Armed Forces as a Political Instrument* (Washington, D.C.: Brookings Institution, 1978), 38–57; Edward Luttwak, *The Political Uses of Sea Power* (Baltimore: Johns Hopkins University Press, 1974), 74–79; and James Cable, *Gunboat Diplomacy: Political Applications of Limited Naval Force* (London: Chatta and Windus, 1971), 23–68.

forces moved to borders or points of likely armed confrontation, naval reinforcements at bases or at sea in region of protégé or adversary; (4) Positioning of military forces for immediate use: Buildup of ground forces on borders or points of likely armed confrontation, buildup of naval forces off the coast of protégé or adversary; (5) Preparation of forces for immediate use: Concentration and alerting of ground and/or naval forces on the border, off the coast of the adversary, or at points of likely armed confrontation; and (6) Mobilization of forces for war: Partial or general mobilization of ground and/or naval forces for combat.

When a policy of strength is adopted, the defender either responds to the military actions of the potential attacker with greater than equal levels of escalation or initiates escalation in the absence of previous military actions. In July 1914 Russian preparations for the mobilization of forces along its borders were initiated in anticipation of such actions by Germany and Austria-Hungary. In a tit-for-tat strategy, the defender responds to the military actions of the potential attacker with equal levels of buildup and preparedness. Germany reciprocated the military preparations of Russia in 1914 by quickly alerting and mobilizing its own forces. With a cautious policy of military escalation, the defender either fails to respond to the military actions of the potential attacker or responds at less than equal levels of escalation. In the Czech crisis of 1938 extensive German military preparations were detected by the British as early as July. Limited British naval measures were not initiated, however, until late September, by which time German forces were mobilized and in position to attack Czechoslovakia.

I have treated the defender's strategy of military escalation as a dummy variable in the statistical analysis. For cases in which the defender adopted a policy of tit for tat a value of 1 was used, whereas for cases in which the defender pursued a policy of caution or strength a value of 0 was coded.

Past behavior of defender. I previously formulated two hypotheses on the past behavior of the defender: (1) The past behavior of the defender would have its greatest impact in cases in which the defender confronted the same potential attacker as in the current case of attempted deterrence (as opposed to the defender's past behavior in confrontations with other states); (2) A past record of bullying or conciliation by the defender in a confrontation with the potential attacker would decrease the probability of deterrence success, whereas a past record of firm-but-flexible bargaining would increase the probability of deterrence success. I have analyzed the past behavior of the defender for two sets of past international confrontations: the most recent past case of attempted extended deterrence by the defender and the most recent past confrontation between the defender and potential attacker.[22]

The outcomes of attempted extended deterrence for the defender were coded as either: (1) *Success*—Defender stands firm in support of protégé and potential attacker refrains from attack; (2) *Failure but armed support*—Deterrence fails and protégé is attacked but defender does intervene with military force to protect protégé; or (3) *Capitulation*—Deterrence fails but defender does not intervene with military force to protect protégé.

The first two categories indicate a record of firmness for the defender; the third indicates a record of weakness. In the statistical analysis I used a value of 1 for each case with one of the three outcomes listed above and a value of 0 for each case with no past attempt at extended deterrence for the defender.

I described the outcomes of the most recent past confrontation between the defender and potential attacker in three ways:[23] (1) *Diplomatic put-down*—The defender adopts a bullying bargaining strategy and/or forces the potential attacker to make critical concessions to avoid an armed conflict; (2) *Stalemate*—The defender and potential attacker avoid a direct military confrontation, but firm-but-flexible bargaining by the defender fails to achieve an agreement that resolves

22. The principal sources used to identify past confrontations between defender and potential attacker were William L. Langer, *An Encyclopedia of World History,* 5th ed., rev. (Boston: Houghton Mifflin, 1972), and the Correlates of War Project data set—"Militarized Disputes, 1816–1976."

23. This categorization of dispute outcomes is adopted from Zeev Maoz, *Paths to Conflict: International Dispute Initiation, 1816–1976* (Boulder: Westview Press, 1982), app. 2, and Russell J. Leng, "Coercive Bargaining in Recurrent Crises," *Journal of Conflict Resolution* 27: 3 (1983):379–420. A fourth outcome—compromise—was possible, but no such cases were identified. Glenn H. Snyder and Paul Diesing, *Conflict among Nations* (Princeton: Princeton University Press, 1977), 248, report a similar pattern.

the underlying issues; and (3) *Diplomatic defeat*—The defender retreats under pressure and concedes on the critical issues to avoid a direct military confrontation.

To determine which outcome applied to the past behavior of the defender, I recorded the specific demands and counteroffers of the defender and potential attacker during the confrontation and then examined the final terms to determine whether the defender had conceded to the demands of the potential attacker.[24] Whenever possible the outcomes of past confrontations were coded according to the potential attacker's perception of the outcome and of the defender's behavior. When such information was not available (in about half of the cases), I used the coding rules as follows: If the defender refused to compromise on the principal issues and/or forced the potential attacker to make critical concessions, the outcome was coded as a diplomatic put-down. In the 1898 colonial conflict, the British forced the French to withdraw from Fashoda, thus denying the French rights to the Nile watershed from the British.[25]

If the defender and its adversary engaged in negotiations without reaching an agreement or reached a limited agreement that did not resolve the principal issues in dispute, the outcome was recorded as a stalemate. In these case both sides tacitly agreed not to press further and the immediate confrontation de-escalated without submission by either side. During 1940 and 1941, Germany and the Soviet Union negotiated over rights to the Petsamo region in Finland. The Soviets initially demanded exclusive rights in the area and protested any German attempt to reach an agreement with the Finnish government. Germany reciprocated the hard-line position of the Soviets by insisting that the Soviets respect the agreement signed with Finland. Negotiations continued for several months but neither side was willing to concede to the demands of the other and no resolution was reached.

I designated an outcome as a put-down, rather than a stalemate, if the defender forced the potential attacker to make critical concessions or rebuffed the potential attacker's proposals for compromise. In the Fashoda confrontation, the British not only rebuffed French proposals

24. On a random sample of twenty cases the intercoder reliability score was r = 0.96.

25. Langer, *Diplomacy of Imperialism*, 537–80, and Sanderson, *England, Europe and the Upper Nile*, 332–62.

for compromise but also forced the French to accept their unyielding position. In the Finnish confrontation, however, the Soviets did not make substantive compromises and were not forced by Germany to retreat from attempts to secure an agreement that would ensure Soviet dominance in the Petsamo region.[26]

A diplomatic defeat occurred when the defender acceded to the principal demands of the potential attacker under the threat of force. To avoid a military confrontation the defender made unilateral concessions on critical issues and accepted an asymmetrical agreement. In the Cyprus crisis of 1967 the leadership of Greece, confronted with a Turkish threat to invade Cyprus, agreed to withdraw over ten thousand troops from Cyprus instead of using force to maintain its position of military strength on the island.[27]

To test the hypothesis that a record of conciliation or bullying with the potential attacker reduces the likelihood of deterrence success, I examined those cases in which either the defender or potential attacker accepted a diplomatic defeat. To test the hypothesis that a record of firm-but-flexible bargaining enhances the likelihood of deterrence success, I analyzed those cases in which the past behavior of the defender is coded as a stalemate.

For purposes of statistical analysis, I treated the outcomes of past confrontations between the defender and potential attacker as a dummy variable. I used a value of 1 when the past behavior of the defender was either diplomatic put-down, stalemate, or diplomatic defeat and a value of 0 when there was no prior confrontation between defender and potential attacker to code.

Data Analysis

I used probit analysis to test the relative explanatory power of each of the hypotheses.[28] Probit analysis is analogous to multiple regression analysis for situations in which the dependent variable is dichotomous.

---

26. See the case study in chapter 6 of the German-Soviet confrontation over Finland and the Petsamo region.

27. Thomas Ehrlich, *Cyprus, 1958–1967: International Crises and the Role of Law* (New York: Oxford University Press, 1974), 90–116.

28. A critical source of measurement error could be caused by the use of objective indicators, rather than the potential attacker's perception of strength or presence, for the

In this study deterrence either succeeds (a value of 1) or fails (a value of 0). The model specified for empirical testing includes four variables:

$$y = c + b_1x_1 + b_2x_2 + b_3x_3 + b_4x_4 + u_t$$

Where

c = constant

x_1 = the balance of military forces between the defender and protege and the potential attacker

x_2 = the value of the protégé to the defender and potential attacker

x_3 = the defender's bargaining strategy

x_4 = the past behavior of the defender

u_t = error term

I used probit analysis to determine which indicators provided the most explanatory power. (Hypotheses 1.1–5.2 represent the expected results.) Multiple equations were then tested with at least one indicator from each set of variables included in each equation. Those indicators that did not reach the 95 percent level of significance were deleted from the equation.[29] To check the final results of probit analysis, I reentered each of the previously deleted indicators individually into the final equation to ensure that the indicator remained insignificant.[30]

The results (tables 2a and 2b) identify the most powerful equation

---

measurement of the independent variables. I have assumed that in a large set of cases the potential attacker's estimates of the variables will not diverge so markedly from objective measurements as to render the operational indicators useless for empirical testing. If subjective estimates do, however, diverge from objective indicators, then the model should have poor predictive value.

29. Significance levels are used even though the hypotheses are tested on fifty-eight cases that represent the complete set of actual historical cases of extended-immediate deterrence from 1885 to 1984. The fifty-eight cases nevertheless constitute a sample of all potential cases of extended-immediate deterrence during that period. For example, historical cases of direct-immediate deterrence could have turned into extended-immediate deterrence cases if a defender had intervened in support of one side. Similarly, cases of extended-general deterrence could have developed into extended-immediate deterrence confrontations if the potential attacker had issued explicit threats against the protégé and the defender then responded in kind. See Eric A. Hanushek and John E. Jackson, *Statistical Methods for Social Scientists* (New York: Academic Press, 1977), 325.

30. Multicollinearity among the indicators of the independent variables for each equation was checked by examining the auxiliary r^2 values for each indicator. Multi-

TABLE 2a. Probit Analysis of the Determinants of Deterrence Outcome

Explanatory Variable	Estimated Coefficient	Significance Level (t statistic)	
Constant	−1.67	—	
Military Balance			
Immediate balance of forces	0.55	>0.95	(1.94)
Short-term balance of forces	0.83	>0.975	(2.27)
Bargaining Behavior			
Firm-but-flexible diplomacy	0.97	>0.975	(2.17)
Tit-for-tat military escalation	0.98	>0.975	(2.12)
Past Behavior[a]			
Defender conciliation	−1.15	0.95	(1.78)
Defender intransigence	−0.86	0.95	(1.77)

[a]Those cases in which the defender and potential attacker were adversaries in a previous confrontation.

TABLE 2b. Ability of Probit Analysis to Predict Deterrence Outcome

		Predicted Deterrence Result[a]	
		Failure	Success
Actual Deterrence Result	Failure	19	5
	Success	4	30

[a]Percentage of predictions correct = 84, N = 58.

collinearity was low with auxiliary r^2 values below 0.3 for almost all indicators. The auxiliary r^2 values for the indicators in table 2a are as follows: immediate balance of forces = 0.13, short-term balance of forces = 0.15, firm-but-flexible diplomacy = 0.03, tit-for-tat military escalation = 0.08, defender conciliation = 0.13, and defender intransigence = 0.12. The estimated coefficient (b) and t-ratio for each of the nonsignificant indicators when included in the final equation (table 2a) are as follows—nuclear weapons: b = 0.52, t-ratio = 1.04; long-term balance of forces: b = −0.23, t-ratio = 0.93; foreign-trade ties: b = 0.06, t-ratio = 0.68; arms-transfer ties: b = −0.02, t-ratio = 0.28; alliance ties: b = −0.77, t-ratio = 1.55; territorial proximity: b = 0.33, t-ratio = 0.65; population size (logged): b = 0.03, t-ratio = 0.23; source of raw materials: b = 0.05, t-ratio = 0.10; deterrence success: b = 0.20, t-ratio = 0.44; deterrence failure but armed support: b = 5.68, t-ratio = 0.01; capitulation: b = 0.61, t-ratio = 0.68; stalemate: b = −0.83, t-ratio = 1.35.

for explaining deterrence outcomes. They indicate that the model provides a strong basis for predicting deterrence outcomes: it predicted correctly in 49 of 58, or 84%, of the cases.[31]

The findings of the probit analysis are summarized below.

1. The balance of military forces between the potential attacker and the defender and protégé was an important determinant of deterrence outcomes. As hypothesis 1.1 predicted, the immediate and short-term balances of military forces had a significant impact on the probability of deterrence success, whereas the long-term balance of forces had no significant impact. As the ratio of immediate and short-term defender and protégé forces to potential attacker forces shifted to the advantage of the former, the likelihood of deterrence success increased. These results support the argument that potential attackers seek quick and decisive results with the use of force at relatively low cost. It follows that the most effective military deterrent is the capacity of the defender to repulse an attack and deny the adversary its military objectives at the outset and early stages of an armed confrontation.[32] The capabilities of the defender and its protégé to prevail in a prolonged struggle are not an effective deterrent because the potential attacker does not initiate the use of force with the intention to engage in a war of attrition. Deterrence based on the threat of denial is much more effective than the threat of punishment in a protracted war.

31. For a case of successful deterrence to be predicted correctly the value of the equation for that case must be equal to or greater than 0.5. Conversely, if a case of failed deterrence is to be predicted correctly the value of the equation for that case must be equal to or less than 0.5.

32. These results generally support the work of John J. Mearsheimer (*Conventional Deterrence* [Ithaca: Cornell University Press, 1983]) and are consistent with the results of Paul Anderson and Timothy J. McKeown ("Changing Aspirations, Limited Attention, and War," *World Politics* 40 1 (1987):17–22). This study's findings on the importance of relative capabilities, however, stands in opposition to much of the empirical work on deterrence and international crisis outcomes, which tends to question the explanatory power of the balance of forces. Examples include Janice Gross Stein, "Extended Deterrence in the Middle East: American Strategy Reconsidered," *World Politics* 39:3 (1987):326–52; and Zeev Maoz, "Resolve, Capabilities, and the Outcomes of Interstate Disputes," *Journal of Conflict Resolution* 27: 2 (1983):195–230. See Jack Levy ("Quantitative Studies of Deterrence Success and Failure," in *Perspectives on Deterrence,* ed. Robert Axelrod, Robert Jervis, Roy Radner, and Paul Stern [Washington, D.C.: National Academy of Sciences/National Research Council, 1988], chap. 6), for a thorough summary and critique of much of the literature.

2. Crisis bargaining behavior had a strong impact on deterrence outcomes. As I argued in hypotheses 4.1 and 4.2, a policy of tit for tat in military escalation and a firm-but-flexible diplomatic posture by the defender were the most effective bargaining strategies for successful deterrence, as compared with more aggressive or accommodative strategies.[33] The results confirm that bargaining strategies that rely on reciprocity most effectively balance deterrence stability and credibility.[34]

3. As hypothesis 5.1 predicted, the defender's past behavior in its most recent confrontation with the potential attacker had a significant effect on deterrence outcomes, whereas the past behavior of the defender in deterrence cases with other states did not. Hypothesis 5.2 was partially supported by the empirical evidence: a record of past conciliation or bullying by the defender reduced the likelihood of deterrence success; a past outcome of firm-but-flexible bargaining between defender and potential attacker, however, did not increase the probability of deterrence success, contrary to the expectations of Hypothesis 5.2.

A potential attacker's calculus of military costs seems to focus on the outcome of the initial engagement with the defender and protégé and the capacity to follow up with superior forces. The following relationship between the immediate and short-term balance of forces emerged. In most cases of deterrence failure either the defender's forces were not in a position to repulse the initial attack, giving the attacker a decisive advantage in the immediate balance of forces, and/or the defender's capacity to mobilize and reinforce local forces

33. These results support the findings on the effectiveness of a mixed strategy in crisis bargaining situations of Leng and Wheeler, "Influence Strategies, Success, and War"; Russell J. Leng and Charles S. Gochman, "Dangerous Disputes: A Study of Conflict Behavior and War," *American Journal of Political Science* 26: 4 (1982):664–87; Charles S. Gochman and Russell J. Leng, "Realpolitik and the Road to War: An Analysis of Attributes and Behavior," *International Studies Quarterly* 27: 1 (1983):97–120; and Snyder and Diesing, *Conflict among Nations,* 183–281.

34. The importance and utility of reciprocity as a general strategy of state policy in international political economy has been argued as well. See Robert O. Keohane, "Reciprocity in International Relations," *International Organization* 40: 1 (1986):1–28; Robert Axelrod and Robert O. Keohane, "Achieving Cooperation under Anarchy: Strategies and Institutions," *World Politics* 38: 1 (1985):226–54; and Stephen D. Krasner, *Asymmetries in Japanese-American Trade: The Case for Specific Reciprocity* (Berkeley: Institute of International Studies, 1987).

did not decisively alter the short-term balance of forces in its favor. Deterrence failed in only 17% of the cases (4/24) where the defender possessed military capabilities comparable or superior to those of the potential attacker in both the immediate and short-term balance of forces. Of those four cases the defender possessed a greater than 2 to 1 advantage at both levels in only one case (the Vietnam War with the United States as defender). Deterrence failed then in only 1 of 24 cases (4%) in which the defender possessed a clear advantage in both the immediate and short-term balance of forces. In most cases of successful deterrence, in contrast, the defender and protégé either maintained a favorable balance of forces with reinforcements or buttressed a rough balance of local forces with superior reinforcement. In 88% (30/34) of deterrence successes the defender and protégé possessed comparable or superior military capabilities in either the immediate or short-term balance of forces.

In tables 3a and 3b I present the impact of changes in the immediate and short-term balance of forces on the probability of successful deterrence when all other variables are held at their mean value. A change in the immediate balance of forces for the defender from a 1 to 4 disadvantage to an equal balance, for example, increases the probability of successful deterrence by 16%, while the change from an equal balance of forces to a 3 to 1 advantage for the defender increases the likelihood of deterrence success by 27%. Similar results are obtained when the short-term balance of forces is examined. The change from a 1 to 4 disadvantage to an equal balance for the defender produces an increase of 15% and the change from an equal balance to a 3 to 1 advantage for the defender results in a 21% increase in the probability of deterrence success.

My results confirm that the bargaining behavior of the defender is critical in determining the outcome of extended deterrence and suggest that potential attackers do pay close attention to the diplomatic and military actions of the defender when estimating intentions and weighing the risks of using force or backing down. The effectiveness of reciprocity as a bargaining strategy is reflected in the 79% rate of deterrence success (27/34) when the defender used a firm-but-flexible diplomatic strategy or tit-for-tat strategy of escalation. Deterrence failed in only 1 of 14 cases (7%) when the defender adopted both firm-

TABLE 3a. Effect of the Immediate Balance of Forces on Outcome of Deterrence

	Change in Probability of Deterrence Success (%)
Defender/Protégé Forces: Potential Attacker Forces	0.25 0.50 — +5[a] 0.75 — +5 1.00 — +6 1.50 — +9 2.00 — +8 3.00 — +10 5.00 — +6

[a]The marginal impact of each variable in tables 3a. and 3b. is calculated by changing its value while holding all other variables in the model at their mean value. The change in the location on the cumulative standard normal distribution produced by this procedure is then converted into the percentage change in the probability of successful deterrence.

TABLE 3b. Effect of the Short-Term Balance of Forces on Outcome of Deterrence

	Change in Probability of Deterrence Success (%)
Defender/Protégé Forces: Potential Attacker Forces	0.25 0.50 — +6 0.75 — +5 1.00 — +4 1.50 — +7 2.00 — +6 3.00 — +8 5.00 — +9

but-flexible and tit-for-tat strategies (the conflict between the Netherlands and Indonesia over West Irian is the exception).

The adoption of a firm-but-flexible diplomatic strategy by the defender increased by 32% the probability of successful deterrence as compared with bullying or conciliation.[35] This strong, positive impact seems to reflect the ability of a firm-but-flexible strategy to reduce the costs of inaction for a potential attacker.[36] By combining firmness with positive diplomatic initiatives, the defender can avoid challenging the bargaining reputation of the attacker. Positive inducements may also provide evidence of tangible gains that the potential attacker can use to mollify elite opposition to backing down or to minimize the backlash of public opinion against concessions to the defender. Offers of conditional accommodation by the defender may also break negotiating deadlocks and promote a diplomatic settlement through trade-offs among issues. In over one-half of the 26 cases in which the defender adopted a firm-but-flexible strategy the defender proposed a trade-off among issues as the basis for negotiations.[37]

35. The marginal impact of adopting (1) a firm-but-flexible diplomatic strategy or (2) a tit-for-tat policy of military escalation or of having a record of either (3) conciliation or (4) intransigence in a past confrontation with the potential attacker is calculated by changing its value while holding all other variables in the model at their mean value. The change in the location on the cumulative standard normal distribution produced by this procedure is then converted into the percentage change in the probability of successful deterrence.

36. The importance of the costs of continued peace in failures of deterrence is emphasized in Bruce Russett, "Pearl Harbor: Deterrence Theory and Decision Theory," *Journal of Peace Research* 4: 2 (1967):89–105, and Robert Jervis, Richard Ned Lebow, and Janice Gross Stein, *Psychology and Deterrence* (Baltimore: Johns Hopkins University Press, 1985), chaps. 3, 5, 9.

37. The results concerning the importance of a firm-but-flexible diplomatic strategy may be spurious because they do not account for the underlying degree of conflict of interest between defender and potential attacker. Richard Ned Lebow, *Between Peace and War: The Nature of International Crisis* (Baltimore: Johns Hopkins University Press, 1981), 23–56, in his analysis of the origins of international crises argues that justification of hostility and spin-off crises are the most difficult confrontations to manage because of either the initiator's determination to go to war from the start of the crisis or the clash of vital, opposing national interests between adversaries. Only four such cases identified by Lebow are included in this study's universe of cases: Austria-Hungary versus Serbia, 1914; Germany versus Poland, 1939; Germany versus France, 1914; Germany versus Belgium, 1914. North Vietnam versus South Vietnam, 1964–65, could be added as a fifth case. Thus, in most cases there was an opportunity for negotiations to influence the outcome of the confrontation. Furthermore, if the degree of conflict of interest could be measured (independent of the deterrence outcome) and incorporated into the analysis, its conclusion would not invalidate the results concerning crisis bargaining but would instead suggest the conditions under which a firm-but-flexible strategy would be more or less likely to succeed.

A strategy of tit for tat not only signals the defender's intention to use force if necessary, it can also influence the immediate balance of forces. The movement of naval and land forces by the defender can erase a local imbalance of forces and establish a formidable trip-wire deterrent capability in which the use of force by the potential attacker against the protégé results in the direct engagement of the defender's forces. *The adoption of a tit for tat policy by the defender increased by 33% the probability of successful deterrence as compared with failing to match or exceeding the military escalation of the potential attacker.*

The importance of the immediate balance of forces and a tit-for-tat policy to the success of extended-immediate deterrence is relevant to assessing the prospects for conventional deterrence in Europe between NATO and the Soviet Union/Warsaw Pact. Soviet military strategy calls for a blitzkrieg conventional attack to break through NATO's forward defense line. The Soviet objective is to neutralize NATO's nuclear forces and to defeat NATO's conventional forces very quickly; the Soviets do not want to become engaged in a protracted armed conflict. The credibility of conventional deterrence therefore depends on NATO's capacity to mobilize sufficient conventional forces at the outset of an armed conflict to repulse the initial Soviet attack. If NATO has the conventional capability to deny the Soviets a blitzkrieg victory, then the prospects for conventional deterrence are good.[38]

Recent studies have cogently argued that NATO has a much stronger conventional capability than is commonly assumed and that NATO has the conventional forces to prevent a Soviet blitzkrieg victory.[39] These

38. Phillip A. Peterson and John G. Hines, "The Conventional Offensive in Soviet Theater Strategy," *Orbis* 27: 3 (1983):695–739; John Hemsley, "The Soviet Ground Forces," in *Soviet Military Power and Performance*, eds. John Erickson and E. J. Feuchtwanger (Hamden, Conn.: Archon Books, 1979), 47–73; Mearsheimer, *Conventional Deterrence*, 165–88; and Michael MccGwire, *Military Objectives in Soviet Foreign Policy* (Washington, D.C.: Brookings Institution, 1987), 67–89.

39. Mearsheimer, *Conventional Deterrence;* Barry R. Posen, "Measuring the European Conventional Balance: Coping with Complexity in Threat Assessment," *International Security* 9: 3 (1984–85):47–88; William Mako, *U.S. Ground Forces and the Defense of Central Europe* (Washington, D.C.: Brookings Institution, 1983); William F. Kaufmann, "Nonnuclear Deterrence," in *Alliance Security: NATO and the No-First-Use Question*, eds. John D. Steinbruner and Leon V. Sigal (Washington, D.C.: Brookings Institution, 1983), 43–90; Joshua Epstein, "Dynamic Analysis and the Conventional Balance in Europe," *International Security* 12:4 (1988):154–65; Mear-

studies assume that NATO would promptly mobilize its forces upon indication of Soviet military preparations for a possible attack. If NATO is to prevent a decisive Soviet advantage in the immediate balance of forces, it must use a tit-for-tat policy of crisis escalation. With any significant delay in NATO mobilization a Soviet blitzkrieg victory is much more likely. Prompt mobilization by NATO, however, may be uncertain in a future crisis.[40] Mobilization will require NATO to disperse its tactical nuclear forces from their peacetime storage sites and to deploy some of them close to the forward defense line in accordance with the policy of flexible response and potential first-use of nuclear weapons. Because of the great dangers of nuclear escalation and the potential threat of a Soviet preemptive strike once such actions have been undertaken, NATO political leaders might delay as long as possible authorization for dispersal of nuclear weapons and conventional mobilization.[41]

For NATO to adopt a tit-for-tat policy of military escalation, political cohesion within the alliance must be high. Cohesion, however, is likely to be strained in a crisis by the extensive integration of nuclear forces into NATO's conventional force structure and operational plans. The threat of first-use and the corresponding nuclear force structure may undermine the effective deterrent strength of NATO's conventional forces.

The final important variable in the outcome of deterrence was the past behavior of the defender. The probit results indicated that if, in the most recent confrontation with the potential attacker, the defender acceded to the demands of the potential attacker, then the defender's bargaining reputation was undermined. In the next confrontation be-

sheimer, "Numbers, Strategy, and the European Balance," *International Security* 12:4 (1988):174–85; and Posen, "Is NATO decisively outnumbered?" *International Security* 12:4 (1988):186–202.

40. Richard K. Betts, *Surprise Attack: Lessons for Defense Planning* (Washington, D.C.: Brookings Institution, 1982), 153–227, and Richard K. Betts, "Conventional Deterrence: Predictive Uncertainty and Policy Confidence," *World Politics* 37: 2 (1985):153–79.

41. Paul Bracken (*The Command and Control of Nuclear Forces* [New Haven: Yale University Press, 1983], 129–78) and Daniel Charles (*Nuclear Planning in NATO: Pitfalls of First Use* [Cambridge: Ballinger, 1987]) examine the potential problems of command and control of NATO nuclear forces.

tween the two states the deterrent threats and actions of the defender lacked credibility. *If the outcome was conciliation by the defender instead of a stalemate or no past confrontation with the potential attacker, then the probability of successful deterrence decreased by 42%.*

A record of intransigence by the defender decreased by 32% the probability of successful deterrence. Although a reputation for unyielding firmness enhances credibility, it undercuts deterrence stability. If in a previous confrontation the defender refused to compromise and forced the potential attacker into a diplomatic defeat, then the potential attacker will be determined to avoid any appearance of retreating under pressure a second time. The past bullying of the defender may suggest to the potential attacker that a diplomatic solution with the defender is unlikely to be reached and that the only way to achieve its objectives is the use of force (the case studies of deterrence failure in chapter 6 examine the impact of past behavior).

These findings concerning past behavior lend ambiguous support to the argument that a state's commitments are interdependent. Weakness in one situation did undermine a state's future credibility; that is, if the defender backed down the likelihood of deterrence success decreased. But firmness in one situation did not necessarily enhance a state's credibility in another; a record of firm-but-flexible bargaining had no positive impact on deterrence outcomes, and past bullying, a negative impact. The past behavior of the defender in confrontations not involving the potential attacker did not significantly affect deterrence outcomes. The potential attacker did not seem to draw conclusions about the future behavior of the defender based on the defender's behavior in disputes with other states.[42] Rather, the past behavior of the defender was taken as an indicator of behavior in the current conflict only when the potential attacker had been directly involved in past confrontations with the defender. Past behavior and reputations are important, then, in continuing rivalries between adversaries who have a history of prior confrontations.

Probit analysis also demonstrated that the possession and capability to deliver nuclear weapons by the defender did not increase the likelihood of extended deterrence success (hypothesis 1.2). It is important,

42. This finding confirms Huth and Russett, ''What Makes Deterrence Work?'' on the impact of past behavior.

however, to distinguish between nuclear and nonnuclear attackers because, of the fifteen cases in which the defender possessed nuclear weapons, only one case included an attacker with nuclear capabilities. The empirical findings of the probit analysis thus relate almost exclusively to the value of nuclear weapons in deterring nonnuclear powers in extended-immediate deterrence confrontations.[43] Latent nuclear threats did not enhance the credibility of a defender's extended deterrent threat to a nonnuclear power. In addition to the risks of increasing the incentives for nuclear proliferation and the political backlash from domestic and international denunciation, two possible reasons for this finding are suggested by detailed examination of the individual cases. First, in most cases the destruction threatened by nuclear weapons would have been out of proportion to the potential attacker's military threat or the issues at stake in the confrontation. Second, in most cases the nuclear power also possessed sufficient conventional military capabilities (naval and land-based) to respond to the potential attacker's threat. Nuclear threat was not credible or relevant to a nonnuclear potential attacker in most cases of extended-immediate deterrence.[44]

The results of probit analysis did not support the hypothesis that strong economic and political-military ties between defender and protégé would enhance deterrence success (hypotheses 2.1–2.3). The existence of a military alliance between defender and protégé did not increase the probability of extended deterrence success. This finding is consistent with other studies that have found that alliance commitments have weak deterrent impact but contrasts with the finding in other studies that alliance ties influence the defender's decision to go to war once the protégé has been attacked. Thus, one source of miscalculation that can lead to the failure of extended deterrence and the outbreak of war is the potential attacker's tendency to discount the importance of alliance ties when it calculates the defender's response. The potential attacker may estimate that it can defeat the protégé before the defender could intervene, or that the defender's intervention would not prevent

43. Jacek Kugler reports a similar finding in ''Terror without Deterrence: Reassessing the Role of Nuclear Weapons,'' *Journal of Conflict Resolution* 28: 3 (1984):470–506.

44. The 1955 Quemoy-Matsu crisis involving the United States and China may be an exception. In the case study in chapter 5 of the off-shore islands crisis I explain why the United States nuclear threat probably contributed to the success of deterrence.

quick defeat of the protégé. In such a case, the defender would be forced to accept the new status quo ante despite the alliance commitment.[45]

The results of the probit analysis also indicated that the strength of foreign trade and arms transfer ties between defender and protégé did not influence extended deterrence outcomes significantly. Earlier studies have reported, however, that strong economic and military ties between defender and protégé were associated with extended deterrence success.[46] These previous studies did not incorporate the bargaining process into the analysis of deterrence cases. The strong impact of bargaining behavior on the potential attacker's estimate of defender intentions and interests might account for the difference in results. The level of arms transfers and foreign trade between defender and protégé represents an indirect basis for estimating the defender's interests at stake. The bargaining behavior of the defender, however, is a more direct indicator of the defender's intent to support the protégé, which the potential attacker is likely to infer reflects the importance of the interests at stake for the defender.[47] The conclusion to be drawn is not that high levels of military cooperation between defender and protégé are unimportant but that the bargaining behavior of the defender provides a more powerful and salient indicator of intentions than do the underlying ties between defender and protégé.

A second reason for this weak correlation would also help to explain why the hypotheses on the strategic value of the protégé to the potential attacker (3.1–3.3) were not supported by the probit analysis. What may have happened in a number of cases is that the protégé was of economic, political, and/or strategic value to both the defender and potential attacker. In such cases the defender's deterrent threat may have been viewed as credible, but the potential attacker also had more

45. The failure of alliances to deter confirms Russett, "The Calculus of Deterrence," and Huth and Russett, "What Makes Deterrence Work?" For the importance of alliance ties in the defender's decision to go to war, see Paul Huth and Bruce Russett, "Deterrence Failure and Escalation to War," *International Studies Quarterly* 32: 1 (1988):40–42.

46. Russett, "The Calculus of Deterrence," and Huth and Russett, "What Makes Deterrence Work?" found that military and economic ties have a positive, significant impact on deterrence outcomes.

47. Multicollinearity was not a problem because the auxiliary r^2 value for the arms transfer and foreign trade variables in the equation were 0.15 ad 0.08 respectively.

to gain by using force to coerce concessions from the protégé. The net effect would be to cancel out any consistent and significant impact for the value of the protégé on deterrence outcomes.

The results of the probit analysis indicate that the outcome of extended-immediate deterrence is influenced by a number of military and political factors that determine whether the military posture and deterrent actions of the defender balance the requirements of deterrence stability and credibility. The attacker's decision to escalate to war is generally based on the expectation of victory at acceptable costs and/or the high costs of continued peace. The decision to step back from a military confrontation, in contrast, is based on the uncertainty of victory, the potentially high costs of military action, and/or the belief that the costs of accommodation or inaction will not be too high. It is important to recognize, however, that probit analysis does not directly test whether the defender's threat of intervention deterred or provoked the potential attacker. Instead, I observed whether deterrence succeeded or failed and from the empirical results inferred that the military balance, crisis bargaining, and past behavior were critical in determining the credibility and stability of deterrence. The next step then is to examine individual cases of extended-immediate deterrence more closely to assess whether the inferences drawn from the results of probit analysis are correct.

5

Case Studies: The Impact of the Balance of Forces and Military Preparedness

In this chapter and the one to follow I analyze individual cases of deterrence success and failure to evaluate the generalizations suggested by the results of the probit analysis. By examining cases of both deterrence success and failure, I identify similarities as well as differences in the causal connections among variables. If the generalizations suggested by the probit analysis are of real value in predicting deterrence outcomes, then the analysis of deterrence successes should document the consistent impact of certain variables, whereas the analysis of deterrence failures should show the changes in the value of those variables and the impact of other variables.

I use three criteria to select cases for individual analysis. First, the case studies used include the historical confrontations and crises from 1885 to 1984 that are recognized by experts as the most important. I examine the crises leading to the outbreak of World Wars I and II as well as the U.S. decision to invade North Korea in 1950. Second, the case studies used represent a diverse set of cases to evaluate how applicable the generalizations of the probit analysis are to state behavior in various geographic regions and time periods. I therefore examine confrontations involving the Great Powers as well as regional powers in Europe, the Middle East and North Africa, Central Asia, and the Far East in the pre–World War I era, the interwar period, and post-1945. Third, the case studies used include individual cases that deviate from the expected results to illustrate some possible limitations and necessary refinements in the generalizations suggested by the probit analysis. Certain aspects of the confrontations leading to the outbreaks of World Wars I and II are useful for this purpose, as is the Quemoy-Matsu crisis of 1955.

The individual case studies are not intended to be comprehensive historical examinations of particular confrontations. I analyze each case with the purpose of assessing the relevance of particular variables on the success or failure of deterrence. When it is not possible to present a detailed analysis of the potential attacker's decision-making process, I reconstruct the broad outlines of the confrontation as it was likely to be evaluated by the potential attacker. On that basis I assess the likely impact of such variables as the balance of military forces, bargaining strategies, and past behavior on deterrence outcomes. In this chapter I examine in detail the potential attacker's assessment of the costs of armed conflict with the protégé and the risks of war with the defender. I then use this analysis to evaluate the generalizations about the impact of the balance of military forces and the defender's policy of military escalation on deterrence outcomes. I discuss diplomacy and negotiations only briefly because many of the cases lacked diplomatic interaction or direct negotiations between defender and potential attacker. Diplomatic strategies and negotiating behavior of the defender was peripheral in influencing the decisions of the potential attacker. I examine three cases of successful deterrence—the Jordanian civil war of 1970, the Chadian civil war of 1983, and the Quemoy-Matsu crisis of 1955—and three cases of deterrence failure—the Czech crisis of 1938, the Polish crisis of 1939, and the Korean War of 1950. A twofold theme emerges from the case studies: First, deterrence failure is likely if the potential attacker believes it can achieve a quick and decisive defeat of the protégé without becoming embroiled in a larger armed conflict with the defender; and, second, a tit-for-tat strategy of military escalation by the defender contributes to deterrence success by erasing an imbalance of local forces that favors the potential attacker and thereby denying the potential attacker a fait accompli.

Cases of Deterrence Success

The Syrian and Israeli confrontation in the Jordanian civil war, 1970. The rapid and decisive military defeat of Arab armed forces in the Six Day War of June 1967 led to Israeli occupation of previously held Arab territories: Sinai, the Golan Heights, the West Bank, and

Jerusalem. Following the war, attempts to conclude a peace agreement failed, and as a result Israel remained in control of the newly occupied territories. The Arab countries, however, refused to accept the new status quo.

In the wake of the political and military deadlock following the Six Day War a militant and increasingly popular Palestinian guerrilla movement began to emerge as a strong force in the Arab world.[1] The guerrilla forces were committed to the formation of an independent Palestinian state via a popular armed struggle against Israel. The *fedayeen,* as they were called in Arabic, established military bases in a number of Arab countries, including Lebanon, Syria, and Jordan. The largest concentration of fedayeen were based in Jordan, where an uneasy partnership between the guerrilla forces and the regime of King Hussein developed.[2]

Tensions between the fedayeen and the Jordanian government centered on the degree of freedom the guerrilla forces were to have in their armed raids on Israeli forces in the occupied territories along the West Bank. Both parties shared the desire to apply military pressure against Israel and to reestablish control of the territories occupied by Israeli armed forces. The Jordanian government, however, viewed the guerrilla attacks of the fedayeen as potentially disruptive to, if not in conflict with, efforts to reach a peace settlement with Israel. King Hussein sought to limit the military operations of the fedayeen for fear that unrestricted guerrilla attacks would cause escalating Israeli reprisals that would threaten Jordanian security and undermine attempts at negotiations. The fedayeen, however, more militant in their opposition to Israel, resisted efforts by the Jordanian government to restrict their military operations and freedom of movement within the country.[3]

In early February 1970 the Jordanian government issued new security regulations in an attempt to maintain law and order within the country. The fedayeen rejected the new security regulations, and a tense confrontation, including armed clashes, developed between the guerrillas and the Jordanian army. Talks between the leadership of the

1. William B. Quandt, Faud Jabber, and Ann Mosely Lesch, *The Politics of Palestinian Nationalism* (Berkeley: University of California Press, 1973), 176–85.

2. Ibid., 52–123, 186–98.

3. Ibid., 195–98.

fedayeen and the government led to an agreement on 22 February.[4] The February accord, however, reduced tensions only temporarily, and by June the fedayeen and the Jordanian army were engaged in further armed clashes. The confrontation rose to a crisis when the fedayeen demanded that King Hussein dismiss a number of military and civilian leaders accused of being anti-fedayeen and disband a recently formed special security force. A cease-fire agreement signed 10 June failed because each side charged the other with violations. By the end of June total casualties for the fedayeen and the Jordanian army were estimated at more than fifteen hundred.[5]

Further attempts to reach a stable cease-fire agreement (10 July, 8 and 10 September) failed, as armed clashes between government forces and the guerrillas continued through August and early September. Threatened with the collapse of his political power and authority and under heavy criticism from the military, King Hussein announced on 16 September the formation of a provisional military government with a mandate to restore law and order within the country. The Hussein government had decided to impose, by force of arms, control over the activities of the fedayeen within Jordan. The guerrilla forces responded by calling for a popular rebellion and began preparations for an armed confrontation. At dawn on 17 September heavy fighting broke out between Palestinian guerrillas and the Jordanian army in and around the capital, Amman. Heavy fighting also broke out in the critical town of Ramtha, located just south of the Syrian-Jordanian border and very close to the most important road junction in northern Jordan. The control of Ramtha and the junction would ensure the guerrilla forces access to supply lines from Syria and the main road leading to Amman.[6] In the first two days of armed clashes the guerrilla forces suffered heavy losses and were on the defensive. United States and Israeli officials were confident that the Jordanian army would defeat the armed resistance of the guerrillas quickly.[7]

4. Daniel Dishon, ed., *Middle East Record, 1969–1970,* vol. 5 (Jerusalem: Israel Universities Press, 1977), 796–99.

5. Ibid., 803–11.

6. British Broadcasting Corporation Monitoring Service (hereafter referred to as BBC), *Summary of World Broadcasts: The Middle East and Africa,* 17 September 1970:3484/A/9–14, 19 September 1970:3486/A/10–21.

7. Alan Dowty, *Middle East Crisis: U.S. Decision-Making in 1958, 1970, and 1973* (Berkeley: University of California Press, 1984), 149–50.

The Syrian regime, headed by President Nureddin al-Atasi, was a strong supporter of the fedayeen in Jordan and opposed the more moderate position of King Hussein in the Arab-Israeli conflict. The decision by the Jordanian government in mid-September to move against the fedayeen therefore led to a quick counterreaction by the Syrian government. On 17 September the Jordanian ambassador in Damascus was summoned to the Syrian foreign ministry and informed that Syria would not remain indifferent or inactive while Palestinian guerrillas were being attacked by the Jordanian army.[8] On 18 September President Atasi declared: "We—government, party, revolution, and people—regard the battle [in Jordan] as our battle. It is a battle for Arab existence, and to safeguard Arab existence; we must give enormously in blood, money, and everything else to consolidate and protect the Palestinian revolution until . . . victory."[9]

Syrian military forces were being prepared for armed intervention and were moving into forward positions along the Jordanian border. On the evening of 18 September Syrian tanks and troops, disguised as forces of the Palestine Liberation Army, began to cross the border into Jordan and take positions just south of Ramtha, while Jordanian forces withdrew to night positions near Irbid. Syrian troops and armor continued to cross the Jordanian border during the night, and on the following day Syrian forces advanced to Irbid.[10]

The Israeli government was watching the deteriorating situation in Jordan with concern. The Hussein regime was regarded by Israeli leaders as one of the more moderate governments in the Arab world, certainly preferable to the leadership of the guerrilla forces. The Israeli government therefore had an interest in ensuring that King Hussein was not replaced by a more militant regime. As Defense Minister Moshe Dayan explained in an interview, Israel would not have minded if Hussein had been replaced by a regime willing to make peace, but the leaders of the fedayeen—Yassir Arafat or Georges Habash—were "unacceptable from the Israeli point of view."[11] Israel considered the maintenance of the Hussein regime in power to be of vital importance.

The Israeli government therefore issued a series of warnings that

8. BBC, *Summary of World Broadcasts,* 18 September 1970:3485/A/20.
9. Ibid., 21 September 1970:3487/A/9.
10. Dishon, ed., *Middle East Record,* 850.
11. Ibid., 855.

the outcome of the civil war in Jordan was closely linked to the security of Israel. On 13 September, for example, Deputy Premier Yigal Allon stated that Israel had "special security interests in Jordan" and that "it must insure them. The situation may arrive when Israel may have to act."[12] On 18 September it was reported that "high-ranking authoritative sources within the Israeli Government said that Israel was keeping open the option of taking action in case of changes in Jordan which could adversely affect Israel's security."[13]

As Syrian forces were being moved into position for intervention in Jordan prior to 18 September, Israel responded with a reciprocal military buildup in preparation for a counterintervention. Israeli tanks and troops began to be moved from the south to northern Israel, and Israeli troops were concentrated in the Bet Shean Valley and in Lower Galilee, facing the Syrian forces in Jordan. The Israeli air force began to carry out reconnaissance flights in Jordanian airspace over the Syrian forces. On the Golan Heights, the western flank of the Syrian invasion force, heavy reinforcements of tanks and troops were moved into forward positions and placed on high alert.[14]

The immediate objective of the Syrian military intervention was to prevent the Jordanian army from reestablishing control over Ramtha and the junction just south and to then consolidate the position of the guerrilla forces in northern Jordan. The Syrian intervention was very similar to a limited aims strategy designed to seize Jordanian territory to establish a secure base for the guerrilla forces in the country. By 21 September the size of the invading Syrian forces was estimated at approximately a division with two hundred T-54 and T-55 tanks, which amounted to almost half of Syria's most capable heavy armor. Opposing the Syrian forces, in and around Ramtha, was only the Jordanian Fortieth Brigade. The other Jordanian armored brigade was deployed in and around the capital.[15]

On 20 September Syrian armed forces went into action against the Jordanian army at the Ramtha junction. The first attack, led by an armored brigade, was repulsed by Jordanian forces. Syria responded by committing another armored brigade to combat and in a second attack forced the Jordanian Fortieth Brigade to withdraw to a defensive line

12. *New York Times,* 17 September 1970, 19.
13. Dishon, ed., *Middle East Record,* 854.
14. Ibid., 854.
15. Ibid., 852.

MAP 1. The Middle East

south of the Ramtha junction in order to prevent a possible advance on the capital. By the morning of 21 September Syrian and guerrilla forces controlled the Ramtha junction and Syrian tanks had entered Irbid.[16]

16. BBC, *Summary of World Broadcasts,* 22 September 1970:3488/A/10–11, A/27–29, 23 September 1970:3489/A/24–25.

The advance of Syrian forces on 20 September had led King Hussein to send two urgent requests for air strikes against the Syrians to the United States that evening, expressing openness to the possibility of Israeli intervention.[17] The distance from the Syrian border to Amman was less than fifty miles, and a rapid attack from Irbid by Syrian forces could have reached the capital within twenty-four hours. The United States contacted the Israeli government late in the evening and discussed the possibility of an Israeli air strike, with National Security Adviser Henry Kissinger tentatively approving such a strike if necessary. Israeli Ambassador Yitzhak Rabin, however, argued that air strikes might not be sufficient and that intervention on the ground might be necessary as well. On 21 September Rabin contacted Kissinger and informed him that based on the latest intelligence Israeli military leaders were certain that air strikes alone would not be sufficient to repulse the Syrians. The Israeli government therefore pressed for explicit assurances from the United States that it would intervene to defend Israel in the contingency of an Egyptian or Soviet counter-response. Evidently, the United States provided Israel with neither a formal, specific assurance of support nor a detailed plan of military actions to be taken in the event of intervention. Contingency plans for Israeli air and armored intervention in Jordan and Syria were nevertheless agreed to. Israeli intervention was to occur if the Syrians reinforced their troops and armor in Jordan and advanced on the capital or if the Syrian air force were committed to battle.[18]

The Israeli government, however, would not directly intervene until absolutely necessary. The risks of escalation were too high to justify immediate action. Instead, Israeli policymakers hoped that further warnings and military preparations would be sufficient to convince the Syrian leadership to withdraw. The Israeli government therefore issued another warning to Syria on 20 September. Acting Prime Minister Allon "expressed the hope that Syria would reconsider her actions before she penetrated 'too deeply' into Jordan." Allon concluded by stating that Israel would "follow developments there [in Jordan] very closely in order to protect Israel's legitimate security interests."[19]

17. Dowty, *Middle East Crisis,* 169–70.

18. Ibid., 171–73; Adam M. Garfinkle, "U.S. Decision Making in the Jordan Crisis: Correcting the Record," *Political Science Quarterly* 100: 1 (1985):117–38; and Dishon, ed., *Middle East Record,* 855.

19. Dishon, ed., *Middle East Record,* 854.

Israeli military preparations continued along both the West Bank and the Golan Heights with heavy reinforcements of troops and tanks. By 21 September Israeli armed forces were poised for immediate intervention if necessary: approximately four hundred tanks and two armored brigades had been fully mobilized on the Golan Heights, more than one third of the army reserves were being mobilized as part of a larger intervention force, and the Israeli air force had been put on full alert.[20]

On 22 September the Jordanian army went on the counteroffensive and King Hussein ordered the air force into action. With air support Jordanian armor halted the Syrian forces in and around Ramtha. On 23 September Syrian forces withdrew from Jordan, and the Jordanian army quickly surrounded the city of Ramtha and established effective control of the area.[21] That day King Hussein offered terms for settlement of the armed conflict with the fedayeen: (1) guerrilla forces withdraw from Amman and all other towns; (2) guerrilla forces occupy bases along the cease-fire line with Israel; (3) the guerrillas respect and abide by Jordanian law; and (4) the Jordanian government would only recognize Yassir Arafat as leader of the PLO.

With the Jordanian army in control of both the Ramtha junction and the capital, Amman, and having lost the direct support of their Syrian ally, the leadership of the Palestinian guerrillas agreed to King Hussein's terms. The terms of a cease-fire agreement were agreed upon in principle on 25 September, and on 27 September the Jordanian government concluded the Cairo Agreement, ending the immediate confrontation.[22]

The threat of Israeli intervention most likely played a critical role in the Syrian decision to withdraw from northern Jordan on 23 September.[23] Militarily, Syrian forces were in a position of local dominance in

20. Ibid., 854–55; William B. Quandt, *Decade of Decisions: American Policy towards the Arab-Israeli Conflict, 1967–1976* (Berkeley: University of California Press, 1977), 117–18; William B. Quandt, "Lebanon, 1958, and Jordan, 1970," in *Force without War: U.S. Armed Forces as a Political Instrument,* Barry M. Blechman and Stephen S. Kaplan (Washington, D.C.: Brookings Institution, 1978), 283; and Henry Kissinger, *White House Years* (Boston: Little, Brown, 1979), 626–28.

21. BBC, *Summary of World Broadcasts,* 24 September 1970:3490/A/12, 25 September 1970:3491/A/9–10.

22. Dishon, ed., *Middle East Record,* 860–70.

23. Israeli deterrent actions may also have influenced Iraq's decision not to become involved in the Jordanian civil war. Approximately seventeen thousand Iraqi troops had been stationed in Jordan since the Arab-Israeli war in 1967, and the Iraqi government had

northern Jordan, as the Jordanian forces were outnumbered by at least 3 to 1 (a division versus a brigade). Syria furthermore had the capability to reinforce with superior manpower, armor, and air support if the conflict were to escalate beyond the engagement of local forces. Syria, for example, had approximately 850 tanks against Jordan's 310 and 210 combat aircraft against Jordan's 38.[24] In a strictly Syrian-Jordanian military confrontation, Syria was in a strong position to establish and maintain control of positions in northern Jordan, if not to advance on the capital and attempt to defeat the Jordanian army.

Israel, however, responded to the Syrian threat with a tit-for-tat policy of military escalation. Within a week, from 15 to 22 September, Israel escalated its military preparations from the buildup of forces along the border, to the positioning of such forces for possible intervention, and finally to their preparation for immediate engagement. These military actions by Israel shifted the balance of military forces against Syria. The mobilization of 400 tanks and two armored brigades for immediate intervention erased Syria's 3 to 1 advantage in the immediate balance of forces in and around Ramtha. Furthermore, the mobilization of army reserves by Israel ensured that if the conflict escalated into a larger Israeli-Syrian war the balance of forces would have shifted decisively against Syria. Fully mobilized, the Syrian army numbered 75,000 men whereas the Israeli army totaled 275,000, and Israeli air power and armored strength greatly outnumbered the Syrian forces as well.[25] The combined effect of the Israeli military preparations was to significantly increase the costs of pursuing a limited aims strategy for Syria and to threaten Syria with a defeat in a war. Outnumbered in the immediate as well as the short-term balance of forces, Syria was not in a position to achieve its objectives in Jordan without incurring substantial military costs.

The Syrian regime had been deeply divided on the decision to

---

been a strong supporter of the guerrilla forces within Jordan. Israeli and United States policymakers were initially more concerned about Iraqi intervention than about the threat posed by Syria when King Hussein formed the military government on 16 September. But the Iraqi forces avoided involvement in the ensuing armed conflict between the Jordanian army and guerrilla forces.

24. *The Military Balance, 1970–1971* (London: International Institute for Strategic Studies, 1970), 41, 44.

25. Ibid., 40–41.

intervene in Jordan.[26] The ruling Baath party was split into civilian and military factions. The civilian wing, led by President Atasi, favored a militant policy toward Israel and ordered the intervention in Jordan in support of the fedayeen. President Atasi and his supporters may have calculated that Israel would be reluctant to enter an intra-Arab conflict and would in addition be deterred by the threat of possible Egyptian and Soviet counterresponses. Israel had retreated from strategic bombing of Egyptian territory earlier that year after the Soviet Union had intervened in support of Egyptian air defenses.[27] Indeed, Israeli leaders were concerned about possible Egyptian and Soviet counterresponses—concerned enough to both press the United States for a formal commitment to defend Israel and delay direct intervention for as long as possible. The military wing of the Baath party, led by Defense Minister and Air Force Commander Hafiz al-Asad, opposed intervention on the grounds that it entailed a serious risk of provoking Israeli intervention and drawing Syria into a disastrous military conflict.[28] But the relatively weak military position of the guerrilla forces and their heavy losses in clashes with the Jordanian army from 14 to 17 September seems to have galvanized the civilian wing to decide in favor of armed intervention. The Syrian military operation to defend and consolidate the position of the guerrilla forces in and around Ramtha was reportedly to be achieved within two or three days.[29]

Although there is debate as to the Soviet role in the initial Syrian decision to intervene, the Soviets pressured Syria to withdraw from Jordan, partly because of Israeli and U.S. military actions that threatened to escalate the civil war into a larger confrontation. The Soviets pressed for an immediate cease-fire agreement between the guerrilla forces and the Jordanian government following the Syrian intervention. President Gamel Nasser of Egypt also pressed for an immediate cease-

26. For a general study of the conflicts within the Syrian political and military leadership, see Nikolaos Van Dam, *The Struggle for Power in Syria: Sectarianism, Regionalism, and Tribalism in Politics, 1961–1978* (New York: St. Martin's, 1979).

27. Alvin Z. Rubinstein, "Air Support in the Arab East," in *Diplomacy of Power: Soviet Armed Forces as a Political Instrument,* ed. Stephen S. Kaplan (Washington, D.C.: Brookings Institution, 1981), 471–88; Lawrence L. Whetten, *The Canal War: Four Power Conflict in the Middle East* (Cambridge: M.I.T. Press, 1974); and Dishon, ed., *Middle East Record,* 43–78.

28. Dishon, ed., *Middle East Record,* 1150.

29. Ibid., 1150–51.

fire and did not attempt to deter Israeli intervention. Both countries viewed the Syrian-Jordanian conflict as a serious threat to Arab unity and therefore to the benefit of Israel.[30] Syria did not receive the support of its two most important allies and faced clear indications from extensive military preparations that Israel would intervene to protect the Hussein regime. The probable calculations of Atasi and his supporters that intervention in the civil war could be limited to a Syrian-Jordanian confrontation in which Syria could achieve its objectives quickly and that Soviet and Egyptian support could be relied on in a larger conflict were therefore mistaken. Asad, who had opposed the initial decision to intervene, refused to commit the forces necessary to defeat the Jordanian army. Asad is reported to have argued that had Syrian "forces succeeded in advancing deep into Jordan they would have been easy prey to a flank attack from Israel." When the Jordanian air force attacked Syrian forces on 22 September, Asad refused to use the superior Syrian air force against Jordan, fearing that this escalation would trigger Israeli intervention (which was correct). Without air support, Syrian forces suffered losses and were forced to withdraw. It was Asad who reportedly ordered the immediate withdrawal of Syrian forces from Jordan on 22 September.[31]

The Israeli capability to intervene quickly with superior forces deterred the military leadership of Syria, led by Asad, from further escalating its military involvement in the Jordanian civil war. Israel's tit-for-tat policy of military preparations convinced the Syrian military leaders that the risks and likely costs of supporting the guerrilla forces were too high. Immediate intervention by Israel on 20 or 21 September might have provoked military response by the Soviets and Egyptians, perhaps triggering a direct U.S.-Soviet confrontation. Conversely, if

30. Ibid., 857–58, 863–71, and Dowty, *Middle East Crisis,* 145–74. United States support for Jordan and Israel probably neutralized the potential opposition of the Soviet Union and isolated Syria in a potential confrontation with Israel. United States actions contributed to deterrence at the level of superpower relations, whereas Israeli actions functioned as a deterrent at the regional or local level. See Quandt, "Lebanon, 1958 and Jordan, 1970," 287.

31. Dishon, ed., *Middle East Record,* 1150. Syria's failure in Jordan precipitated a new confrontation between the civilian and military wings of the Baath Party in October and November 1970. On 18 October Atasi resigned as President and Prime Minister, and on 16 November, following the conclusion of the Tenth National Congress, a new government led by Asad was formed.

Israel had not quickly alerted and reinforced its forces Syria—particularly President Atasi and his supporters—might have been tempted to reinforce Syrian armed forces in Jordan and even to advance on the capital, which would most likely have triggered a belated Israeli intervention. In either scenario the Jordanian civil war might have escalated into another Arab-Israeli war and a superpower confrontation in support of regional allies. Israeli military preparations and capabilities in defense of Jordan successfully balanced the requirements of deterrence credibility and stability. As the results of the probit model suggested, a policy of tit for tat in military escalation by the defender coupled with the defender's advantage in the immediate and short-term balance of forces was an effective deterrent.

Franco-Libyan confrontation in Chad, 1983. The involvement of Libya and its leader, Colonel Moamer Qaddafi, in the internal affairs of neighboring Chad is long-standing. In June 1973 Libyan forces occupied the Aouzou Strip in northern Chad (which is believed to be rich in minerals, uranium in particular) and Libya has controlled the territory since that time despite the protests of successive Chadian governments.[32] Since its independence in 1960 Chad has been divided by deep political cleavages that have enabled external powers to intervene in the struggle for political power between competing domestic groups. During the 1970s Libya supplied military arms and provided financial support and training bases for rebel forces in the continuing civil war in Chad.[33] In 1978 and 1979 Libya intervened with limited military forces in support of rebel groups, but the interventions did not have a decisive impact on the civil war.[34] Underlying the involvement of Libya in the political affairs of Chad is Qaddafi's larger goal of creating an "Islamic state of the Sahara" that would include Libya, Chad, Mali, and Niger.[35] Libyan support for rebel forces escalated in December 1980

---

32. Colin Legum, ed., *Africa Contemporary Record, 1974–1975* (London: Rex Collings, 1975), B568.

33. For an analysis of the origins of the civil war in Chad see Rene Lemarchand, "Chad: The Roots of Chaos," *Current History* 80: (1981):414–38.

34. P. Edward Haley, *Qaddafi and the United States since 1969* (New York: Praeger, 1984), 96–110.

35. Colin Legum, ed., *Africa Contemporary Record, 1980–1981* (New York: Holmes and Meier, 1981), A36.

when large-scale military intervention by Libyan military forces (totaling 4,000–5,000 troops) enabled Qaddafi's Chadian ally, Weddeye Goukouni, to overrun the capital, Ndjamena, and to defeat his rival, Hissene Habré. In January 1981 Qaddafi announced plans to merge Libya and Chad.[36]

As the former colonial ruler, France has maintained close ties with Chad since its independence. Chad is viewed by the French as an important strategic buffer, shielding the French-protected states of the Central African Republic and Cameroon to the south. France has provided economic and military aid to successive Chadian regimes in an attempt to establish a stable government within the country.[37] French military forces have also been stationed in Chad as a deterrent to external intervention and to support the government against rebel forces within the country. In August 1979, however, France agreed in the Lagos Accord to withdraw its troops from Chad and to have a peacekeeping force from the Organization of African Unity (OAU) serve as a replacement. The French agreed to withdraw their forces based on the expectation that Libya would not attempt to intervene and that Nigeria would actively support Chad until the OAU peacekeeping presence was established within the country. French military forces were withdrawn from Chad by May 1980. The French policy of supporting a greater role for African states in resolving the Chadian civil war collapsed, however, when Nigeria did not assume an active role in protecting Chad and the OAU could not agree on the formation of a peacekeeping force. A military vacuum therefore developed in Chad, and Libya, contrary to French expectations, quickly capitalized on the situation by moving into Chad with its own military forces in December 1980.[38]

The Libyan military intervention in Chad was a clear setback for French policy in Africa. The French government was criticized domestically and by its African allies for failing to honor its security commitments in the region. French intelligence sources had closely monitored

36. Ibid., A35–A46; Haley, *Qaddafi and the United States,* 198–218; and *Keesing's Contemporary Archives, 1981* (London: Longman, 1981), 30694–96.

37. David S. Yost, "French Policy in Chad and the Libyan Challenge," *Orbis* 26: 4 (1983):965–71.

38. Legum, ed., *African Contemporary Record, 1980–1981,* A42, and Haley, *Qaddafi and the United States,* 198–202.

Libyan military movements throughout the summer and fall 1980, and President Giscard d'Estaing had attempted to enlist OAU support in opposing a potential Libyan intervention. By early December, French military forces were placed on alert and were prepared to intervene in Chad. On 13 December a verbal warning was issued by the French government to Libya. Unable, however, to secure OAU support for intervention, France decided not to intervene unilaterally and informed the Libyan government of this decision on 23 December. The French government requested that Libya respect Chad's independence, but Libyan forces soon completed the assault on Ndjamena that had been in progress since early December.[39]

When it became known that the merger had been unilaterally imposed on Goukouni, neighboring African states, led by Nigeria, strongly criticized the plan and demanded Libyan withdrawal. In November 1981 Libyan military forces withdrew from Chad at the request of Goukouni.[40] Goukouni's Transitional National Union Government (GUNT), however, quickly proved incapable of consolidating power, and a small OAU peacekeeping force was unable to prevent resumption of the civil war. In June 1982 Habré's Forces Armées Nationales Tchadiennes (FANT) overran Ndjamena and forced Goukouni and GUNT into exile, reversing the defeat of December 1980.

By spring 1983 Goukouni's forces, resupplied by Libyan arms, were prepared to confront the Habré regime. In May the GUNT launched a major offensive (2,000–3,000 troops) southward from its base in northern Chad toward Faya-Largeau, the major crossroads of northern Chad. By late May western sources reported the buildup of Libyan air and ground forces in the Aouzou Strip along the Chad-Libyan border.[41] Faya-Largeau fell to the GUNT forces on 24 June. The Chadian government charged that Libyan troops were supporting the GUNT forces at Faya-Largeau, and French Foreign Minister Claude Cheysson warned on that same day that France would not remain indifferent to Libyan involvement in Chad. On 28 June French Presi-

39. Legum, ed., *African Contemporary Record, 1980–1981,* A42; and Yost, "French Policy in Chad," 971–74.

40. Rene Lemarchand, "Chad: The Road to Partition," *Current History* 83: (1984):115, and Haley, *Qaddafi and the United States,* 204–13.

41. *United States Foreign Broadcast Information Service: Middle East and North Africa,* 1 June 1983:Q6.

dent Francois Mitterand accused Libya of direct intervention and announced that France would begin an immediate airlift of military arms to the Chadian government.[42] The Libyan government and Qaddafi denied the charges of direct intervention and warned that French intervention in Chad would provoke a confrontation with Libya.[43] GUNT forces pressed ahead and captured Abéché (an important base from which FANT had received arms and supplies in 4the past) in early July.[44]

Habré's FANT army (approximately 3,000 troops) began a counteroffensive on 8 July and quickly recaptured Abéché as GUNT forces retreated to Faya-Largeau. Advancing northwest against little opposition, Habré's forces drove out GUNT forces and reestablished control over territories that had just previously been captured by the rebel forces. On 30 July FANT forces recaptured the critical area of Faya-Largeau.[45]

The success of Habré's counteroffensive led to direct military intervention by Libya in support of the GUNT forces. Western intelligence reports indicated that on 24 July Libyan aircraft, capable of airlifting troops and providing tactical air support, had been moved from positions in southern Libya into northern Chad. On 31 July Libyan aircraft began to strike FANT positions at Faya-Largeau and points south, and by 9 August Libyan tanks and ground forces were reported to be advancing on Faya-Largeau. Faced with superior military forces, Habré's FANT forces were forced to withdraw from Faya-Largeau and points south beginning on 10 August. By mid-August GUNT and Libyan forces were advancing southward beyond Faya-Largeau. The intervention of Libyan forces (2,000–3,000 troops) had shifted the balance of local military strength against the forces of Habré and put the rebel forces of GUNT in a favorable position to repeat their assault on the capital as in December 1980.[46]

In an attempt to deter an advance on the capital, the French govern-

42. Robert Fraser, ed., *Keesing's Contemporary Archives, 1983* (London: Longman, 1983), 32591–92, and Colin Legum, ed., *Africa Contemporary Record, 1983–1984* (New York: Holmes and Meier, 1985), B350.

43. Fraser, ed., *Keesing's, 1983*, 32592, and *FBIS*, 7 July 1983:Q1–2.

44. Legum, ed., *African Contemporary Record, 1983–1984*, B348–50.

45. Fraser, ed., *Keesing's, 1983*, 32592.

46. Ibid.; Haley, *Qaddafi and the United States*, 318–19.

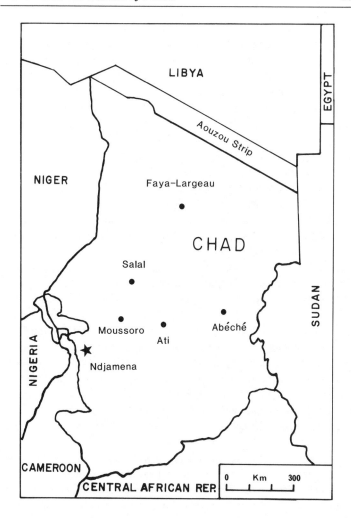

MAP 2. Central Africa

ment countered the buildup of Libyan forces in Chad and their advance southward with a reciprocal military escalation in support of Habré's FANT forces. At an emergency meeting of the French cabinet on 4 August President Mitterand decided to commit French forces to the defense of the Habré regime. On the following day orders were issued that preparations be made within forty-eight hours for the airlifting of French troops to Chad—Operation Manta.[47] Between 10 and 13 August over 1,000 French troops were airlifted to the Chadian capital from military bases in France and the Central African Republic. On 13 August a detachment of 180 paratroops was moved from the capital to positions at Abéché, the point most likely to be attacked next. The commander of the French troops in Chad, Brig. Gen. Jean Poli, warned, "If we are attacked, we shall defend ourselves." On the following day an additional 1,000 French troops, equipped with helicopters and antiaircraft guns, took positions at Salal, Ati, Moussoro, and Mao with the stated purpose of forming a defensive line (the Red Line, as it came to be called) to oppose further advance by Libyan and rebel forces. French military sources also reported that a squadron of Jaguar fighter aircraft were "standing by for any eventuality at a base in the Central African Republic."[48]

Within less than a week France had responded to the threat of a Libyan advance on the capital with a reciprocal buildup of ground forces in Chad. During late August further reinforcements of French troops were airlifted to Chad and deployed in forward positions along the Red Line. The total number of French troops on the ground in Chad by the end of August was approximately 3,000 with at least ten combat aircraft stationed in Ndjamena prepared to provide tactical support.[49] To underscore the military actions taken by France, President Mitterand warned in an interview published in *Le Monde* on 25 August, "If threatened, our troops will riposte and in order to defend themselves effectively, they will not limit themselves to purely defensive retaliation."[50]

Operation Manta was a quick and effective response to the direct Libyan intervention in Chad and the immediate threat of an advance on the capital, Ndjamena. The formation of a defensive line by French troops at forward positions ensured that any further advance by Libyan and rebel forces would result in a direct confrontation with French

47. Legum, ed., *African Contemporary Record, 1983–1984*, B350–51.
48. Fraser, ed., *Keesing's, 1983*, 32593, and Haley, *Qaddafi and the United States*, 319–21.
49. Legum, ed., *African Contemporary Record, 1983–1984*, A210, and Lemarchand, "Chad: The Road to Partition," 116.
50. Fraser, ed., *Keesing's, 1983*, 32593.

forces. The defensive line therefore acted as a potent trip-wire force that greatly enhanced the credibility of France's deterrent warnings. Furthermore, Operation Manta had a decisive impact on the local balance of forces. The deployment of 3,000 French ground troops at forward positions in Chad created a rough parity in the immediate balance of forces, and the trip-wire role of these forces ensured that France would reinforce with superior forces if the conflict escalated to a larger armed confrontation. Thus, as with the threat of Israeli counterintervention in the 1970 Jordanian case, a French policy of tit for tat in military escalation signaled not only France's determination to support Chad but also the capability to deny Libya a quick military victory at relatively low cost.

In December 1980 Qaddafi had pressed ahead and overrun the capital in a matter of weeks despite a French warning and the alerting of French forces. Qaddafi had presented France with a fait accompli; however, there had been no French forces in Chad at that time, much less in forward positions prepared to repulse a Libyan advance. Qaddafi may have initially believed that the French warnings in late June 1983 were a bluff and that France would not intervene as it had in December 1980. In early July 1983 the French had refused a request by the Chadian government for direct intervention and had instead limited their support to the provision of military arms and equipment. French military actions in August, however, greatly altered the strategic situation confronting Libya. It was no longer possible for Libyan and GUNT forces to take the capital without provoking direct armed clashes with the French. In August 1983 the balance of immediate military forces did not favor Libya, and the costs of an offensive to take the capital were much too high. Qaddafi drew back from further military escalation. A military stalemate resulted: Libyan and rebel forces would not cross the Red Line despite statements by rebel leaders of their intention to continue fighting until they controlled all of Chad, while France stated that it had no intention of compelling Libya to withdraw its forces from Chad despite the urging of FANT leaders to drive all Libyan forces out of Chad. Sporadic clashes were reported between opposing sides in early September, but no major military operations were undertaken.

As the stalemate developed in Chad diplomatic initiatives were undertaken to construct a long-term political solution to the civil war.

Libya and France made unofficial contacts in mid-August, and in late August Mitterand proposed a form of federation in Chad as a political solution.[51] Further progress was reported in late September when Goukouni dropped the demand for French withdrawal as a precondition to negotiations with Habré. The Chadian government in turn dropped its preconditions for negotiations and agreed to attend a meeting with all of the rebel factions represented.[52] The proposed meeting scheduled for early 1984 did not take place, and negotiations between the government and rebel forces were not attempted again until 1986. The stalemate in Chad persisted as Libyan forces continued to occupy Northern Chad. France continued to support Chad and reintroduced French troops in 1986 after their withdrawal in 1984. In early 1987 the stalemate ended when government forces decisively defeated Libyan forces and compelled them to withdraw from Northern Chad back across the border into Libya.

The off-shore islands crisis, 1955. The military defeat of the nationalist forces by the communists in 1949 forced Chiang Kai-shek to evacuate mainland China and to establish a rival government on Taiwan, an island located about a hundred miles off the mainland coast. Chinese nationalist forces also occupied a number of much smaller islands located directly offshore (fewer than ten miles from the coast). Control over these offshore islands had assumed a symbolic as well as strategic importance in the continuing struggle between the Chinese nationalist and communist forces.

Militarily, control of the offshore islands provided the nationalist forces with a forward defensive position from which to repulse a communist invasion of Taiwan. Conversely, nationalist control over the offshore islands could also serve as a bridgehead or forward base from which nationalist forces could launch an invasion of the mainland. Chinese nationalist forces had also used their control of the offshore islands to place economic and political pressure on the People's Republic of China (PRC). From their positions on the Quemoy and Matsu

51. Ibid.

52. Legum, ed., *African Contemporary Record, 1983–1984,* A210, and *New York Times,* 26 November 1983, 3.

islands the nationalist forces were able to institute a partial blockade of the ports of Amoy and Foochow. The nationalists had used these islands as bases for launching covert operations against the mainland.

Nationalist control of the offshore islands was also a symbol of the weakness of the communist government since, historically, the off-shore islands had been under the control of the mainland government. Continued occupation of the offshore islands was an open challenge and act of defiance by the nationalist forces. The PRC had strong incentives to wrest control of the offshore islands from Chinese na-tionalist forces. Strategically, control of such offshore islands as Quemoy and Matsu would remove a potential military threat to the security of the PRC. In addition, control of the offshore islands by the PRC would decrease the immediate threat of subversion and espionage and would deal a sharp blow to the morale of the nationalist regime, since control of the islands kept alive their hope of an eventual return to the mainland.[53]

The critical question confronting the PRC leadership in considering an attack on the nationalist-held offshore islands was the reaction of Taiwan's closest supporter, the United States. In January 1950 Presi-dent Harry S. Truman announced the U.S. decision not to provide military aid to the Chinese nationalists and not to become involved in the civil war.[54] The outbreak of the Korean War in June 1950, how-ever, resulted in a reconsideration of that policy, and on 27 June

53. Some analysts have argued that the PRC did not intend to seize Quemoy and Matsu but was attempting to prevent the United States and Taiwan from signing a mutual defense pact. The best statement of this position is Thomas E. Stolper, *China, Taiwan, and the Offshore Islands* (Armon, N.Y.: M. E. Sharpe, 1985). I accept the argument that the PRC wished to prevent the signing of the defense pact, but I argue that another critical objective was to eliminate the growing military threat posed by the buildup of Chinese nationalist forces on the offshore islands. PRC leaders strongly denounced the decision by the Eisenhower administration in 1953 to discontinue opposition to nationalist attempts to invade the mainland, and during 1954 nationalist forces began to be deployed in strength for the first time on Quemoy and Matsu. I believe that the PRC viewed the buildup of nationalist forces on the offshore islands as a potentially serious threat and sought to wrest control of the islands from nationalist forces before a large-scale nationalist military presence was established.

54. U.S. Department of State, *Foreign Relations of the United States [FRUS], 1950,* vol. 6 (Washington, D.C.: Government Printing Office, 1976), 264, and *Depart-ment of State Bulletin,* 22: 550 (1950):79.

Truman ordered the U.S. Seventh Fleet be sent to the Taiwan Straits to neutralize the threat of any military action in the area temporarily.[55] Following the intervention of the PRC in the Korean War in autumn 1950 and the prolonged stalemate in the war, the temporary neutralization order of Truman developed into a U.S. commitment to defend Taiwan against a PRC invasion. Truman's original neutralization order of June 1950 had not extended the reach of the U.S. Seventh Fleet to include the defense of offshore islands held by Chinese nationalist forces. The Truman and then Eisenhower administrations had not, however, explicitly excluded the offshore islands from the protection of the Seventh Fleet either.[56]

To determine the strength of, and if possible to erode, any commitment that the United States might have to defending the offshore islands, the PRC initiated a limited probe and a policy of controlled pressure in autumn 1954.[57] Beginning in mid-August, intelligence reports indicated the buildup of People's Liberation Army (PLA) troops and the movement of jet fighters along the Fukien coastline opposite offshore islands under the control of nationalist forces, and repeated threats to liberate Taiwan were issued by the PRC leadership. On 3 September batteries from the shore began to shell Quemoy Island.[58]

The response of U.S. policymakers was to avoid any clear commitment to the defense of the offshore islands. On 24 August Secretary of State John Foster Dulles stated that "United States armed forces would be justified in defending against Communist attack some of the small islands between Formosa and the Chinese mainland."[59] Throughout autumn 1954 the Eisenhower administration reiterated the U.S. com-

---

55. U.S. Department of State, *Foreign Relations of the United States [FRUS]*, *1950*, vol. 7 (Washington, D.C.: Government Printing Office, 1976), 202–3, and Rosemary Foot, *The Wrong War: American Policy and the Dimensions of the Korean Conflict, 1950–1953* (Ithaca: Cornell University Press 1985), 63–66.

56. U.S. Department of State, *American Foreign Policy, 1950–1955—Basic Documents*, vol. 2 (Washington, D.C.: Government Printing Office, 1957), 2468–75.

57. The concepts of limited probe and controlled pressure are drawn from Alexander George and Richard Smoke, *Deterrence in American Foreign Policy: Theory and Practice* (New York: Columbia University Press, 1974), 540–47.

58. U.S. Department of State, *Foreign Relations of the United States [FRUS]*, *1952–1954*, vol. 14, pt. 1 (Washington, D.C.: Government Printing Office, 1985), no. 263, 550; no. 270, 556–57; no. 275, 566.

59. Ibid., no. 275, 562.

mitment to the defense of Taiwan, but whether this included any of the offshore islands was uncertain. At a press conference announcing the signing of a defense treaty between the United States and the Republic of China on 1 December, Dulles stated that "the position on the offshore islands is unaffected by this treaty. Their status is neither promoted by the treaty nor is it demoted by the treaty."[60]

Military preparations by the PLA continued along the Fukien coastline, but the specific focus of military pressure was the offshore islands north of Matsu, in particular the Tachen Islands. Beginning 1 November PRC air and artillery strikes were targeted at these northern islands.[61] United States policymakers, however, avoided any direct mention of the Tachen Islands in their policy statements throughout autumn 1954, and in negotiations with the Chinese nationalists on a mutual defense pact (which was concluded in December) the United States refused to extend the security commitment to the offshore islands.[62]

Military pressure by the PRC escalated with heavy air attacks beginning on 10 January 1955, and on 18 January an amphibious invasion force of approximately 4,000 PLA troops with air support overwhelmed the poorly defended island of Yikiang, seven miles north of the Tachens.[63] Secretary Dulles downplayed the importance of the Tachens to the defense of Taiwan by describing them on that day as marginal at best.[64] Air and artillery strikes by the PRC continued to hit the Tachens and on 5 February nationalist forces began to evacuate the islands with the assistance of U.S. naval forces.[65]

Military pressure by the PRC had isolated a vulnerable position in the chain of offshore islands occupied by the nationalist forces, and PLA forces seized the islands when it became clear that the United States

60. *Department of State Bulletin*, 31: 807 (1954):896.

61. J. H. Kalicki, *The Pattern of Sino-American Crises: Political Military Interactions in the 1950s* (Cambridge: Cambridge University Press, 1975), 137, and George and Smoke, *Deterrence in American Foreign Policy,* 285.

62. *FRUS, 1952–1954,* vol. 14, pt. 1, no. 396, 904–5.

63. U.S. Department of State, *Foreign Relations of the United States [FRUS], 1955–1957,* vol. 2 (Washington, D.C.: Government Printing Office, 1986), no. 6, 10–11; no. 21, 53–54.

64. U.S. Department of State, *American Foreign Policy, 1950–1955,* vol. 2, 2482–83.

65. *FRUS, 1955–1957,* vol. 2, no. 57, 163–64; no. 58, 164–65.

would not oppose an attack. Whether Quemoy and Matsu would be left open to an invasion was the next question addressed by PRC military pressure. Throughout autumn 1954 U.S. policymakers had avoided any explicit commitment to the defense of Quemoy and Matsu. At a high-level meeting of foreign policy advisers at the White House on 19 January and at a National Security Council meeting the following day U.S. policymakers concluded that it was time for the United States to clarify its position on the defense of the remaining offshore islands.[66] In an attempt to bolster the credibility of a U.S. potential intervention the United States government issued a series of verbal warnings. On 24 January President Dwight D. Eisenhower called on Congress to authorize the President to use force in defense of Taiwan. As Eisenhower stated, ''A suitable congressional resolution would clearly and publicly establish the authority of the President as Commander in Chief to employ the Armed Forces of this Nation promptly and effectively. . . . it will reduce the possibility that the Chinese Communists, misjudging our firm purpose and national unity, might be disposed to challenge the position of the United States, and precipitate a major crisis which even they would neither anticipate nor desire.''[67]

A special national intelligence estimate presented on 25 January reflected the President's concern. The intelligence estimate argued that the PRC would continue to apply pressure on the offshore islands and might be tempted by a favorable balance of local military forces to seize further offshore islands even if a clear U.S. commitment existed.[68] On 29 January Congress passed the Formosa Resolution, which authorized the President ''to employ the Armed Forces of the United States as he deems necessary for the specific purpose of securing and protecting Formosa . . . this authority to include the securing and protection of such related positions and territories of that area now in friendly hands.''[69] Although the Formosa Resolution and statements by U.S. policymakers strengthened the credibility of the U.S. position, no explicit statement of intent to defend the Quemoy and Matsu islands was issued. The ambiguity in policy statements reflected crosscutting

---

66. Ibid., no. 20, 50–52, no. 23, 69–82.
67. U.S. Department of State, *American Foreign Policy, 1950–1955*, vol. 2, 2484–85.
68. *FRUS, 1955–1957*, vol. 2, no. 40, 125–28.
69. U.S. Department of State, *American Foreign Policy, 1950–1955*, vol. 2, 2487.

pressures that concerned Eisenhower and his advisers. The President was not confident of public support for a stronger position, and the British government had repeatedly voiced its opposition to a U.S. commitment to the offshore islands. Eisenhower was also concerned that a firm U.S. commitment would embolden the nationalist government to apply more aggressive military pressure against the mainland from the offshore island positions. Eisenhower and Dulles were strongly in favor of defending Quemoy and Matsu, but because of the opposition of important allies like Great Britain and the uncertainty of domestic political support the President decided on a more cautious declaratory policy.[70]

To enhance the credibility of the verbal warnings the United States began reinforcing naval and air strength in the Taiwan Straits and the Far East in late January. On 22 January three aircraft carriers were ordered to be dispatched to the Taiwan Straits from Manila, and on 27 January two wings of F-86 Sabre jets were flown to Taiwan from Okinawa and Clark Air Force Base in the Philippines. In the following two weeks a squadron of B-26 Bombers was moved to bases in South Korea, and the Seventh Fleet patrolling the straits was further reinforced with destroyers and cruisers.[71]

In early February intelligence reports indicated that junks were being built up opposite Matsu and that PLA forces were being moved into positions along the coastline. In mid-February a national intelligence estimate warned that, because the PRC might not understand which offshore islands the United States would defend, the circumstances under which the United States would defend them, or the extent to which such a defense would be carried out, the PRC was likely to take military action against the offshore islands to test the U.S. commitment.[72] On 24 February Chinese nationalist forces began to evacuate Nanchi Shan Island, north of Matsu.

By March the confrontation between the PRC and the United States over the offshore islands was in danger of escalating to a direct armed clash. The buildup of the PLA forces necessary for an assault on

70. *FRUS, 1955–1957,* vol. 2, no. 97, 238–40; no. 99, 243–47; no. 110, 270–72; no. 129, 308–9; no. 177, 418–22, no. 189, 445–46.

71. Ibid., no. 122, 299, and George and Smoke, *Deterrence in American Foreign Policy,* 288.

72. *FRUS, 1955–1957,* vol. 2, no. 102, 250; no. 108, 268; no. 111; 273–76.

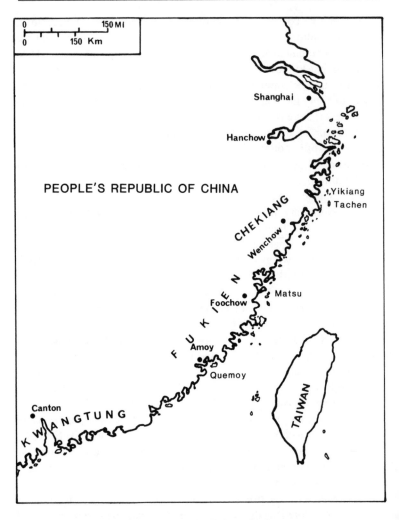

MAP 3. The Coastline of China and the Taiwan Straits

Quemoy and Matsu—the construction and enlargement of jet airfields along the coast, the emplacement of additional guns and artillery along the coast, the stockpiling of ammunition and supplies, and the concentration of troops, aircraft, and naval vessels—had been steadily proceeding for months. Heavy shelling of Quemoy Island was reported throughout the month, with naval clashes between PRC and nationalist forces occurring on several occasions. By mid-March U.S. intelligence sources concluded that the PRC had sufficient military forces in position along the coastline to seize the Quemoy and Matsu islands if defended only by Chinese nationalist forces.[73]

The increased military pressure by the PRC on Quemoy and Matsu beginning in March led to an escalation in verbal warnings by the United States. On 3 March Secretary of State Dulles warned the PRC that retaliatory strikes by the United States might extend to hitting targets along the mainland coastline: "It cannot be assumed that the . . . aggressor would enjoy immunity with respect to the areas from which he stages his offensive."[74] In a meeting on 6 March President Eisenhower and Dulles discussed the possible use of nuclear weapons and decided that a veiled verbal threat of nuclear use should be issued.[75] Consequently, Dulles further escalated the threat of U.S. retaliation when he threatened the PRC implicitly with the use of tactical nuclear weapons at a press conference on 8 March. He warned that U.S. naval and air forces were "equipped with new and powerful weapons of precision, which can utterly destroy military targets without endangering civilian centers."[76] Eisenhower repeated Dulles's threat at a press conference a week later on 16 March, stating that he would authorize the use of tactical nuclear weapons against military targets along the Chinese coastline in a general war in Asia.[77] The threat of tactical nuclear air strikes was backed up with the presence of F-86 Sabre jets in Taiwan, which were capable of delivering nuclear weapons.

United States military leaders perceived the buildup of PRC military forces, in particular air power along the coastline, as a serious threat.

73. Ibid., no. 125, 302–3; no. 150, 357–58; no. 153, 366–67; no. 158, 376–80; no. 161, 385–86; no. 196, 465–66; no. 199, 471.

74. *New York Times,* 4 March 1955, 5.

75. *FRUS, 1955–1957,* vol. 2, no. 141, 336–37. Dulles and Eisenhower also discussed the potential use of tactical nuclear weapons at White House meetings on 10 and 11 March. See Richard K. Betts, *Nuclear Blackmail and Nuclear Balance* (Washington, D.C.: Brookings, 1987), 57–58.

76. *Department of State Bulletin,* 32: 821 (1955):459–60.

77. *Public Papers of the Presidents of the United States: Dwight D. Eisenhower, 1955* (Washington, D.C.: Government Printing Office, 1959), 332.

By late March and early April some military officials were arguing for preventive military action against PRC positions along the coastline. Dulles met with the secretary of defense and members of the Joint Chiefs of Staff on 26 March to discuss policy options regarding the defense of the offshore islands and Taiwan. Adm. Arthur Radford expressed deep concern over the continuing buildup of PRC airfields along the coast and proposed that the United States demand that the buildup cease. If the PRC refused, he proposed, the United States should then approve preventive air strikes by the Chinese nationalist air force against PRC military bases along the coast. On 8 April the commander in chief, Pacific, sent a telegram to the chief of naval operations outlining the potential dangers of the PRC buildup of air power and advocating that the Chinese nationalist air force had the capability to successfully attack PRC bases in a preventive strike.[78] Eisenhower and Dulles, however, believed that preventive air strikes were potentially provocative actions in a tense situation. Dulles in particular argued that preventive air strikes would undermine both diplomatic efforts underway and the possibility of progress at the upcoming Bandung Conference among Asian countries. The President agreed with Dulles and refused to authorize Chinese nationalist air strikes. Eisenhower summarized his position when he stated, ''It is oftentimes necessary to take heavy liabilities from a purely military standpoint in order to avoid being an aggressor and the initiator of a war. This is a price which often has to be paid and which may have to be paid in this case.''[79]

The defense of Quemoy and Matsu put the United States in a difficult military position. The local balance of ground forces along the coastline opposite Quemoy and Matsu favored the PRC (more than 200,000 PLA troops against 50,000–60,000 nationalist troops), and the PRC could have mobilized even larger forces. Thus, both the immediate and short-term balance of forces favored the PRC. The results of probit analysis predict that successful deterrence in such circumstances is unlikely. Nevertheless, deterrence succeeded and the PRC refrained from an attack on Quemoy and Matsu. The explanation is that the PRC's advantage in ground forces was offset by the decisive U.S. advantage in naval and air strength in the Taiwan Straits area. The United States

78. *FRUS, 1955–1957,* vol. 2, no. 170, 402–3, no. 196, 465–66, no. 199, 471–73.

79. Ibid., no. 201, 476. See also no. 207, 491–95.

could employ such forces quickly to repulse a PRC amphibious attack as a result of the naval and air reinforcement in the region in late January and early February. Lacking the necessary naval and air strength to support amphibious operations against well-defended islands, the PRC could not effectively bring to bear its advantage in ground forces. Thus, whereas in the Jordanian and Chadian cases a tit-for-tat policy of military escalation in the buildup of ground forces acted as a deterrent-by-denial capability, in the Taiwan Straits it was the movement and tit-for-tat buildup of U.S. naval and air power that effectively contributed to deterrence. PRC military pressure against the offshore islands was an example of a confrontation in which the potential attacker's immediate objectives were limited to seizing disputed territory without becoming engaged in a general war with a powerful adversary. United States naval power was critical in frustrating this limited aims strategy because it could be deployed quickly enough to inflict heavy losses on PLA forces as the outset of an attack on the offshore islands. In more general terms, this suggests that naval power is most effective as an extended deterrent when the capability exists to intervene and decisively influence the course of land-based operations at the outset.

The U.S. threat to use tactical nuclear weapons may have also had a deterrent impact because air strikes against PRC military targets on the coastline would have escalated a localized armed conflict over the offshore islands into a larger conflict with direct attacks on mainland territory. Although the results of probit analysis indicated that the possession of nuclear weapons by the defender was not in general a significant deterrent, the U.S. threat to use nuclear weapons in the offshore islands crisis may have been perceived as credible by PRC policymakers. United States declaratory policy at the time was massive retaliation, which threatened communist countries with the potential use of nuclear weapons in situations where the United States and its allies lacked adequate land forces to act as a deterrent. This was exactly the situation that confronted the United States in spring 1955 when the United States and the Chinese nationalists could not match the PLA in deployable manpower strength in the Taiwan Straits. The Eisenhower administration's policy of massive retaliation was reinforced by implicit as well as explicit threats of nuclear use by U.S. policymakers during the crisis. United States aircraft capable of carrying out tactical air strikes had also been moved to Taiwan at the height of the confrontation. Furthermore, tactical nuclear strikes against PRC shore batteries and coastal airfields would have neutralized the crucial air and artillery support that a PLA amphibious attack would have required. The United States could threaten to use tactical nuclear weapons with impunity because the PRC lacked any nuclear retaliatory capability and the Soviet Union had not issued a counterthreat or offered support to the PRC in the confrontation.[80]

The PRC withdrew its threat to use armed force to seize the offshore islands and signaled its willingness to consider negotiations. United States policymakers had proposed a cease-fire and negotiations on several occasions since January. The PRC had repeatedly rebuffed such offers, but by the end of March a favorable military solution to the offshore islands conflict no longer seemed possible. Accordingly, Chou En-lai signaled the change in the PRC's position in a surprise speech at the Bandung Conference on 23 April when he declared that his country had no desire to go to war with the United States and would be willing to negotiate.[81] This reversal in PRC policy in April is especially important in view of the requests by U.S. military leaders in late March and early April for preventive air strikes against PRC military bases along the coastline. If those requests had been approved by President Eisenhower and executed, the PRC would probably have reacted forcefully in retaliation. Furthermore, if the PRC had proposed negotiations and expressed the desire to avoid war just after it had been attacked in preventive air strikes, its political and military leadership would have faced charges of intimidation and weakness in the face of U.S. provocation. Eisenhower's decision not to support the preventive air strike requests reflects an understanding of the need to carefully balance military considerations with the requirements of crisis diplomacy and deterrence stability. The United States reacted cautiously but positively to the PRC initiative in the weeks that followed.[82] By the end

80. Harold C. Hinton, ''Sino-Soviet Relations in a U.S.-China Crisis: The Chinese Attitude,'' in *Sino-Soviet Relations and Arms Control,* ed. Morton H. Halperin (Cambridge: M.I.T. Press, 1967), 186.

81. *FRUS, 1955–1957,* vol. 2, no. 77, 202–3; no. 143, 338–39; no. 216, 506; U.S. Department of State, *American Foreign Policy, 1950–1955,* vol. 2, 2484–85, 2493; and *Department of State Bulletin,* 32: 816 (1955):251–68.

82. *FRUS, 1955–1957,* vol. 2, no. 217, 507–9; no. 231, 531–34, no. 251, 566–67; and *Department of State Bulletin,* vol. 32, no. 828 (1955):754–59.

of April military activity along the Fukien coastline had de-escalated, and by mid-May a tacit cease-fire had been established in the Taiwan Straits. The immediate confrontation had passed.

Cases of Deterrence Failure

The Czech crisis of 1938 and the Polish crisis of 1939. At a high-level policy conference on 5 November 1937 attended by the German foreign minister and the leaders of the armed forces, Adolph Hitler discussed what he believed to be the critical problem of lebensraum for the German nation and the need for territorial expansion in Eastern Europe. Hitler argued that, because Britain and France were likely to oppose Germany's expansionist aims in Eastern Europe, war against the Western powers would be necessary before Germany began its final drive to the east. To prepare for war with the Western powers, Hitler believed it would be to Germany's advantage to eliminate as military threats both Austria and Czechoslovakia. Czechoslovakia, in particular, was viewed by Hitler as a potential threat to Germany in a war with Britain and France. Hitler believed that it might be possible to annex both Austria and Czechoslovakia without provoking Western intervention. He therefore stressed the importance of Germany being prepared to take advantage of favorable international conditions, even though German rearmament was years from being completed, to achieve the elimination of Austria and Czechoslovakia in the near future.[83]

Convinced that Britain and France would not intervene and assured by Mussolini that Italy would not oppose a German invasion of Austria, Hitler ordered German troops to cross the Austrian border on 12 March 1938. Austria was officially annexed to the German Reich on the following day without opposition from the Western powers.[84] With the annexation of Austria, Czechoslovakia was surrounded on three sides

---

83. U.S. Department of State, *Documents on German Foreign Policy [DGFP], 1918–1945*, ser. D, vol. 1 (Washington, D.C.: Government Printing Office, 1949), no. 19, 29–39.

84. Telford Taylor, *Munich—The Price of Peace* (New York: Doubleday, 1979), 331–76, and Gerhard L. Weinberg, *The Foreign Policy of Hitler's Germany: Starting World War II, 1937–1939* (Chicago: University of Chicago Press, 1980), 261–312.

by Germany. Hitler then turned his attention to the destruction of Czechoslovakia. To this end, political and military pressure were applied to compel the Czech government to relinquish frontier regions that were populated by large numbers of Germans—the Sudetenland districts.

On 28 March 1938 Hitler informed Konrad Henlein, the leader of the Sudeten German party, that "he intended to settle the Sudeten German question in the not too distant future."[85] The threat, or the actual use, of military force against Czechoslovakia, however, was far riskier than the Austrian anschluss. Czechoslovakia was more powerful militarily than Austria and had military alliance ties with the Soviet Union and France, while Britain had treaty obligations to France. Hitler was aware that plans for the destruction of Czechoslovakia carried a risk of provoking western intervention and precipitating a general European war. The position of Britain was critical because France would not actively intervene with military force unless assured of the full support of the British, whereas the Soviet Union would come to the defense of Czechoslovakia only if France lived up to its alliance commitment to the Czechs.[86]

The basis of British policy toward Czechoslovakia was presented in a speech by the prime minister in the Commons on 24 March 1938. Chamberlain stated that Britain could not give an a priori guarantee that it would commit its armed forces to the defense of Czechoslovakia, since this would place Britain in a position where it would be obligated to go to war irrespective of the circumstances that precipitated the conflict. Britain, Neville Chamberlain argued, must maintain control over the final decision of war or peace in areas where vital interests were not directly involved. The prime minister concluded, however, with the warning that

> where peace and war are concerned, legal obligations are not alone involved, and, if war broke out, it would be unlikely to be confined to those who have assumed such obligations. It would be quite impossible to say where it would end and what Governments might

85. *DGFP, 1918–1945,* ser. D, vol. 2 (Washington, D.C.: Government Printing Office, 1949), no. 107, 198.

86. Taylor, *Munich,* 381, and Norman Rich, *Hitler's War Aims: Ideology, the Nazi State, and the Cause of Expansion* (New York: W. W. Norton, 1973), 104–5.

become involved. The inexorable pressure of facts might well prove more powerful than formal pronouncements, and in that event it would be well within the bounds of probability that other countries, besides those which were parties to the original dispute, would almost immediately become involved. This is especially true in the case of two countries like Great Britain and France, with long associations of friendship, with interests closely interwoven, devoted to the same ideals of democratic liberty, and determined to uphold them.[87]

The British position was therefore ambiguous. On one hand, the prime minister refused to pledge unconditional British support for Czechoslovakia because vital national interests were not directly at stake. On the other hand, Chamberlain argued that if war broke out Britain might intervene in support of Czechoslovakia because of its French alliance commitments. Indeed, the French government informed Germany in early April of its intention to defend Czechoslovakia.[88] The critical question for Hitler was whether this British warning was a bluff.

Hitler's concern for avoiding western intervention was reflected in his thinking on the military aspects of the planned operation (Case Green) against Czechoslovakia. Gen. Wilhelm Keitel of the German army took notes during an important meeting on 21 April in which Hitler discussed the prospects for Case Green. Hitler rejected a surprise attack without justification against Czechoslovakia because it would incite western public opinion against Germany and could lead to a serious international situation. Hitler proposed two alternative scenarios for military action against Czechoslovakia: a period of diplomatic confrontation that would gradually escalate to a crisis and then war, or lightning-swift action as a result of an incident, such as the assassination of the German ambassador during anti-German demonstrations. Decisive and quick results with the use of force were essential if outside intervention was to be forestalled. As Keitel recounts, Hitler argued that "the first 4 days of military action are, politically speaking,

---

87. E. L. Woodward and Rohan Butler, eds., *Documents on British Foreign Policy [DBFP], 1919–1939*, 3d ser., vol. 1 (London: His Majesty's Stationary Office, 1949), no. 114, 97.

88. *DGFP, 1918–1945*, ser. D, vol. 2, no. 117, 214; no. 120, 217–23.

decisive. In the absence of outstanding military successes, a European crisis is certain to arise. Fait accomplis must convince foreign powers of the hopelessness of military intervention."[89] In Hitler's judgment the risk of Western intervention depended primarily on the length of time required to defeat Czechoslovakia. If the German army could rapidly overrun Czech defenses, then Britain and France would face the collapse of Czech armed resistance and the alternative of initiating a prolonged war of attrition against Germany to restore Czech independence. Hitler was convinced that the Western powers would not be willing to incur such costs in defense of an ally who was already defeated.[90] In a meeting with the German military command on 28 May Hitler argued that the destruction of Czechoslovakia could be accomplished in a short, successful, and isolated war.[91] In a military directive two days later Hitler ordered preparations for Case Green to begin so that in the event of a favorable political or military opportunity armed intervention and success could be achieved.[92]

Hitler's estimation of the British position was essentially correct. Within the British government a series of studies indicated that Britain was in no position to contest a German attack on Czechoslovakia. For example, a Chiefs of Staff report presented on 21 March concluded that "no military pressure we can expect by sea, or land or in the air can prevent Germany either from invading and overrunning Bohemia or inflicting a decisive defeat on the Czechoslovakian Army. If politically, it is deemed necessary to restore Czechoslovakia's lost integrity this aim will entail war with Germany, and her defeat may mean a prolonged struggle."[93]

The French government was duly informed of Britain's appraisal. On 24 March an official memo was presented to the French which argued that there was little the Western powers could do to prevent the occupation of Czechoslovakia by Germany. In meetings between the political leaders of the two governments in London on 28–29 April,

89. Ibid., no. 133, 240.

90. Taylor, *Munich*, 381, and Williamson Murray, *The Change in the European Balance of Power, 1938–1939: The Path to Ruin* (Princeton: Princeton University Press, 1984), 173.

91. Weinberg, *Foreign Policy of Hitler's Germany*, 371.

92. *DGFP, 1918–1945*, ser. D, vol. 2, no. 222, 358–62.

93. As quoted in Taylor, *Munich*, 631.

Chamberlain informed the French prime minister and foreign minister that in the event of war the primary mission for British forces would be home defense and protection of trade routes and that only two British divisions could be sent to France. Chamberlain also stressed the weak military position of Czechoslovakia: ''In the judgment of His Majesty's Government, if he might be allowed to state the problem quite crudely, that the result of their combined military and political examination of the issues at stake was that, if the German Government decided to take hostile steps against the Czechoslovak State, it would be impossible, in our present military situation, to prevent those steps from achieving immediate success.''[94]

Chamberlain therefore thought it was necessary to pressure Czechoslovakia into making far-reaching concessions on the Sudeten question. The prime minister was determined to reach a peaceful solution so that the unattractive alternative of providing armed support to Czechoslovakia could be avoided. Thus, while the French government in April and May made clear its intention to defend Czechoslovakia if attacked,[95] the British emphasized in contacts with the German government the desire to achieve a peaceful solution to the conflict.[96]

During June and July the British continued to express interest in a general settlement and avoided stronger deterrent actions for fear that they might provoke Hitler.[97] On 8 June British Foreign Secretary Viscount Halifax assured the German ambassador that Czechoslovakia had not received a blank check of support from the British, and in Berlin on 10 June the British ambassador delivered the same message to Foreign Minister Joachim von Ribbentrop, stating that the British government would do nothing to increase Czech intransigence.[98] On 11 June Halifax informed the British ambassador in Czechoslovakia to advise the Czech government not to call up reservists for their annual training in advance as planned since this would be provocative to Germany.[99] Many German diplomats and policymakers concluded

---

94. *DBFP, 1919–1939*, 3d ser., vol. 1, no. 164, 214; see also no. 106, 85–86.

95. Weinberg, *Foreign Policy of Hitler's Germany*, 341–43.

96. *DGFP, 1918–1945*, ser. D, vol. 2, no. 139, 246–47; no. 145, 255–56; no. 149, 261–62; no. 150, 262–63; no. 154, 269–71; no. 157, 274–75.

97. Weinberg, *Foreign Policy of Hitler's Germany*, 373, 393, 395–96.

98. *DGFP, 1918–1945*, ser. D, vol. 2, no. 245, 396–98; no. 251, 409–10.

99. *DBFP, 1919–1939*, 3d ser., vol. 1, no. 397, 467. See also no. 404, 474–75.

therefore that the British warning of possible intervention was a bluff. In a report to his government in June the German ambassador argued that British policy was driven by the desire to reach a lasting solution in order to free Britain from having to honor its commitment to France. In mid-July State Secretary Ernst von Weizsäcker reported that the British still strongly desired to avoid war and were willing to put pressure on Czechoslovakia to make concessions.[100]

Negotiations between Henlein, representing the Sudeten Germans, and the Czechoslovakian government remained deadlocked throughout the summer 1938. By late July reports of widespread German military preparations were received by the British. The British ambassador in Berlin reported that the German army had been ordered to hold itself short of actual mobilization in readiness for all eventualities. In August British intelligence sources reported the calling up of reservists, the holding of maneuvers at the level of divisional formations, the large-scale building of fortifications on the western frontier, and warnings that Hitler intended to attack Czechoslovakia by the end of September.[101]

The British government's immediate reaction to these reports of extensive German military preparations was to deliver a protest. In mid-August the British ambassador informed German Foreign Minister Ribbentrop that because the recent military actions of Germany threatened Czechoslovakia, increased tensions, and undermined efforts at negotiations Germany should modify its military actions. Ribbentrop countered with the charge that British support for Czechoslovakia had only increased Czech intransigence and he refused to discuss German military actions. To signal further British concern the chancellor of the exchequer, Sir John Simon, reiterated Chamberlain's warning of 24 March in a speech delivered on 27 August.[102]

On 30 August a high-level meeting of the British government was held to discuss the Czech situation, and a number of stronger deterrent measures were considered: threatening that if Germany invaded Czech-

100. *DGFP, 1918–1945*, ser. D, vol. 2, no. 250, 403–4; no. 292, 488–90. See also no. 259, 420–22; no. 266, 432–34; no. 309, 509–10.

101. *DBFP, 1919–1939*, 3d ser., vol. 2, no. 553, 13–16; no. 558, 21–22; no. 564, 27–28; no. 573, 39–40; nos. 575–81, 41–49; no. 605, 76–77; no. 635, 103–5; no. 658, 125–26; no. 660, 127; no. 770, 236–38.

102. Ibid., no. 608, 78–80; no. 661, 128.

oslovakia, Britain would declare war on Germany; making naval preparations and moving the British fleet; and summoning Parliament into special session. These proposed actions, however, were rejected by a majority of cabinet members as too provocative among other reasons, and it was decided that the best policy would be to continue "to keep Germany guessing as to our intentions."[103] Accordingly, the British ambassador delivered another warning regarding the probable attitude of Britain in the event of German aggression against Czechoslovakia.

The British policy of verbal warnings but no active military response to Germany's buildup of military force reinforced Hitler's prevailing judgment that the Western powers were not likely to intervene in support of Czechoslovakia. On 30 August Hitler is reported to have stated, "England bluffs and plays for time. . . . A British attack is not to be expected."[104] The unpreparedness of British forces for war also contributed to Hitler's belief that the British were not likely to intervene. A memorandum delivered to Mussolini in early September summarized Hitler's appraisal of the British military position: "(a) the navy is at present inadequate to meet the needs of the British Empire in the event of war, (b) the weakness of air armament, especially anti-aircraft, (c) the weakness and unpreparedness of the Regular Army for use at the present time in a European theater of operation." Hitler concluded, "Great Britain is therefore trying to prevent or postpone at all costs any European conflict."[105]

German military preparations continued unabated, and by the beginning of September the invasion plans were complete. On 3 September Chief of Staff, Gen. Franz Halder, presented Case Green to Hitler. The plan called for thirty-seven out of forty-eight regular divisions and almost all of the army's armored and motorized strength to be committed against Czechoslovakia. The main attack would entail a pincer operation that would cut Bohemia and Moravia from Slovakia and encircle the Czechoslovakian army, preventing its retreat to the interior of the country. Hitler criticized the plan as being too obvious and not designed to achieve decisive results quickly enough. He demanded that the main thrust come from Bavaria with the objective of capturing

103. Taylor, *Munich,* 665–67, and Weinberg, *Foreign Policy of Hitler's Germany,* 421.

104. As quoted in Taylor, *Munich,* 721.

105. *DGFP, 1918–1945,* ser. D, vol. 2, no. 415, 671.

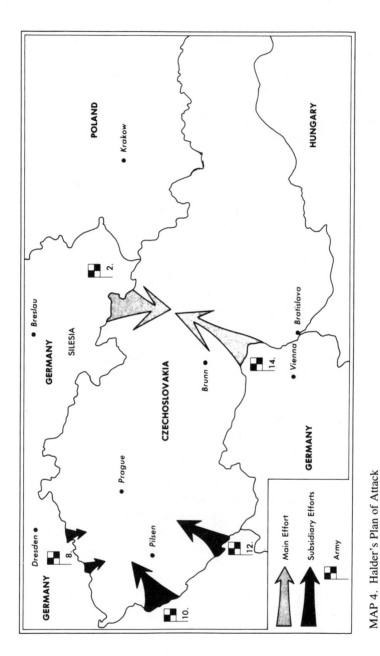

MAP 4. Halder's Plan of Attack

Williamson Murray, *The Change in the European Balance of Power, 1938–1939: The Path to Ruin*, 227. Copyright © 1984 by Princeton University Press. Reprinted by permission of Princeton University Press.

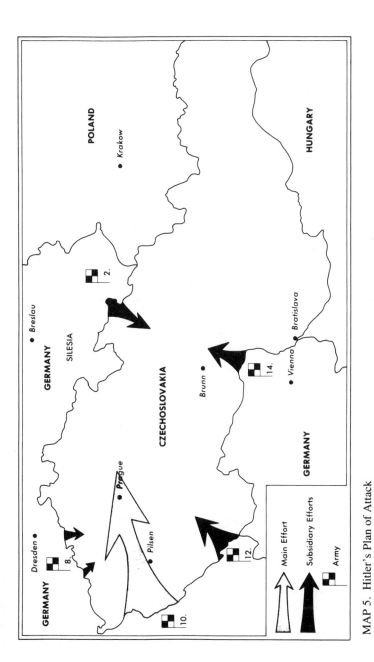

MAP 5. Hitler's Plan of Attack

Williamson, Murray, *The Change in the European Balance of Power, 1938–1939: The Path to Ruin*, 228. Copyright © 1984 by Princeton University Press. Reprinted by permission of Princeton University Press.

Prague, the capital, in the first few days of the war. Hitler argued that the fall of Prague would result in the collapse of Czech resistance and would undermine British and French willingness to intervene.[106] At a second meeting on 9 September Hitler again demanded that the main attack be directed at Prague and forced the army leadership (which favored the pincer operation) to accept his revised plan. Once again Hitler emphasized the critical importance of the rapid defeat of Czech forces for political reasons. Hitler explained to Halder, "There is no doubt that the planned pincer movement is the most desirable solution and should take place. But its success is nevertheless too uncertain for it to be depended on. Especially as a rapid success is necessary from a political point of view. The first week is politically decisive, within which a far-reaching territorial gain must be achieved."[107]

By 9 September intelligence reports of German troop concentrations near the Czech border led the British government to decide that a stronger warning should be sent to Germany. The warning was to be read to Foreign Minister Ribbentrop, and it was to be requested that the warning be transmitted to Hitler without delay. But the warning was never presented because the British Ambassador, Sir Nevile Henderson, strongly opposed it and convinced the British cabinet that it would provoke Hitler and worsen the situation. The only step agreed to was limited precautionary naval measures: the activation of a small number of minelayers and minesweepers currently held in reserve status.[108]

Within Czechoslovakia events had reached a breaking point. Following Hitler's Nuremberg speech on 12 September, riots broke out in Czechoslovakia that forced the Czech government to declare martial law. Henlein responded by suspending negotiations and submitting a six-hour ultimatum to the Czech government.[109] At a high-level meeting that evening, Duff Cooper, first lord of the admiralty, proposed that the British fleet be mobilized as a clear signal to Germany of British intentions. Chamberlain, however, presented an alternative policy ini-

---

106. Ibid., no. 424, 686–87, and Murray, *Change in the European Balance*, 225–26.

107. *DGFP, 1918–1945,* ser. D, vol. 2, no. 448, 729, and Murray, *Change in the European Balance,* 226–29.

108. *DBFP, 1919–1939,* 3d ser., vol. 2, no. 815, 277–78, and Taylor, *Munich,* 673–74, 728.

109. *DGFP, 1918–1945,* ser. D, vol. 2, no. 467, 751–52.

tiative, a proposal to travel to Germany to negotiate directly with the German leader. The British cabinet, except for Cooper, supported Chamberlain's proposal, and more extensive British military counter-measures were put on hold pending the outcome of diplomatic negotiations. The possibility of mobilizing the fleet to increase the diplomatic leverage available to Chamberlain was not seriously considered.[110]

By mid-September German mobilization measures were nearing completion and Hitler was aware that Britain and France had been closely following German military preparations. The lack of an effective Western military response (a policy of caution in military escalation) indicated to Hitler that the repeated warnings of the British and French were bluffs. As Telford Taylor states, "The realists in Berlin would look beyond the words spoken to the steps taken by the western powers. They knew that by this time the French and British had a pretty good idea of the scope of the Wehrmact's moves toward mobilization. If . . . Britain was only mobilizing a few minesweepers, and France was avowedly doing much less than Germany, it was plain that neither France nor Britain was preparing for a swift and vigorous military response to Green."[111]

The lack of military preparations by Western powers indicated not only a lack of resolve on their part but also their inability to aid Czechoslovakia at the outset of an armed confrontation. It was this lag in the reaction time of the Western powers that Hitler planned to exploit. Even if the Western powers did decide to intervene (which Hitler did not think likely), Hitler believed that Germany could defeat Czechoslovakia so rapidly that outside intervention would seem futile. The cautious policies of military escalation by Britain and France played right into the hands of Hitler's strategy for a rapid offensive attack.

By late September the German army was prepared for Case Green. Thirty-seven divisions were in position to attack, whereas Czechoslovakia had mobilized approximately thirty divisions. This modest German numerical advantage in the immediate balance of forces was enhanced by the fact that all of the German divisions were regular units,

110. Taylor, *Munich,* 677–80; Weinberg, *Foreign Policy of Hitler's Germany,* 430; and ibid., no. 469, 754.
111. Taylor, *Munich,* 729.

whereas a sizable number of the Czech forces were reserve units. In the west Germany had only five regular divisions deployed against France with four reserve and one landwehr division providing backup support.[112]

Although the French government had repeatedly expressed its intention to honor the alliance commitment to Czechoslovakia, the French military had no plans for effectively intervening on behalf of the Czechs. It was widely believed that an offensive against German forces along the Westwall would be ineffective and that heavy losses would be suffered. The French shared the British perception that little could be done militarily to prevent Germany from overrunning Czechoslovakia.[113] The French government thus found itself in a policy dilemma. French honor and prestige were at stake in the defense of Czechoslovakia. But military intervention by the French could not prevent the defeat of Czechoslovakia and would engage France in a lengthy war with Germany in which victory was by no means certain. The French government had not informed the British of its lack of military plans or of its pessimistic assessment of the military situation. French intentions were somewhat clarified on 12–13 September when the French prime minister and foreign minister sent urgent messages to the British government urging action to avert war.[114] The lack of French military plans became clear at a high-level meeting in London on 25–26 September when Chamberlain pressed the French on the exact military operations to be undertaken if Germany invaded Czechoslovakia. The French, reluctant to admit that they had no real plans for defending Czechoslovakia, would provide only evasive and general answers that greatly alarmed the British.[115]

British military preparations between 23 and 28 September signaled a stiffer stance to Germany. On 23 September the following naval measures were taken: recalling men from leave, bringing up all crews to full strength, and manning the Suez Canal defenses. Army preparations included calling up the home army units for air and coastal defense and alerting the Royal Air Force fighter command. On 28 Sep-

112. Murray, *Change in the European Balance*, 231, 240.

113. Weinberg, *Foreign Policy of Hitler's Germany*, 398–401.

114. Ibid., 428–29.

115. *DBFP, 1919–1939*, 3d ser., vol. 2, no. 1093, 534, and Murray, *Change in the European Balance*, 242.

tember orders were issued to mobilize the British fleet.[116] Chamberlain, however, was still determined to avoid war by pressuring Czechoslovakia to accept Hitler's new demands presented at Godesberg on 22 September for the immediate occupation of the Sudetenland regions.[117] The costs of coming to the defense of Czechoslovakia were too high. Halifax explained to the cabinet in mid-September: "He had no doubt that if we were involved in war now we should win it after a long time," however he then noted that he "could not feel we were justified in embarking on an action which would result in such untold suffering."[118] Under the threat of a general European war Chamberlain, with the support of the French, agreed at the Munich Conference on 29 September to the virtual break-up of Czechoslovakia. Hitler's only concession was to delay occupation from 1 October to 10 October.[119]

War was avoided but the vital interests of the Czech state were sacrificed. The German annexation of the Sudetenland was a tremendous blow to Czechoslovakia: sixteen thousand square miles of territory were lost, and 86 percent of its chemical industry, 80 percent of its textiles, 70 percent of its iron and steel capacity, and 70 percent of its electric power were lost. Most disastrous to the future security of the country was that, in relinquishing almost all of its frontier districts, Czechoslovakia lost virtually its entire system of frontier fortifications.[120] The Munich agreement crippled Czechoslovakia economically and left it militarily vulnerable to attack. Hitler called off the invasion of Czechoslovakia because the Western powers had capitulated to his far-reaching demands under the threat of war. Hitler had achieved his primary goal—the elimination of Czechoslovakia as a potential military threat—without having to use military force. He completed the destruction of the Czech state in the months following the Munich agreement. In March 1939 German forces occupied the remainder of Czechoslovakia without opposition from France or Great Britain.

116. Taylor, *Munich,* 813, 862–63, 881–82.
117. *DBFP, 1919–1939,* 3d ser., vol. 2, no. 1033, 463–73; no. 1048, 482–83; no. 1053, 485–87; no. 1057, 489–90; no. 1073, 499–508.
118. As quoted in Murray, *Change in the European Balance,* 217.
119. *DBFP, 1919–1939,* 3d ser., vol. 2, no. 1224, 627–29; no. 1227, 630–35; no. 1228, 635–40; no. 1229, 640–41.
120. Rich, *Hitler's War Aims,* 109–10.

The failure of deterrence in the Czech crisis is consistent with the results of probit analysis. The British and French were unwilling to fight a protracted war in support of Czechoslovakia but still hoped to deter Germany from an attack through verbal warnings. Hitler was unimpressed by this policy of verbal bluff. The lack of British and French resolve, evident in the cautious policies of military escalation that the two countries pursued, undermined the credibility of British and French warnings of intervention. In the three cases of successful deterrence examined in this chapter, in contrast, the defenders were determined to protect their protégés and demonstrated their resolve by a tit-for-tat policy of military escalation.

The case studies of successful deterrence demonstrated that a tit-for-tat policy of escalation was effective because it erased the potential attacker's advantage in the immediate balance of forces and established a trip-wire ensuring that further reinforcements would be committed to battle by the defender if the local conflict escalated to a larger war. A critical weakness in the cautious policies of military escalation pursued by Britain and France was that Germany maintained an advantage in the immediate balance of forces and that no trip-wire deterrent force was in position to repulse immediately a German attack. Because Britain and France recognized their inability to prevent Germany from overrunning Czechoslovakia, they did not prepare their armed forces for early intervention. As a result, the deterrent effect of their capacity to augment the local balance of forces through mobilization was absent. Germany's advantage in the immediate balance of forces negated the deterrent impact of Britain and France's combined advantage in short-term mobilized armed strength.[121] Hitler's plan for a rapid defeat of Czechoslovakia and the lack of a western military response countering that plan convinced Hitler to gamble that the Sudetenland question could be escalated to the very brink, and if necessary to the outbreak, of war without provoking immediate opposition by Britain and France.

The next state Hitler sought to eliminate as a threat to Germany in a

---

121. The strict limitations placed on the size of the German army following World War I severely constrained the wehrmact's mobilization capacity because of a lack of trained reserves. The German army was thus poorly prepared (as were Britain and France) to fight a general European war in 1938. Murray, *Change in the European Balance*, 239–63, and Matthew Cooper, *The German Army, 1933–1945: Its Political and Military Failure* (New York: Stein and Day, 1978), chap. 12.

war against Britain and France was Poland. Germany had presented proposals to the Polish government in October 1938 for the return of the city of Danzig to Germany, an extraterritorial road and railway across the corridor to East Prussia, and Poland's adherence to the Anti-Comintern Pact. Poland would, in return, be granted special rights in Danzig, a German guarantee of Poland's western border, and an extension of the 1934 German-Polish Nonaggression Pact.[122] Subsequent meetings were held in November, December and January 1939 with the Polish government refusing to accept the German proposals.[123] Hitler initially believed that Poland could be pressured to accept Germany's position, but the Polish refusal to concede increasingly shifted Hitler's thinking toward plans to use military force against Poland.[124] On 21 March 1939 Ribbentrop presented Germany's negotiating position as demands to the Polish government for Danzig and extraterritorial routes across the corridor in exchange for a guarantee of Poland's western frontier. The Polish government responded with a show of military force in the corridor and a firm but diplomatically polite refusal on 26 March. Anticipating Poland's firm position, Hitler had on the previous day stated in a military directive to the commander in chief of the army that although he did not intend to settle the Polish question by force work on military plans for an attack should begin nevertheless.[125]

The German occupation of Prague resulted in a British reassessment of policy toward Germany. The change in British perceptions of Hitler's intentions was reflected in Chamberlain's speech at Birmingham on 17 March when the prime minister asked in reference to Prague, "Is this the last attack upon a small state, or is it to be followed by others? Is this, in fact, a step in the direction of an attempt to dominate the world by force?"[126] At a cabinet meeting on 18 March Chamberlain argued for a new approach toward Germany. The prime minister declared that Britain should resist any further aggression in

122. *DGFP, 1918–1945,* ser. D, vol. 5, no. 81, 104–7.

123. Ibid., no. 101, 127–29; no. 112, 142–43; no. 113, 144–45; no. 115, 146–47; no. 116, 147–49; no. 119, 152–58; no. 120, 159–61; no. 121, 161–62; no. 122, 162; no. 125, 166–67; no. 126, 167–68.

124. Weinberg, *Foreign Policy of Hitler's Germany,* 489.

125. Great Britain Foreign Office, *DGFP, 1918–1945,* ser. D, vol. 6 (London: His Majesty's Stationary Office, 1956), no. 61, 70–72; no. 99, 117–19; no. 101, 121–24; no. 103, 127.

126. As quoted in Weinberg, *Foreign Policy of Hitler's Germany,* 540.

Eastern Europe and warn Germany of its intention to do so. The cabinet supported Chamberlain in this change in British policy.[127] A number of Eastern European states were contacted about the possibility of forming a coalition to resist the German threat. Poland was viewed as a key state not only because Germany was exerting pressure on Poland over Danzig and the corridor but also because Poland was valuable as an ally since it could threaten Germany directly in the east along the German-Polish border. On the evening of 30 March the British government proposed to Poland an interim and unilateral pledge (including France) to guarantee Poland's independence pending negotiations on a bilateral defense pact. The Polish foreign minister quickly agreed to the British offer.[128] On the following day in Parliament Chamberlain announced the pledge of support to Poland: ''In the event of any action which clearly threatened Polish independence, and which the Polish Government accordingly considered vital to resist with their national forces, His Majesty's Government would feel themselves bound at once to lend the Polish Government all support in their power.''[129]

The British guarantee to Poland did not, however, deter Hitler from proceeding with plans to attack Poland. He had not ruled out the possibility of Poland capitulating to Germany. On 3 April Hitler issued a directive on the plans for attack against Poland—Operation White—if relations with Poland deteriorated further. In the directive Hitler called on the military to be prepared for an attack any time after 1 September. As with the plans for the attack on Czechoslovakia in autumn 1938, the primary objective was the rapid and decisive defeat of the Polish army, enabling Germany to present the Western powers with a fait accompli.[130] The German ambassador was instructed to adopt an intransigent position in talks with Poland and to refuse to discuss the German demands until Poland changed its position.[131] The primary objective of German policy was to isolate Poland politically and militarily from the Western powers.

The British government attempted to convince Hitler that the

127. Ibid., 542–44.

128. Christopher Thorne, *The Approach of War, 1938–1939* (London: Macmillan, 1967), 119, and Murray, *Change in the European Balance*, 289.

129. E. L. Woodward and Rohan Butler, eds., *DBFP, 1919–1939*, 3d ser., vol. 4 (London: His Majesty's Stationary Office, 1951), no. 582, 552; no. 584, 554.

130. *DGFP, 1918–1945*, ser. D, vol. 6, no. 149, 186–87; no. 185, 223–28.

131. Ibid., no. 159, 195; no. 169, 205–7.

pledge to Poland was a firm commitment. Throughout the spring and summer of 1939 British diplomatic efforts repeatedly emphasized Britain's willingness to support a compromise solution to the German-Polish talks on Danzig and the corridor but stressed that if Germany refused to compromise and resorted to the use of force Britain would fully support Poland. The British ambassador, who had been recalled from Berlin on 17 March and returned on 25 April, lost no time in expressing Britain's position when he met with the German state secretary on the following day. So there would be no mistaking British intentions, Henderson informed the state secretary that conscription would be introduced in accordance with Britain's new European commitments.[132] Hitler proceeded with further pressure in an attempt to isolate Poland. On 28 April he announced that neither the Anglo-German Naval Agreement of 1935 nor sections of the 1937 Naval Agreement between the two countries were any longer in effect because of the British guarantee to Poland. Hitler also sent a memorandum to the Polish government denouncing the 1934 German-Polish Nonaggression Pact for the same reason.[133] Poland officially responded to the abrogation of the 1934 Pact on 5 May by rejecting the German arguments contained in the 28 April memorandum and by maintaining its firm position in support of its interests in Danzig and the corridor. The Polish government, however, did not rule out further negotiations if Germany was willing to reciprocate compromise.[134]

In reaction to reports in early May that German officials did not believe Britain would intervene in support of Poland, the British government instructed the British ambassador in Berlin to reiterate the seriousness of the British pledge.[135] Accordingly, Henderson met with the German state secretary on 15 May and warned that the British government was determined to uphold the guarantee to Poland and that Britain was confident of victory in the event of war.[136] In London

132. E. L. Woodward and Rohan Butler, eds., *DBFP, 1919–1939,* 3d ser., vol. 5 (London: His Majesty's Stationary Office, 1952), no. 284, 320–21; no. 288, 337; no. 289, 337–39.

133. *DGFP, 1918–1945,* ser. D, vol. 6, no. 276, 347–51; no. 277, 351–52; no. 282, 357.

134. Ibid., no. 334, 430–31.

135. *DBFP, 1919–1939,* 3d ser., vol. 5, no. 365, 424; no. 431, 478.

136. Ibid., no. 525, 562–63; and *DGFP, 1918–1945,* ser. D, vol. 6, no. 385, 502–3.

Foreign Secretary Halifax informed the German ambassador on 18 May that Britain was absolutely determined to resist German aggression and that Britain was no longer willing to negotiate a settlement under the threat of German arms. In a meeting with Field Marshal Hermann Göring on 27 May Henderson stated that there had been a complete change in British policy as a result of Germany's occupation of Prague and that any further aggression by Germany would be resisted by Britain.[137]

By late May Hitler was convinced that Poland would have to be defeated militarily. There were no indications that the Polish government would capitulate to Germany's demands and the British guarantee was viewed as encouraging Poland to stand firm. At a conference with the military on 23 May Hitler characterized Poland as unreliable and likely to side with Germany's adversaries in a war and declared that Poland had to be eliminated at the first suitable opportunity.[138] Military plans for Operation White continued throughout June with Hitler taking an active part.[139]

The British government continued to issue warnings to convince Germany that the guarantee to Poland reflected a true change in British policy. In a speech on 29 June Halifax stated, "If the security and independence of other countries are to disappear, our own security and independence will be gravely threatened. We know that, if international law and order is to be preserved, we must be prepared to fight in its defence. . . . The threat of military force is holding the world to ransom, and our immediate task is . . . to resist aggression."[140] In reaction to increased military activity in Danzig in late June and early July the British prime minister issued another warning to Germany.[141] In a statement before the House of Commons on 10 July Chamberlain warned that an attempt to settle the Danzig issue by a fait accompli was mistaken since "the issue could not be considered as a purely local matter . . . but would at once raise graver issues affecting Polish

137. *DBFP, 1919–1979*, 3d ser., vol. 5, no. 559, 601–3; no. 658, 713–15.

138. *DGFP, 1918–1945*, ser. D, vol. 6, no. 433, 574–80.

139. Weinberg, *Foreign Policy of Hitler's Germany*, 583–84.

140. As quoted in Thorne, *Approach of War*, 159.

141. E. L. Woodward and Rohan Butler, eds., *DBFP, 1919–1939*, 3d ser., vol. 6 (London: His Majesty's Stationary Office, 1953), no. 155, 177–79; no. 198, 224; no. 219, 242.

national existence and independence. We have guaranteed to give our assistance to Poland. . . . and we are firmly resolved to carry out this understanding.''[142]

Military preparations in Danzig continued throughout July and the mobilization of the German army was in progress by early August.[143] Halifax repeated the warning that Britain was determined to support Poland in a meeting with the German ambassador on 10 August but the repeated British warnings since May had not deterred Hitler. On 11 August Hitler met with the League of Nations high commissioner to Danzig and made statements that he clearly intended to have the commissioner pass on to the British. Hitler informed M. Burckhardt that the next provocation by Poland would result in Germany launching a large-scale military attack against Poland. The objective would be to gain a free hand in the east against Russia. If the western powers failed to understand this and intervened, Germany would be compelled to defeat the Western powers before attacking the Soviets. Hitler hoped to isolate Poland from Britain and France by revealing his true aims.[144] On the following day Italian Foreign Minister Count Galeazzo Ciano met with Hitler and noted in his diary that the German leader was determined to strike. According to the official German record of the meeting, Hitler argued that Poland would always side with the opponents of Germany and Italy and that the elimination of Poland would thus be to the Axis powers' advantage before war with the Western powers.[145]

On 14 August Hitler held a meeting with the leadership of the German armed forces. Hitler began by noting that any political and military success involved some risks of general war. He then proceeded to explain why the British were unlikely to intervene in support of Poland. On general political grounds he argued that the British, realizing that any war against Germany would be long and difficult, would stand to lose a great deal with small gains. Britain would be unlikely to incur such costs in the defense of another state. ''The men I got to know at Munich are not the kind to start a new World War,'' Hitler stated. He

142. *DGFP, 1918–1945,* ser. D, vol. 6, editor's note, 898.

143. *DBFP, 1919–1939,* 3d ser., vol. 6, no. 353, 586–87; no. 660, 698–99.

144. Rich, *Hitler's War Aims,* 126.

145. U.S. Department of State, *DGFP, 1918–1945,* ser. D, vol. 7 (Washington, D.C.: Government Printing Office, 1956), no. 43, 39–49; no. 47, 53–56.

then presented a detailed appraisal of the military situation. British armaments and preparations were in the developmental stage. British naval strength would not be increased before a year or two, and three years were needed for Britain to build an adequate antiaircraft force. An increase in British ground forces would require months of training before a sizable number of effective units could be organized. Hitler concluded that Britain was not in a position to intervene immediately in the effective defense of Poland. A British-French attack against the Westwall was very unlikely, a British-French attack through Belgium and Holland would not help Poland. The only military option was to blockade Germany and Hitler was confident that Germany could withstand such a policy. Hitler believed that the military weakness of Britain undermined its verbal deterrent actions and that the British were bluffing. Britain might recall its ambassador and embargo trade in response to a German attack on Poland, but armed intervention was unlikely. Operation White was thus to be carried out to shatter Polish armed resistance within a week to two weeks of initiation.[146]

In meetings with the German state secretary on 15 and 18 August the British ambassador reiterated that Britain was determined to carry out its guarantee to Poland. Weizsäcker informed Henderson that Germany had no faith in these verbal warnings.[147] Hitler held a conference on 22 August with the German military command concerning the planned attack on Poland. Hitler argued that the attack was necessary because Poland could not be relied on to remain neutral in a conflict with the Western powers. To protect Germany's flank, Poland would have to be eliminated first. As Hitler had argued at the 14 August conference, Britain's political leadership lacked the resolve and character to carry out the threat of intervention in support of Poland. Germany was in a strong military position to defeat Poland rapidly, and the Western powers could do nothing to prevent a German victory. Only in three to four years would Britain be prepared for a war against Germany. Final preparations were issued for Operation White with the target date of 26 August for the attack.[148]

For the attack on Poland, Germany assembled more than fifty-four divisions into two army groups—south and north—totaling more than

146. Ibid., app. 1, 551–56.
147. Ibid., no. 66, 72–74; no. 114, 123.
148. Ibid., app. 1, 557–60.

1.5 million troops. Poland was in an extremely difficult strategic position. German territory surrounded Poland on three sides, and no natural barriers protected Poland's exposed borders. Polish terrain was ideal for armored operations except in the far southeast of Poland in the Carpathian Mountains. The Polish army consisted of thirty infantry divisions with the mobilization of reserves adding another fifteen divisions. But the most important weakness of the Polish army was the lack of modern equipment and arms. The Polish army possessed no counterpart to German motorized and mechanized forces, and Germany had superiority in air power.[149]

The British government began to call up reserves for the armed forces on 22 August, and a letter from Chamberlain reaffirming Britain's pledge to Poland was presented to Hitler on 23 August despite news that a German-Soviet agreement was about to be signed. "Whatever may prove to be the nature of the German-Soviet Agreement, it cannot alter Great Britain's obligation to Poland which His Majesty's Government have stated in public repeatedly and plainly and which they are determined to fulfill. . . . If the case should arise, they are resolved, and prepared, to employ without delay all the forces at their command, and it is impossible to foresee the end of hostilities once engaged."[150]

Hitler denounced the letter after the British ambassador presented it to him and warned Henderson that Germany would not back away from war if Britain intervened.[151] The official German response was contained in a letter from Hitler presented to Chamberlain on 24 August.[152] On 23 August Hitler issued the order to launch the attack against Poland on the twenty-sixth.[153] Hitler's calculation that Britain would back down in the end was shattered when late in the afternoon on 25 August Britain and Poland formally ratified their mutual security pact. Hitler had issued the final orders for Operation White just hours earlier, but he quickly decided to postpone the attack against Poland temporarily to try to prevent British intervention.[154] Hitler hoped that a proposal submit-

149. Murray, *Change in the European Balance,* 322–23.

150. E. L. Woodward and Rohan Butler, eds., *DBFP, 1919–1939,* 3d ser., vol. 7 (London: His Majesty's Stationary Office, 1954), no. 145, 127.

151. Ibid., no. 200, 161–63.

152. *DGFP, 1918–1945,* ser. D, vol. 7, no. 201, 216–19.

153. Ibid., app. 1, 560.

154. Weinberg, *Foreign Policy of Hitler's Germany,* 637–39.

ted to the British government earlier that afternoon for an alliance if Britain refrained from intervention would be tempting enough to drive a wedge between Britain and Poland.[155]

The British cabinet discussed Hitler's proposal in meetings on 26 and 27 August. The attempt by Hitler to split Britain from Poland was recognized and the cabinet decided to reject the German proposal. An alternative proposal that was the reverse of Hitler's offer was developed. Only after a peaceful negotiated settlement of the German-Polish question would a general settlement in Anglo-German relations be considered.[156] The British ambassador was to deliver the formal British response on his return to Berlin on 28 August.[157]

Hitler had, however, already reached a final decision. Hitler had informed the commander in chief of the army that Operation White would be initiated against Poland on 1 September even at the risk of war with Britain.[158] When Henderson delivered the British reply to Hitler late on 28 August,[159] Hitler decided to make one last effort to secure British nonintervention. The following day Hitler formally replied to the British government, referring to the British statement that Poland was prepared to engage in direct negotiations by demanding that a Polish plenipotentiary arrive in Berlin on 30 August.[160] If Poland refused the demand Hitler hoped to pin blame for the outbreak of the war on a Polish refusal to negotiate. Conversely, if Poland agreed to negotiate directly Germany would present unacceptable demands but attempt to blame Polish intransigence. In either case Hitler hoped to isolate Poland from the British.[161] The British government viewed the demand by Hitler as extreme, and in a stormy meeting with Hitler on the evening of 29 August Henderson stated that Britain would not pressure Poland to negotiate on such terms.[162] At a midnight meeting on 30 August Henderson presented the formal British reply, and Rib-

155. *DGFP, 1918–1945*, ser. D, vol. 7, no. 265, 279–81, and *DBFP, 1919–1939*, 3d ser., vol. 7, no. 283, 227–29.

156. Weinberg, *Foreign Policy of Hitler's Germany*, 642–43.

157. *DBFP, 1919–1939*, 3d ser., vol. 7, no. 426, 330–32.

158. *DGFP, 1918–1945*, ser. D, vol. 7, app. 1, 565, and Weinberg, *Foreign Policy of Hitler's Germany*, 643–44.

159. *DBFP, 1919–1939*, 3d ser., vol. 7, no. 455, 351–55.

160. *DGFP, 1918–1945*, ser. D, vol. 7, no. 421, 413–15.

161. Weinberg, *Foreign Policy of Hitler's Germany*, 644.

162. *DBFP, 1919–1939*, 3d ser., vol. 7, no. 504, 391; no. 508, 393.

bentrop responded that the nonarrival of the Polish plenipotentiary nullified the German proposal for negotiations. By 6:30 A.M. on 31 August the German high command received the final order from Hitler to commence the attack against Poland on 1 September.[163] The Second World War was about to begin.

British deterrent actions in 1939 sharply contrasted British policy in the Czech crisis of 1938. Throughout the spring and summer of 1939 the British issued repeated warnings to the German government that the pledge to Poland would be carried out without exception. Furthermore, the British government refused to pressure Poland to concede to the demands of Germany. Hitler, nevertheless, launched the attack on Poland. As the results of probit analysis on past behavior suggest, British weakness in the Czech crisis convinced Hitler that the British guarantee was likely to be a bluff. British past behavior undermined the credibility of the change in British policy that resulted from Germany's occupation of Prague in March 1939. Hitler does not seem to have believed that the apparent change in British policy would be sustained when challenged by another crisis and the threat of war. Hitler's statements at the 14 and 22 August conferences about the weakness of Britain's political leadership reflect this belief.

As with the Czech crisis of 1938, the Western powers' lack of military capabilities to defend their protégé and reliance instead on the threat of defeat in a war of attrition failed to deter Hitler. The Czech and Polish cases nicely illustrate the finding of probit analysis that a deterrent-by-denial military capability is much more potent than a deterrent-by-punishment capability. But it can be asked whether Hitler could have been deterred in 1939 even if the military balance had been different. Hitler was determined to dominate Central and Eastern Europe, and a general European war probably could not have been avoided unless the Western powers had been willing to acquiesce to such German domination. Hitler believed that the Western powers would eventually oppose his plans, and he sought to eliminate potential threats to his flank in Eastern Europe before defeating the Western powers. Hitler would have preferred to have defeated Poland in a isolated war, but the threat of British intervention did not fundamentally challenge his long-term goals. Hitler's determination to dominate Europe made successful extended deterrence very difficult for the

163. *DGFP, 1918–1945,* ser. D, vol. 7, no. 461, 451–54, and app. 1, 569.

Western powers, and the military weaknesses of Britain and France ensured the failure of deterrence in 1939. The Western powers were in no position to intervene effectively in the defense of Poland, and Hitler realized this. Germany could defeat Poland without becoming immediately engaged in a two-front war with the Western powers. Because British and French rearmament programs were only in the early stages, Germany was in a relatively favorable military position to wage war against the Western powers after defeating Poland. Even if Britain and France in 1939 had possessed much stronger military capabilities and had demonstrated the intent to use force by a tit-for-tat policy of military escalation, Hitler might not have been deterred.[164] Strong military capabilities and military actions that signal the intent to use those capabilities will generally, as the results of the probit analysis indicate, contribute to deterrence success. The case of Hitler, however, suggests that if political leaders are fanatically devoted to expansionist aims the threat of suffering heavy military losses to achieve those aims may not be a powerful enough deterrent.

The U.S. decision to cross the thirty-eighth parallel, 1950. On 25 June 1950 North Korean armed forces crossed the thirty-eighth parallel and invaded the Republic of Korea (ROK) in an attempt to overthrow the regime of Syngman Rhee and unify Korea under communist rule. Outnumbered and unprepared for the attack, ROK forces suffered a series of rapid defeats and the capital, Seoul, fell within four days of the initial attack. The South Korean army was forced to retreat swiftly southward to avoid complete defeat.[165]

The North Korean government, with the support of the Soviet Union, had anticipated the rapid defeat and collapse of armed resistance in South Korea and did not expect the United States to intervene in defense of the ROK.[166] But the Truman administration reacted vig-

164. Under such conditions the German high command might have been deterred. Whether the leadership of the armed forces would have summoned the courage to confront Hitler or have possessed the ability to remove Hitler from power is another question.

165. Roy A. Appleman, *United States Army in the Korean War: South to the Naktong, North to the Yalu* (Washington, D.C.: Office of the Chief of Military History, Department of the Army, 1961), 7–35.

166. Adam B. Ulam, *Expansion and Coexistence: Soviet Foreign Policy, 1917–1973* (New York: Praeger, 1974), 518–19, and Allen S. Whiting, *China Crosses the*

orously to the news of North Korean invasion. United States naval and air units were committed to the defense of South Korea on 27 June, and President Truman ordered on 30 June that U.S. ground forces be committed as well.[167]

The U.S. intervention had no immediate impact on the battle on the ground in Korea because time was required to organize and send reinforcements to the Far East. By the end of July, ROK and U.S. ground forces were in jeopardy of being driven off the Korean peninsula. Substantial reinforcement began to arrive in South Korea at the beginning of August, and ROK and U.S. forces established a stable defensive line around the southern port city of Pusan by mid-August, thus securing a base for further reinforcements of men and materials.[168]

With the North Korean offensive stymied, U.S. policymakers turned their attention to plans for a counteroffensive. The initial objective of the Truman administration in defending South Korea had been to repulse the North Korean invading forces and compel their withdrawal across the thirty-eighth parallel. But from the outset of the U.S. intervention officials had been considering the complete defeat of the North Korean army and the unification of Korea under the auspices of elections sponsored by the United Nations (U.N.). John Allison, director of the Office of Northeast Asian Affairs, argued in a memorandum to Assistant Secretary Dean Rusk dated 1 July, "If we can . . . we should continue right on up to the Manchurian and Siberian border, and, having done so, call for a UN-supervised election for all of Korea." United States military leaders supported a more ambitious policy. A Defense Department memorandum of 31 July referring to General MacArthur, commander of U.N. forces in Korea, argued that "(1) The unified command should seek to occupy Korea and to defeat North Korean armed forces wherever located north or south of the 38th parallel. (2) To achieve this objective, the Commanding General of the unified command should be directed to take necessary military action in Korea, without regard to the 38th parallel."[169]

United States officials were also publicly hinting at a possible

Yalu: The Decision to Enter the Korean War (Stanford: Stanford University Press, 1980), 38–40.

167. *FRUS, 1950,* vol. 7, 155–61, 170–71, 178–83, 200–3, and 211.

168. Appleman, *United States Army in the Korean War,* 248–436.

169. *FRUS, 1950,* vol. 7, 272, 509. See also 528–35.

change in policy. At the United Nations, U.S. ambassador Warren Austin argued in a Security Council debate on 17 August that the General Assembly had endorsed the goal of a free, independent, and unified Korea in a number of past resolutions. He went on to state that now was the time to realize this objective. "The Security Council has set as its first objective the end of the breach of the peace. This objective must be pursued in such a manner that no opportunity is provided for another attempt at invasion. . . . The United Nations must see that the people of Korea attain complete individual and political freedom."[170]

President Truman indicated his support for this larger political and military objective in a national broadcast on 1 September when he stated, "We believe that Koreans have a right to be free, independent, and united."[171] On 7 September Secretary of State Acheson declared that to repulse the North Korean invasion was certainly not the only task of the United Nations forces.[172]

In August a series of memorandums and draft papers were circulated within the U.S. government asking whether U.S. ground forces should cross the thirty-eighth parallel and considering the risks of Soviet or Chinese communist intervention to oppose such a crossing. Intelligence reports noted the movement of Chinese forces from Central China to Manchuria, and an army intelligence assessment of 30 August estimated PLA troop strength in Manchuria at approximately 240,000.[173] On 9 September the National Security Council sent NSC 81/1—a study of the policies the United States should adopt after U.S. forces had reached the thirty-eighth parallel—to President Truman (Truman had requested a study on this question on 17 July). The NSC study recommended that General MacArthur be authorized to cross the thirty-eighth parallel, to pursue and complete the destruction of enemy forces, and to prepare for the occupation of North Korea. But NSC 81/1 recommended that MacArthur be given only provisional approval to cross the parallel because U.S. policymakers were concerned that

170. *United Nations Security Council: Official Records,* 488th sess., 17 August 1950, no. 30.
171. *Public Papers of the Presidents of the United States: Harry S. Truman, 1950* (Washington, D.C.: Government Printing Office, 1965), 609.
172. *Department of State Bulletin,* 23: 585 (1950):463.
173. *FRUS, 1950,* vol. 7, 600–3, 617–23, 635–39, 646–48, 653–66, 671–79.

crossing the parallel might provoke Soviet or PRC intervention in support of North Korea. United States officials recognized that military operations in North Korea carried serious risks. The NSC study thus provided approval for U.S. crossing of the thirty-eighth parallel only if "at the time of such operations there has been no entry into North Korea by major Soviet or Chinese Communist forces, no announcement of intended entry, nor a threat to counter our operations militarily in North Korea."[174]

President Truman approved the recommendations of NSC 81/1 on 11 September, thereby approving tentative plans to cross the thirty-eighth parallel and occupy North Korea. The final decision would depend on the perceived risk of Soviet or Chinese communist military intervention. The unification of Korea with U.S. arms was to be pursued as long as it did not entail a serious risk of provoking a general war.

The leadership of the PRC had not been closely involved in planning the North Korean invasion and had anticipated the rapid collapse of the South Korean regime following the North Korean attack. The most important military problem confronting the Chinese leadership in the spring and summer of 1950 was the projected invasion of Taiwan, which was occupied by nationalist forces. Communist armed forces were being concentrated and trained in southeast China opposite Taiwan for an amphibious attack. But the unexpected intervention of the United States in support of South Korea tempered the PRC's optimism about a rapid victory for North Korean arms. The communist press still predicted ultimate victory but voiced increasing concern about the necessity of a prolonged war to defeat the enemy. At this time there were no public statements of a PRC intent to intervene, but the PRC's increased concern about the course of the Korean War was reflected in the movement of approximately eight divisions from south and southeast China to Manchuria in order to reinforce the Fourth Field Army already stationed there.[175]

The failure of the North Korean offensive to deliver a knockout blow to ROK and U.S. forces at Pusan by mid-August, coupled with Ambassador Austin's statement at the United Nations that the time was

174. Ibid., 716.
175. Whiting, *China Crosses the Yalu*, 18–22, 54–57, 64–67.

right for the unification of Korea, led to a decisive change in the PRC's policy toward the Korean War. The PRC had from the outset of the war maintained a low profile, leaving it to the Soviet Union to assume the diplomatic lead in supporting North Korea at the United Nations and internationally. By mid-August, efforts by the Soviet representative in the Security Council to establish a basis for peace talks had proven unsuccessful. Furthermore, the likely shift in the balance of forces on the ground in Korea to the advantage of the ROK, as large-scale U.S. reinforcements began to arrive, indicated a dangerous reversal in the course of the war from the perspective of the PRC. The leadership of the PRC decided that its country would have to assume a more active diplomatic role in support of North Korea to deter the United States from pursuing a policy of total victory in the war.[176]

On 20 August Foreign Minister Chou En-lai addressed a cable to the United Nations acknowledging the importance of North Korea to the PRC: "Korea is China's neighbor. The Chinese people cannot but be concerned about (a) solution of the Korean question." On 26 August an article in the communist press further developed the link between threats to North Korea and the security of the PRC: "The barbarous action of American imperialism and its hangers-on in invading Korea not only menaces peace in Asia and the world in general but seriously threatens the security of China in particular. . . . It is impossible to solve the Korean question without the participation of its closest neighbor, China. . . . North Korea's friends are our friends. North Korea's enemy is our enemy. North Korea's defense is our defense." At the beginning of September a militant domestic propaganda campaign attempted to prepare the population for a possible military confrontation with the United States. Armed conflict with the United States was not linked directly to the defense of North Korea.[177]

The Inchon landing on 15 September and the rapid collapse of the North Korean army in the last two weeks of September brought the question of whether the United States should cross the thirty-eighth parallel to the forefront. The risky but carefully planned Inchon offensive encircled the North Korean army through a daring, difficult amphibious landing north of the battlefront. Caught between U.S. forces moving southward from Inchon and U.S. and ROK forces advancing

176. Ibid., 72–80.
177. As quoted in ibid., 79, 84–85, 99–100.

northward from Pusan in a counteroffensive strike, the North Korean army was to be entrapped and destroyed. The military operation was a considerable though not complete success, with an estimated 25,000–30,000 North Korean troops managing to slip back across the thirty-eighth parallel into North Korea. Nevertheless, the North Korean army had been shattered and was on the brink of complete defeat.[178] On 26 September U.S. troops from the south of Korea established contact with units from Inchon. Two days later Seoul was liberated, and by the end of September U.S. and ROK forces were approaching the thirty-eighth parallel and were in a position to swiftly complete the destruction of the North Korean army.

The PRC responded to the rapid turn of events in Korea during late September by escalating its efforts to deter a U.S. invasion of North Korea. The government issued a series of increasingly stiff warnings. On 22 September a spokesman for the Ministry of Foreign Affairs stated, ''We clearly reaffirm that we will always stand on the side of the Korean people . . . and resolutely oppose the criminal acts of American imperialist aggressors against Korea.'' On 25 September Gen. Neih Jung-chen, acting chief of staff of the PLA, indirectly conveyed another warning in a conversation with the Indian ambassador to the United Nations, K. M. Panikkar. Neih stated that China would not ''sit back with folded hands and let the Americans come up to the [Sino-Korean] border.'' He added, ''We know what we are in for but at all costs American aggression had to be stopped.''[179] A third warning was issued when Chou En-lai declared in an official speech on 30 September, ''The Chinese people absolutely will not tolerate foreign aggression, nor will they supinely tolerate seeing their neighbors being savagely invaded by the imperialists.''[180] Along with these verbal warnings, the PRC undertook military preparations to signal its resolve. Beginning in mid-September large-scale reinforcements of troops were dispatched to Manchuria (estimated troop strength in Manchuria increased to approximately 320,000 by mid-October), and troops in Manchuria began to be moved to positions along the Sino-Korean border.[181]

178. Appleman, *United States Army in the Korean War*, 488–541, 573–606.
179. As quoted in Whiting, *China Crosses the Yalu*, 105, 107.
180. *People's China*, vol. 11, no. 8 (Peking: Foreign Languages Press, 1950):9.
181. Whiting, *China Crosses the Yalu*, 111.

The verbal warnings of the PRC were viewed as empty bluffs by U.S. policymakers. The PRC warnings lacked credibility for a number of reasons. First, for months the PRC had been issuing threats to attack Taiwan despite the presence of the U.S. Seventh Fleet in the Taiwan Straits. Because the PRC had not attempted any military action, the threats to intervene in Korea were discounted by U.S. policymakers. Second, the warnings of the PRC were viewed as an attempt to influence the upcoming General Assembly vote on the resolution authorizing U.N. forces to cross the thirty-eighth parallel. By emphasizing the potential dangers of a U.S. crossing of the thirty-eighth parallel the PRC, it was believed, was attempting to persuade U.N. members to vote against the resolution. Third, internal political and economic problems were so pressing for the PRC that war with the United States would be too heavy a burden.[182] Fourth, the military preparations of the PRC lagged behind the rapidly changing military situation on the ground in Korea. While the buildup of PLA forces in Manchuria signaled the PRC potential to intervene in Korea, U.S. and ROK forces concentrated on the thirty-eighth parallel were prepared for immediate invasion of North Korea. United States policymakers were focusing their attention on the immediate costs and dangers of crossing the thirty-eighth parallel. If PRC military actions were to have deterred a U.S. invasion, PLA troops should have been moved into North Korea and deployed near the thirty-eighth parallel in late September or early October. Without a trip-wire deterrent force in position, U.S. policymakers were tempted to gamble on a rapid, decisive thrust across the parallel to defeat the North Korean army. On 27 September the Joint Chiefs of Staff transmitted, with Truman's approval a new directive to MacArthur on military operations in North Korea. MacArthur was authorized to cross the thirty-eighth parallel and seek the complete destruction of the North Korean army if there had been: (1) no entry into North Korea by major Soviet or PRC forces, (2) no announcement of intended entry, and (3) no threat to counter U.S. forces in North Korea. The directive considerably reduced the impact of the last two requirements when it further explained, ''(4) In the event of the open or covert employment of major Chinese Communist units south of the 38 parallel, you should continue

182. *FRUS, 1950,* vol. 7, 849, 852, 868–69, 885; Harry S. Truman, *Years of Trial and Hope,* vol. 2 (Garden City, N.Y.: Doubleday, 1956), 362; and Foot, *Wrong War,* 80–81.

the action as long as action by your forces offers a reasonable chance of successful resistance. (5) In the event of an attempt to employ small Soviet or Chinese Communist units covertly south of the 38 parallel, you should continue the action.''[183]

The 27 September directive, in effect, sanctioned a U.S. crossing of the parallel if the immediate balance of forces remained in the United States' favor (there had been no significant prior entry of PRC forces, only small units) and the costs of a military victory were not too high (thus even if opposed by major PRC forces MacArthur was authorized to continue to attack as long as the chances of success remained good). Given the decisive advantage in the immediate balance of forces along the thirty-eighth parallel (more than 100,000 U.S. and ROK forces against two North Korean divisions), United States policymakers were confident of a rapid military victory. The weakened state of North Korean defenses also led U.S. leaders to believe that North Korea could be overrun before the PRC could intervene effectively. The very weakness of the North Korean army and the lopsided balance of local forces led U.S. officials to calculate that the PRC would not intervene in support of a lost cause. United States policymakers argued that if the PRC had not intervened under more favorable circumstances in July or August to help North Korea achieve complete victory why would the PRC intervene under far less favorable conditions in October with the North Korean army almost completely defeated? This type of miscalculation is not uncommon, because policymakers often fail to appreciate that adversaries are willing to use force to prevent or minimize losses. United States policymakers not only discounted the probability of PRC intervention, they also estimated that if the PRC did intervene it would not be decisive. The combined effect of these calculations created the perception among U.S. policymakers that the unification of Korea was an attractive and relatively low-cost military operation.[184] A

183. *FRUS, 1950*, vol. 7, 781–82. See also 792–93.

184. Robert J. Donavan, *Tumultuous Years: The Presidency of Harry S. Truman, 1949–1953* (New York: W. W. Norton, 1982), 285; James F. Schnable, *United States Army in the Korean War: Policy and Direction—The First Year* (Washington, D.C.: Office of the Chief of Military History, United States Army, 1972), 201–2; Martin Lichterman, ''To the Yalu and Back,'' in *American Civil-Military Decisions: A Book of Case Studies,* ed. Harold Stein (Birmingham: University of Alabama Press, 1963), 596; Richard E. Neustadt, *Presidential Power: The Politics of Leadership from F.D.R. to Carter* (New York: John Wiley and Sons, 1980), 100–2; and Foot, *Wrong War*, 80, 86.

memorandum presented to the White House on 12 October by the Central Intelligence Agency summarized the general consensus at the highest levels of the U.S. government, outlining several reasons that the PRC was not likely to intervene and concluding, ''While full-scale Chinese Communist intervention in Korea must be regarded as a continuing possibility, a consideration of all known factors leads to the conclusion that barring a Soviet decision for global war, such action is not probable in 1950. During this period, intervention will probably be confined to continued covert assistance to the North Koreans.''[185]

The United States pushed ahead with its plans to cross the thirty-eighth parallel despite PRC threats of intervention. On 29 September the Joint Chiefs of Staff approved the plan MacArthur had submitted for military operations north of the thirty-eighth parallel. On the following day Ambassador Austin pressed for U.N. support of plans to unify Korea: ''The opportunities for new acts of aggression should be removed. . . . The aggressor's forces should not be permitted to have refuge behind an imaginary line. . . . The artificial barrier which has divided North and South Korea has no basis for existence in law or reason.''[186] General MacArthur issued an ultimatum demanding the unconditional surrender of the North Korean army on 1 October, and later that day ROK forces crossed the thirty-eighth parallel. The PRC issued its final and most explicit threat of intervention. Chou En-lai summoned Panikkar to a midnight meeting at the Ministry of Foreign Affairs and declared that China would enter the war if U.S. troops invaded North Korea. On 7 October the General Assembly passed a resolution authorizing military operations in North Korea, and U.S. forces began to cross the thirty-eighth parallel that day.[187] The PRC's attempt at extended deterrence had failed.

During late September the military position and balance of forces shifted rapidly and decisively in favor of the United States and the ROK. Military preparations by the PRC did not keep pace with the rapidly changing military situation within Korea. It is not clear whether the PRC could have moved its armed forces into North Korea before the U.S. crossing of the thirty-eighth parallel or whether problems of logistics and organization prevented PLA deployment in North Korea before the

185. *FRUS, 1950,* vol. 7, 934.
186. *Department of State Bulletin,* 23: 588 (1950):579.
187. *FRUS, 1950,* vol. 7, 913. See also 839, 850, 904–6.

beginning of October. In any event, only a week after U.S. armed forces had crossed the parallel PLA forces began to cross into North Korea.[188] While the PLA had been preparing for a potential intervention, the altered balance of forces along the battlefront had placed the United States in a position to complete the destruction of the North Korean army in a rapid offensive attack. The lack of a trip-wire deterrent—the capability of the defender to engage immediately the armed forces of the potential attacker—seems crucial to understanding why the PRC attempt at extended deterrence failed. The failure of the PRC to deploy its forces in North Korea before the U.S. crossing of the thirty-eighth parallel resulted in the underestimation by U.S. policymakers of the PRC's resolve and capability to intervene effectively. The decisive United States advantage in the immediate balance of forces counteracted the potential deterrent force represented by the PRC's capability to mobilize and reinforce the North Korean army with superior forces in a general war.

The U.S. decision to cross the thirty-eighth parallel with the intent of reunifying Korea was based on the assumption that a return to the status quo would not ensure long-term peace and stability in the Korean peninsula.[189] Perhaps there were domestic political pressures to push north and payoffs for the Truman administration behind the reunification of Korea. The Truman administration had been under strong criticism from the Republican party following the loss of China to the communists in 1949. The administration was attacked for appeasing communism in Asia and for permitting vital U.S. interests to be sacrificed. The Truman administration's foreign policy record in Asia promised to be a central issue for the Republican party in the upcoming mid-term elections.[190] The rollback of communism in Asia through the reunification of Korea represented a major foreign policy success for Truman's administration that could be used to silence the critics who were charging the administration and the Democratic party with appeasement of communism in Asia. The domestic political payoffs were

188. Whiting, *China Crosses the Yalu,* 116.

189. Foot, *Wrong War,* 71–72.

190. Ibid., 69–70; Richard Ned Lebow, *Between Peace and War: The Nature of International Crisis* (Baltimore: Johns Hopkins University Press, 1981), 174–76, and Richard E. Neustadt and Ernest R. May, *Thinking in Time: The Use of History for Decision Makers* (New York: Free Press, 1986), 34–48.

considerable and probably provided a strong incentive for the Truman administration to pursue a total victory.

As NSC directive 81/1 indicated, President Truman was not prepared to push for reunification of Korea at the cost of general war with the Soviet Union or the PRC. The military costs of achieving reunification were an important constraint on whether such an objective would be pursued. The decisive change in the balance of forces on the ground in Korea in late September enabled the Truman administration to press ahead with the larger objective of reunification, anticipating that the military costs would be acceptable and, in fact, quite low. Domestic political and economic problems can increase the willingness of policymakers to accept more risk in decisions to use force,[191] but domestic, or even international, pressures are not powerful enough to obviate considerations of the military costs of foreign policy goals. The Truman administration's goals in the Korean War expanded when military conditions were favorable in September and October 1950 but quickly reversed when PRC intervention convinced the United States that the military costs of reunifying Korea were too high.

191. I draw this conclusion from the important work of Lebow, *Between Peace and War,* 57–97, 273–81.

6

Case Studies: The Impact of Diplomacy and Past Behavior

In this chapter I analyze four case studies, comparing the effectiveness of diplomatic strategies and the impact of the defender's past behavior on deterrence outcomes. Whereas the case studies in chapter 5 focused on the military calculations that influenced the decisions of a potential attacker, the analysis in this chapter focuses on the role of more broadly defined political and reputational variables in the outcome of deterrence. Military calculations were not unimportant in the cases examined in this chapter, but estimates of the costs and the likelihood of victory in war were not central to understanding why the potential attacker did or did not challenge the defender's deterrent threat.

The purpose of analyzing individual cases of attempted deterrence is to continue evaluating and illustrating the generalizations suggested by the results of probit analysis. Two cases of successful deterrence are examined in this chapter: the Anglo-Russian confrontation over Afghanistan in 1885 and German support for Finland in the dispute with the Soviet Union in 1940–41. Two cases of deterrence failure are also examined: the outbreak of the Russo-Japanese War in 1904 and the outbreak of World War I. A central theme developed in the case studies is that deterrence success may often depend less on the potential attacker's expectation of high costs in the use of armed force than on the potential attacker's belief that the domestic political and the international costs of continued peace will not be prohibitively high. A defender's willingness to consider compromise through firm-but-flexible diplomacy can be instrumental in convincing the potential attacker that there is an acceptable alternative to using military force to achieve foreign policy objectives.

Cases of Deterrence Success

Anglo-Russian conflict over Afghanistan in 1885. For two decades beginning in the 1860s Russia steadily extended the borders of its empire in central Asia with military campaigns and conquests. Pushing eastward from the trans-Caspian region, Russian armed forces defeated the previously independent Turkoman tribes. Within two decades Russia had extended its territorial borders approximately six hundred miles in central Asia. The extension of Russian political rule was accompanied by the development of a railway system that significantly enhanced the reach and potential strength of the Russian army in central Asia.[1]

The geographic expansion of the Russian Empire in central Asia and the growth of the railway system linking the new territories to European Russia was viewed by British policymakers in London and New Delhi as a potential threat to the British Empire in India. British officials increasingly viewed Afghanistan as a critical buffer state—a protective shield for the defense of India against Russian expansionism. To halt the advance of Russia in central Asia, British policymakers concluded that the frontiers of Afghanistan bordering Russia should be well-defined and recognized in an international agreement. Negotiations with Russia to demarcate Afghanistan's northern frontier were initiated in the late 1860s and continued intermittently for more than a decade. Little progress was achieved, as the Russian government sidestepped repeated British protests and was unwilling to define its frontier in central Asia because the authority and control of the Afghan state did not seem to extend into many of the border regions.[2]

The Russian occupation of Merv, just north of the Afghan frontier, in February 1884 alarmed the British, but the Liberal government of Gladstone reacted cautiously. The British presented another protest to the Russian government with a proposal to resume negotiations on the demarcation of Afghanistan's northern frontier. The new round of negotiations soon became deadlocked, and Russian military forces

---

1. Rose Louise Greaves, *Persia and the Defense of India, 1884–1892* (London: Athlone Press, 1959), 55–61, and David Gillard, *The Struggle for Asia, 1828–1914: A Study in British and Russian Imperialism* (London: Methuen, 1977), 115–33.

2. Firuz Kazemzadeh, *Russia and Britain in Persia, 1864–1914: A Study in Imperialism* (New Haven: Yale University Press, 1968), 3–99.

began to move into the disputed frontier regions.[3] At this time the British suffered a major setback in the Sudan when Khartoum fell to dervish forces in late January 1885. In February the British military attaché in St. Petersburg reported strong support within the Russian military for a policy of military advance unencumbered by negotiations and formal obligations.[4] Later that month the Russian ambassador in London, M. De Staal, advised his government to stand firm in the negotiations and assumed that the British would eventually accept Russia's terms. Staal reported to St. Petersburg in mid-March that the Gladstone government was likely to pursue a policy of appeasement.[5] Russian forces defeated Afghan troops in an armed clash at Panjdeh on 30 March 1885, inflicting heavy losses and forcing the retreat of the Afghan forces. Reports in early April indicated the advance of Russian troops at two other critical points along the Afghan border.[6] Russia seemed prepared to settle the border dispute by unilateral action and the use of armed force (Afghan defenses were outnumbered by superior Russian forces along the disputed frontier).

The Russian attack at Panjdeh and the further advance of Russian troops precipitated a major crisis in relations between the British and Russian governments. The British government reacted vigorously to the news of the Panjdeh incident. In an address to Parliament the prime minister described the Russian attack as a ''grave occurrence'' and requested eleven million pounds in war credits. In addition, the government ordered that official announcements declaring the outbreak of war be printed in anticipation of armed conflict with Russia.[7] The British government also decided to mobilize and dispatch two army corps to Quetta, just south of the Indo-Afghan border.[8] On 26 April British

---

3. David Gillard, ed., *British Documents on Foreign Affairs: Reports and Papers from the Foreign Office Confidential Print*, pt. 1, ser. B, vol. 12 (University Publications of America, 1985), no. 10, 100–33.

4. Great Britain Foreign Office (hereafter referred to as F.O.) 65/1236, enclosure no. 27. See also Peter Morris, ''The Russians in Central Asia, 1870–1887,'' *Slavonic and East European Review* 53: 133 (1975):528.

5. A. Meyendorff, *Correspondance Diplomatique de M. de Staal, 1884–1900*, vol. 1 (Paris: M. Rivière, 1929), no. 19, 158–60, no. 30, 172.

6. Gillard, *British Documents on Foreign Affairs*, no. 19, 158; no. 22, 159, and F.O. Confidential Print 5140/44, 54, 65.

7. Gillard, *Struggle for Asia*, 145.

8. India Office, Military Department, Military Collection Papers, L/Mil/7/1261: M–11649, 11622, 1434, and L/Mil/7/1262:M–12822.

naval forces occupied Port Hamilton along the Korean coast in antic-ipation of operations against the Russian naval base at Vladivostok.[9] Russia continued to reinforce its military positions along the Afghan border throughout April and prepared naval forces at Odessa for imme-diate action.[10]

The escalating military confrontation threatening war between Rus-sia and Britain was coupled with an increase in diplomatic exchanges between the two countries. The report of the Russian attack at Panjdeh resulted in an uproar in Britain and created strong political pressures on the Gladstone government to adopt an intransigent and belligerent position toward Russia. The amir of Afghanistan had informed the British that the Panjdeh territory was not vitally important but had insisted that retention of the Zulfiqar Pass and other points along the northern frontier were of strategic importance. In a very important but unofficial meeting between the Russian ambassador and the Foreign Secretary, Lord Granville, and Ambassador Lord Kimberley on 14 April the British proposed a compromise settlement. Granville began by stating that if Russia agreed to withdraw its troops from the disputed frontier regions the prospects for a settlement would be favorable. Lord Kimberley then explained that the Zulfiqar Pass and other points along the frontier had to remain in Afghan possession and proposed that if Russia agreed to this Britain would see that the territories held by the Saryk Turkomans were awarded to Russia. Kimberley also hinted confidentially to the ambassador that concessions on Panjdeh were possible if Russia accepted the frontier line as defined by Britain at other points. The Russian ambassador indicated his support for the proposed tradeoff without the official approval of his government.[11]

On 16 April the Russian foreign minister indicated in a note to the British government his tentative support for the British proposal to exchange Panjdeh for the Zulfiqar Pass and other points along the frontier.[12] The British proposal called for reciprocal concessions in the interests of a negotiated settlement. The critical question for the Rus-

9. Greaves, *Persia and the Defense of India,* 73.

10. F.O. Confidential Print, 5140/70, 95, 156a, 166, 189 and F.O. 65/1240/1241, 1242, 1243.

11. F.O. Confidential Print, 5140/99, and Meyendorff, *Correspondance Diplo-matique,* no. 50, 189–91.

12. Meyendorff, *Correspondance Diplomatique,* no. 52, 192.

sians was how firm was the British position on the Zulfiqar Pass and other points along the frontier. The Gladstone government had been very quick to grant the Panjdeh, and the Russians seem to have calculated that with continued military pressure and a firm bargaining position the British proposal would be turned into a far more advantageous agreement in which the British were forced to make additional concessions. There was a widespread belief within the Russian military that the British government was not eager to enter another foreign conflict after the military setbacks in the Sudan. But the Russian ambassador informed his government that the setbacks in the Sudan might lead the Liberal government to adopt a stronger stance on Afghanistan to avoid another foreign policy defeat.[13]

On 18 April the Russian government issued an official statement declining to withdraw its troops from the disputed territories before negotiations and refusing to participate in a joint investigation of the Panjdeh incident.[14] Granville reciprocated the firm position of the Russian government by informing Staal the following day, that his government could not accept the report of the local Russian commander on the Panjdeh incident and stressing the necessity of an investigation. Granville concluded that if Russian forces withdrew from the disputed territories, a satisfactory settlement might be reached. The Russian government stood firm. On 21 April the Russian foreign minister maintained in two notes to the British foreign minister that Russia could not withdraw its troops and that Afghanistan had provoked the Panjdeh confrontation. In an attempt to break the deadlock over the Panjdeh incident several days later, Granville proposed that although an investigation into the incident was essential it might be possible to invite a third party to act as an impartial judge.[15]

The British insistence on the withdrawal of Russian forces and an investigation of the Panjdeh incident convinced the Russian government to retreat from its stiff position and follow up the British proposal for compromise. On 1 May the Russian ambassador proposed to Granville the neutralization of Panjdeh pending demarcation of the frontier. The British foreign secretary accepted the proposal on the understand-

13. Ibid., no. 29, 168–71; no. 43, 183–85.

14. F.O. 65/1241/152b, and ibid., no. 61, 199–200; no. 76, 207–8.

15. F.O. Confidential Print, 5140/128c, 136, 151.

ing that no Russian or Afghan troops would remain in or enter Panjdeh during the negotiations. The Russian foreign minister presented a note to the British government on the next day proposing third party arbitration of the Panjdeh incident. Granville promptly accepted the Russian proposal for arbitration.[16]

Talks convened immediately between the British foreign secretary and the Russian ambassador on delimiting the frontier. A draft proposal for the demarcation of the Afghan frontier was provisionally agreed upon by 8 May. In accordance with the original British proposal of 14 April, Afghanistan retained those territories that its ruler considered strategically vital and over which he exercised effective political control. The border was to extend as far north as Maruchak and to include the command of the strategic passes at Zulfiqar, Gulran, and Maruchak. In return the Russians were to receive Panjdeh and the territory north of Maruchak extending east and west.[17] The draft proposal was thus a compromise in which the Russians received the territory it considered important—Panjdeh—while Afghanistan retained all those points essential to a strategically defensible frontier.

Further negotiations on the demarcation of the border moved to St. Petersburg. The Russian foreign minister raised no serious objections to Afghanistan retaining control of the Zulfiqar Pass but proposed that the boundary exclude Maruchak from Afghan territory. Lord Kimberley insisted that his government could not accept this proposal. On 21 May the Russians questioned Afghan control of the Zulfiqar Pass for the first time and maintained that Maruchak should be ceded to them. The British responded quickly on 22 May, reiterating that Afghanistan must retain complete control of the Zulfiqar Pass and Maruchak. The Russian government pressed further on the issue of the Zulfiqar Pass: the Russian foreign minister informed the British ambassador that his country could not give up control of the road to Al-Robat just east of the pass and within Afghan territory as proposed by the British.[18]

Negotiations on the Panjdeh incident and the neutralization of the territory were also running into serious difficulties. The Russian government proposed on 7 May that the king of Denmark act as arbitrator.

16. Ibid., 5140/187, 188, 190, 196.
17. Ibid., 5140/217.
18. Ibid., 5140/243, 285, 339, and Meyendorff, *Correspondance Diplomatique,* no. 95, 219; no. 98, 221; no. 100, 222; no. 101, 222–24.

MAP 6. Central Asia

The British responded with a counterproposal that the emperor of Germany be asked to arbitrate instead, but the Russians would not agree.[19] In mid-May the Russians objected to the movement by the Afghan government of more troops into positions near Panjdeh. Meanwhile, the British charged the Russians with maintaining troops in the disputed territory in violation of the neutralization agreement.[20]

In another attempt to break the impasse, the British foreign secretary informed the Russian ambassador on 30 May that his government would accept the Russian proposal that the king of Denmark be asked to arbitrate the Panjdeh incident.[21] On 8 June the Russian government responded with its own compromise, stating in a note that it accepted the British interpretation of the neutralization agreement on the Panjdeh and thus ending the controversy over the presence of Afghan and Russian troops in the area.[22]

The negotiations on the demarcation of the frontier remained deadlocked as the British stood firm on the Zulfiqar Pass. Although the Russians raised no objections initially to the British position that the pass must be retained by Afghanistan, the Russian government began to raise more and more questions about the issue. By the beginning of June the Russian position was that the integrity of its communications lines in the Zulfiqar Pass were as important as Afghan claims to control of the pass based on strategic grounds. In a note sent to the Russian ambassador on 4 June, Granville expressed his appreciation of Russia's desire to preserve its communications lines in that area but stated firmly that the command of the Pass must be retained by the Afghans.[23] The British deeply resented the Russian objections, believing that the Russians were attempting to renege on the agreement approved in the Russian note of 16 April—that the British would concede the Panjdeh if Afghanistan were allowed to retain control of the Zulfiqar Pass and other critical areas. The British believed that they had lived up to their part of the bargain and that it now remained for the Russian government to live up to its end of the deal and concede the pass to the Afghans. The

19. F.O. Confidential Print, 5140/241, 256.
20. Ibid., 5140/310, 311; F.O. 65/1244/33; F.O. 65/1243/57, 87; and Meyendorff, *Correspondance Diplomatique,* no. 119, 234–36.
21. F.O. Confidential Print, 5140/329.
22. Ibid., 5140/371, 372.
23. Ibid., 5140/437, 353.

British were prepared to reach an agreement based on mutual compromise but not unilateral concessions.

The impasse over the Zulfiqar Pass continued for the duration of June, and the election of a new Conservative government in Britain at the end of the month further delayed the negotiations. Renewed Russian military activity near the area of dispute accompanied the deadlock in the negotiations. Intelligence reports indicated that from late June to mid-July Russian troops at the Zulfiqar Pass were reinforced to an estimated strength of 3,000 men.[24] Russian diplomatic pressure was also maintained. On 9 July Staal delivered a note to the new foreign secretary, Lord Salisbury, stating that his government was "not prepared to agree that the whole of the Zulfiqar Pass should be included in Afghan territory" and proposing that negotiations on the remainder of the frontier continue while a decision was reached on the pass. But, Salisbury refused to continue negotiations on the remainder of the frontier because concessions on Panjdeh and other areas were to be conditioned on similar concessions by Russia with respect to the Zulfiqar Pass. On 17 July Salisbury wrote a stiff note informing the Russian government that the British did not accept Russian objections to Afghan control of the Zulfiqar Pass and that any settlement must be based on the original agreement to exchange Panjdeh for the Zulfiqar Pass.[25]

Russian intransigence at the bargaining table backed up by increased military preparations along the Afghan border were designed to force the British to concede on the question of the Zulfiqar Pass. In mid-July the Russian foreign minister informed Staal that it was up to the British government to break the stalemate in the negotiations.[26] But the diplomatic and military pressure failed to force the new Conservative government into further concessions. The new Prime Minister and Foreign Secretary Salisbury had demonstrated his firm resolve in the 1878 crisis with Russia and was a much tougher opponent than Gladstone. Staal reported to his government on 19 July that the new British government was resolved to act with greater firmness than the previous Liberal government, and that there was strong support within Parliament and in the public for this firm stand. In early August the Russian

24. Ibid., 5171/32, 53.

25. Ibid., 5171/39, 68, and Meyendorff, *Correspondance Diplomatique,* no. 131, 246, no. 132, 246–48.

26. Meyendorff, *Correspondance Diplomatique,* no. 136, 249.

ambassador advised his government to compromise because the Salisbury government was not going to concede.[27] It seems that the firm
stand of Salisbury convinced the Russian government that any settlement accepted by the British would require Russia to concede the
Zulfiqar Pass. On 24 August the Russian government presented a new
proposal in which Afghanistan retained complete command of the pass.
Salisbury informed the Russian ambassador on 3 September that the
British government accepted the new Russian proposal. On the following day the foreign secretary and Russian ambassador drew up an
agreement for the demarcation of the Afghan frontier, and a week later
the two countries signed a protocol on the Afghan northern border.[28]

The firm-but-flexible bargaining strategy of Britain was central in
resolving the boundary dispute with Russia and in preventing the
escalation to an armed confrontation. The British proposal of 14 April,
presented at the height of the crisis with military preparations by both
sides escalating, represented a basis for a diplomatic settlement of the
conflict. The terms proposed by the British contained some clear gains
for Russia and would not threaten the bargaining reputation of the
Russian government. Furthermore, British initiatives on the controversy over the Panjdeh incident broke a stalemate and induced Russian
cooperation, by enabling the moderate faction within the Russian leadership, headed by the Foreign Minister N. K. Giers, to convince the
military leadership to back down from a military confrontation with the
British without loss of face.[29] The Russian government and particularly
the War Ministry was prepared to claim as much territory in the
disputed frontier regions as was possible in order to prevent Afghanistan from becoming an effective buffer state for British India. The
military leadership was determined to incorporate at least some sections of the Panjdeh territory following the defeat of the Afghan forces.
The British and Afghan governments were concerned primarily about
establishing borders that were strategically defensible. A trade-off was
possible because the Panjdeh was not considered strategically vital.
Russian prestige and interests in the Panjdeh could be satisfied without
sacrificing Afghanistan's security interests. Although the Liberal government was under heavy domestic political pressure not to make any

27. Ibid., no. 137, 249–50, no. 142, 251–52.
28. F.O. Confidential Print, 5171/203, 259.
29. Morris, ''The Russians in Central Asia,'' 528–29.

concessions to Russia following the attack at Panjdeh, Gladstone recognized the potential for a satisfactory settlement and proposed the Panjdeh/Zulfiqar Pass trade-off despite the immediate domestic political costs incurred. The British determination to stand by the terms of the Panjdeh/Zulfiqar Pass exchange convinced the Russians that the British were not going to make further concessions and were serious about supporting their protégé, Afghanistan. The firm-but-flexible strategy of Britain represented the right combination of accommodation and intransigence necessary to convince a potential attacker that a defender is both interested in a diplomatic solution and determined to stand firm and fully support the vital interests of an ally.

As the hypothesis on bargaining strategies and the results of probit analysis indicated, bargaining strategies that rely on either intransigence or accommodation alone do not contribute to successful deterrence. The most effective bargaining strategy combines elements of both. In this case, accommodative moves by the British in the early stages of the negotiations (April and May) followed by a tit-for-tat policy of cooperation for the remainder of the negotiations (June through August) proved effective. The credibility of the firm British stand in the negotiations from June onward was enhanced by Salisbury's reputation for resolve from the 1878 crisis with Russia over the Turkish Straits. The effectiveness of the firm-but-flexible strategy depends critically on the nature of the potential attacker's goals. If the potential attacker has unlimited goals or will accept nothing less than the complete satisfaction of its demands, the defender's offer of reciprocal compromise will not be sufficient.[30] In such a situation the only potential deterrent would be a decisive advantage in the balance of military power for the defender, which would convince the potential attacker that its goals could not be achieved by the use of force. The Russian government was prepared to seize as much of the disputed territory as was possible, and Afghan defenses were not strong enough

30. Robert Axelrod makes a similar point in his study of bargaining strategies in prisoner's dilemma games: "What is effective depends not only upon the characteristics of a particular strategy, but also upon the nature of the other strategies with which it must interact." See *Evolution of Cooperation* (New York: Basic Books, 1984), 30. Robert Jervis, *Perception and Misperception in International Politics* (Princeton: Princeton University Press, 1976), chap. 3, also emphasizes that the effectiveness of a strategy depends on the adversary's intentions.

to deny the Russians the territory they desired. But the Russian government was not willing to risk war with the British to occupy all of the disputed territory. If the British government had been unwilling to compromise on Panjdeh, Russia would probably have gone to war. Russia was prepared to use force to achieve its minimal objectives—control of the Panjdeh—but was not willing to risk a larger armed conflict to achieve its maximum goals—seizure of all disputed territories. A bullying diplomatic strategy by Britain would probably have provoked war with Russia, whereas British concessions on the Zulfiqar Pass and other points on the frontier would have sacrificed Afghanistan's security to avoid a confrontation with Russia. The Afghan case illustrates what the results of probit analysis for a firm-but-flexible strategy suggest: potential attackers are often not committed to unlimited goals but are motivated by a mix of objectives; a carefully designed policy of conditional compromise can induce the potential attacker to accept limited gains that do not undermine the vital interests of the protégé and the defender.

Britain's credibility was also enhanced by the strength of the economic and military ties between Britain and India and the linkage between the securities of Afghanistan and India. The British threat to defend Afghanistan was credible not because of the intrinsic importance of Afghanistan to Britain but rather because Afghanistan shared a border with India, the most important colony in the British Empire. Afghan control of the Zulfiqar Pass was critical to the British because if Herat, the city to the south of the pass, were militarily vulnerable then the value of Afghanistan as a buffer state for India would be considerably reduced. The British threat to defend Afghanistan was, in fact, a threat to use military force to protect British interests in India. British-Indian troops concentrated at Quetta acted as a deterrent, as did the possibility of the British sending its fleet into the Black Sea.[31] The hypotheses formulated in chapter 3 took only the strength of direct economic and military ties between defender and protégé into account. The broader regional interests at stake for the defender thus may not have been adequately taken into account. Although the direct ties between defender and protégé may not be extensive, the strength of economic and military ties to countries in proximity to the protégé may

31. See Gillard, *Struggle for Asia,* 147, for a discussion of why Britain's threat to force the straits was credible despite Turkey's obligation by treaty not to allow British warships to pass the straits.

be sufficiently strong that the defender's threat to use force in the region is still quite credible.

German-Soviet conflict over Finland, 1940–1941. To meet the demands of the German war economy and to insulate the country from the effects of an economic blockade by the British, Germany pursued a policy of economic exploitation of occupied and neighboring countries, ensuring the supply of raw materials and natural resources.[32] The occupation of Denmark and Norway in spring 1940 established German dominance in the Arctic region and extended German power to the borders of Finland. Rich deposits of nickel ore had been discovered in an area of northern Finland bordering Norway and the Soviet Union and known as Petsamo. Adequate supplies of nickel were critical to the German armaments industry, and in spring 1940 German policymakers placed top priority on acquiring rights to the output of nickel ore from Petsamo. Secret negotiations were initiated with the Finnish government in June 1940. By the end of June the basic terms of an agreement had been approved by the Finnish and German governments, but the official signing of the agreement was delayed until the German company invited to participate in the concession had worked out the details with the Finnish government.[33]

In the early summer of 1940, however, the Soviet Union intervened and revealed an interest in the Petsamo mines. On 23 June Soviet Foreign Minister Vyacheslav Molotov requested that the Finnish government "grant the nickel concession to the Soviet Union, or agree to the establishment of a Finnish-Russian company."[34] The Soviets had not indicated an interest in the area previously, and had, in fact, agreed in the Treaty of Moscow signed in March to return the Petsamo area to Finland after the conclusion of the Soviet-Finnish War, even though Soviet forces had occupied the territory and were in complete control.

The German invasion of Norway in April 1940, however, signifi-

32. Alan S. Milward, *War, Economy, and Society, 1939–1945* (Berkeley: University of California Press, 1977), 132–68.

33. H. Peter Krosby, *Finland, Germany, and the Soviet Union, 1940–1941: The Petsamo Dispute* (Madison: University of Wisconsin Press, 1968), 13, 27–30, and U.S. Department of State, *Documents on German Foreign Policy [DGFP], 1918–1945,* ser. D, vol. 10 (Washington, D.C.: Government Printing Office, 1957), no. 221, 288.

34. *Finland Reveals Her Secret Documents on Soviet Policy, March 1940–June 1941: Official Blue-White Book of Finland* (hereafter referred to as *Blue-White Book*), (New York: Wilfred Funk, 1941), no. 14, 50–51.

cantly increased the German military threat to the Soviet Union's northern frontier, and the Petsamo region served as the northernmost buffer between German-occupied Norway and the Soviet border in the Kola Peninsula. After Germany's occupation of Norway, the Petsamo area took on far greater strategic significance for Soviet security than was the case when the peace treaty was signed in Moscow in March. Soviet leadership feared that Germany might use Finnish territory as a forward base from which to launch an attack in the north on the Soviet Union. Indeed, the Soviets went to war against Finland in the winter of 1939–40 to extend their border westward at the expense of Finland.[35] Because the secret protocol to the German-Soviet Nonaggression Pact of August 1939 had placed Finland within the Soviet sphere of influence,[36] the Soviets had assumed that they retained complete freedom of action in dealing with Finland and that Germany would not obstruct Soviet designs in Finland. Thus, when Germany informed the Soviet government that negotiations were in progress with Finland regarding the Petsamo concession, the Soviets reacted angrily. On 17 July Molotov informed the German ambassador that the Soviet government considered the Petsamo area "its exclusive domain . . ." and the German interest in the concession unwarranted.[37]

The Soviets did not press their demands on Finland through diplomatic channels in the weeks to follow. In the beginning of August they initiated a violent propaganda campaign against the Finnish government, and large-scale Soviet troop movements from bases in the recently annexed Baltic States to positions along the Finnish-Soviet border were reported. Intelligence estimates of the number of Soviet divisions near the Finnish border by the end of August were between twenty and twenty-five. Reports also indicated that the Soviets were preparing to deliver an ultimatum to the Finnish government.[38] The Soviets were prepared to use force if necessary to ensure Finnish

35. Max Jakobson, *The Diplomacy of the Winter War: An Account of the Russo-Finnish Conflict, 1939–1940* (Cambridge: Harvard University Press, 1961), and Vaino A. Tanner, *The Winter War: Finland against Russia, 1939–1945* (Stanford: Stanford University Press, 1957).

36. U.S. Department of State, *DGFP, 1918–1945,* ser. D, vol. 7 (Washington, D.C.: Government Printing Office, 1956), no. 229, 246–47.

37. *DGFP, 1918–1945,* ser. D, vol. 10, no. 182, 237.

38. Krosby, *Finland, Germany, and the Soviet Union,* 60–61; U.S. Department of State, *Foreign Relations of the United States, 1940,* vol. 1 (Washington, D.C.: Govern-

MAP 7. Northern Europe and the Soviet Union

ment Printing Office, 1959), 338, 340; and Military Archives, Navy and Old Army Branch, Military Intelligence Division Files, Record Group 165, Entry 65: 2037–100/45, National Archives.

acceptance of the new Soviet demands on Petsamo, if not to annex Finland completely. In a meeting with the foreign minister of Lithuania prior to the annexation of the Baltic states in June 1940, Molotov stated, ''You must take a good look at reality and understand that in the future small nations will have to disappear. Your Lithuania along with other Baltic nations, including Finland, will have to join the glorious family of the Soviet Union.'' Shortly after the Baltic states had submitted to Soviet ultimatums, Molotov noted in a speech to the Supreme Soviet that, although significant successes had already been achieved, ''we do not intend to rest satisfied with what we have attained.''[39] Stalin had been very careful to move in the Baltic states and Romania in June 1940 at a time when German armed forces were committed to combat in the west against France. By mid-September Hitler's plans for the invasion of Britain were canceled because the German air force was unable to establish air supremacy over the English Channel.[40] Stalin may have delayed plans for military action against Finland in order to assess German intentions once German armed forces were no longer committed to military operations in the West.

Hitler had reached a decision to defend the Petsamo area from a Soviet attack to insure Germany's access to the nickel ore from Petsamo. Accordingly, a directive was issued in mid-August to the commander in chief of the German army in Norway to build up forces in northern Norway immediately in order to prepare for the possible occupation of Petsamo in response to a Soviet attack across the border. Military plans for the swift occupation of Petsamo—Operation Reindeer—were formulated, and orders were issued for the concentration of a sufficiently large German force in northern Norway, in the Kirkenes, to carry out this mission.[41]

On 30 August the Soviets resumed diplomatic pressure on Finland when Molotov informed the Finnish envoy, Juho Kusti Paasikivi, that the Soviet government required a quick reply to the following demands: (1) Finland would transfer the mining concession for Petsamo to a Soviet-controlled company; (2) all other interested parties would have

39. Krosby, *Finland, Germany, and the Soviet Union,* 57.

40. J. R. M. Butler, *Grand Strategy,* vol. 2 (London: His Majesty's Stationary Office, 1957), 267–94.

41. Krosby, *Finland, Germany, and the Soviet Union,* 70–72, and *DGFP, 1918– 1945,* ser. D, vol. 10, no. 280, 405–6; no. 325, 460.

to be excluded from the new concession; (3) Germany could retain its 60 percent share of the current production of the Petsamo concession until the end of 1940; (4) beginning in 1941 the current Soviet share of 40 percent would be increased.[42]

The Finnish and German governments were in close consultation on the Petsamo question, and Germany was immediately informed of the Soviet demands. The German ambassador, Friedrich W. Von Schulenburg, was instructed to meet with Molotov at once to discuss the Petsamo concession. Schulenburg reciprocated the hard-line position of the Soviets when he told Molotov that Germany's claim to at least 60 percent of the Petsamo nickel ore output was indefinite and that it expected the Soviets to respect this agreement. Molotov did not respond directly to the ambassador's statement of Germany's position and ended the meeting by proposing that Schulenburg take up the matter with the Soviet foreign trade minister.[43]

In a meeting on 13 September Paasikivi informed the Soviet foreign minister that Finland could not agree to the Soviet demands presented on 30 August. Molotov persisted and presented the new argument that the existing Petsamo concession agreement conflicted with the 1920 and 1940 Soviet-Finnish peace treaties. He argued that no countries other than the Soviet Union had any rights to be in the Petsamo area and called on the Finnish government to reconsider its entire position. In two subsequent meetings on 23 and 30 September Molotov continued to press the Finnish government to accede to Soviet demands.[44]

While Germany and Finland maintained close contacts on the diplomatic negotiations with the Soviet Union, cooperation also developed at the military level. In early September German troops began to be transported across Finland en route to the Kirkenes area of northern Norway (a total of four divisions[45] would be stationed there), and on 22 September the Finnish government officially announced a military agreement permitting the transit of German troops. During September

42. Krosby, *Finland, Germany, and the Soviet Union*, 73.

43. U.S. Department of State, *DGFP, 1918–1945*, ser. D, vol. 11 (Washington, D.C.: Government Printing Office, 1961), no. 26, 34–35.

44. Krosby, *Finland, Germany, and the Soviet Union*, 75, 77, 79, and *Blue-White Book*, no. 27, 61–62.

45. U.S. Department of State, *Foreign Relations of the United States, 1940*, vol. 1, 348–49.

Germany began to deliver arms to the Finnish government, and on 1 October an official agreement was signed by the two countries.[46]

The Finnish government attempted to put off any formal reply to Soviet insistence on compliance with their demands. On 9 October Molotov demanded a reply to the Soviet proposals, and by the end of October the Soviets were prepared to wait no longer. In a meeting with Paasikivi on 30 October, the Soviet first deputy minister for foreign affairs, charged the Finnish government with delaying the Petsamo question and demanded a reply to the Soviet demands within two to three days. The Soviet official warned that if the Soviet Union received no answer it "would be compelled to take measures which the situation demanded."[47] Finland quickly responded that it had undertaken obligations involving the Petsamo concession and could not reach a new agreement with the Soviet Union. If the Soviets could obtain the consent of Germany as well as Britain and the Anglo-Canadian trust, which maintained an interest in the concession, then a new agreement could be concluded. The Soviets responded by falsely claiming that Germany had already consented to the transfer of the concession to a Soviet-Finnish company.[48].

The time had come for Germany to clarify its position on the Petsamo question in direct talks with the Soviets. The impact of German reinforcement of troops in northern Norway and the recent military cooperation between Germany and Finland would be strengthened if Germany signaled its clear support for Finland on the diplomatic level and restated its position on the Petsamo question. On 13 November Molotov was invited to a meeting with Hitler. Hitler used the opportunity to express Germany's support for Finland. He began the meeting by stressing Germany's vital economic interests in Finland, in particular the delivery of nickel ore from Finland. Hitler then discussed the potential dangers of another war in the Baltic region, which he argued would force Germany to intervene, and asked Molotov if the Soviets intended to go to war against Finland. Molotov replied evasively that everything would be all right if Finland would give up its ambiguous

46. *DGFP, 1918–1945,* ser. D, vol. 11, no. 86, 148–49; no. 139, 232–33, and Military Archives, Navy and Old Army Branch, Military Intelligence Division Files, Record Group 165, Entry 65: 2491–37/13, National Archives.

47. *Blue-White Book,* no. 38, 73.

48. Ibid., no. 38, 73–74; no. 42, 76.

attitude and reach an agreement. Molotov stressed the importance of the terms of the secret protocol that assigned Finland to the Soviet sphere of influence and therefore the right of the Soviet Union to settle the dispute with Finland as it had in Bessarabia and the Baltic states (by occupation and annexation of territory). But Hitler emphasized Germany's opposition to another Russo-Finnish war.[49]

On 25 November the German government delivered a note to the Soviet government presenting Germany's position on the Petsamo question. Germany agreed to the Soviet demand for the transfer of the Petsamo concession to a mixed Finnish-Soviet company if the Soviets would agree to the following four conditions: (1) the German claim to 60 percent of the output for an unlimited period of time is upheld; (2) the Soviet government recognizes the existing agreements between Germany and Finland with respect to the deliveries of the output; (3) the payments for these deliveries continue to be made through a German-Finnish clearing house; (4) the Finnish-Soviet company assumes the place of the Petsamo Nickel Company in the existing agreements between the latter company and the current German company.[50]

The German offer proposed a concession on the ownership of the Petsamo mining company for which the Soviet government would have to make a number of important, but less critical concessions regarding the obligations of the new company to respect existing agreements. The proposal was an attempt to package an agreement that would satisfy the Soviets while protecting the vital interests of Germany in continued access to the nickel ore output from Petsamo. Because the Soviets wanted the ownership rights to the concession company and complete freedom of action to operate the company, the German proposal was a difficult offer to accept. On 25 and 26 November Molotov responded to the German proposal with a minimal concession. The Soviet foreign minister agreed to provide Germany with 60 percent of the nickel ore output until the end of 1942 (not indefinitely as proposed by Germany) but rejected the proposal to take on any obligations arising from current German-Finnish agreements.[51]

The Soviets continued to press their demands, testing whether the Finnish government could be forced into substantial concessions and

49. *DGFP, 1918–1945,* ser. D, vol. 11, no. 328, 550–57.
50. Ibid., no. 355, 611–12.
51. Ibid., no. 405, 716–17.

what support Germany would offer. At the first meeting of a mixed Soviet-Finnish commission formed to discuss the Petsamo concession, the Soviets presented a proposal that reflected Molotov's firm position at the end of November. The Soviet proposal called for control of 51 percent of the capital stock in the new company, a controlling voice in the selection of the board of directors, and exclusive control of the business management.[52] The Finnish government again delayed an official response as long as possible.

The Soviets increased the pressure in January with a violent press campaign against the Finnish government and an economic embargo on trade with Finland. On 14 January the Soviets informed Paasikivi that a reply should be submitted without delay and warned that if Finland refused to accept a settlement the Soviet Union "would find ways to settle the matter." Shortly thereafter Finnish intelligence sources reported increased Soviet military activity along the border.[53]

In response to the increased pressure by the Soviets and their intransigent bargaining position, Hitler decided to send the Soviets another note reaffirming Germany's determination to protect its interests in any settlement of the Petsamo concession. A stiff note was delivered to the Soviet Foreign Ministry on 30 January: "we could agree to modification of the concession arrangement only on condition that the German-Finnish agreements . . . would be fully recognized by the Soviet government and by the future concession company. We could not consent to any impairment of our nickel interests based on these agreements because of the importance of this metal for Germany."[54]

The Soviets continued in talks with German representatives to refuse to assume responsibility for any obligations resulting from current German-Finnish agreements. In negotiations with the Finnish government throughout February the Soviets persisted in pressing for an agreement that would ensure Soviet control of the decisions of a new concession company. Germany was unwilling to back down and reciprocated the intransigent Soviet position in the negotiations. On

52. Krosby, *Finland, Germany, and the Soviet Union*, 105–6.

53. Ibid., 111–12, 116, and *Blue-White Book*, no. 60, 89.

54. *DGFP, 1918–1945*, ser. D, vol. 11, no. 717, 1207–8, U.S. Department of State, *DGFP, 1918–1945*, ser. D, vol. 12 (Washington, D.C.: Government Printing Office, 1962), no. 4, 4–5.

10 February the German ambassador met with Molotov and reiterated Germany's position as outlined in the detailed proposal of 25 November 1940.[55] Negotiations remained deadlocked throughout February, and the Soviets issued a third warning to Finland on the eighteenth stating that their demands were "categorical and definitive" and that since Finland refused to accept them "the matter will now take its course with all its consequences."[56]

Further efforts by Germany and the Soviet Union to reach an agreement were futile because neither side was prepared to make another concession. On 28 February the Soviets offered to guarantee Germany 60 percent of the output until the end of 1947, providing that after that date further study would determine what share Germany would receive. Germany responded on 11 March with a note rejecting the Soviet proposal; a Soviet proposal of 24 March was similarly unacceptable to Germany.[57] By the end of March negotiations on the Petsamo question were at a total impasse. Confronted with Germany's firm refusal to back down in its support for Finland in the negotiations, the Soviets chose not to take the risk of provoking German intervention by pursuing a unilateral solution to the dispute with force. After 24 March the Soviets no longer actively pursued the Petsamo question. Soviet efforts to pressure Finland into an agreement by relying on an intransigent bargaining position coupled with repeated warnings and the reinforcement of Soviet troops along the Finnish border had been successfully resisted by Finland with the support of Germany.

It is important to recognize that, to a much greater extent than in the other cases analyzed in these chapters, the extended deterrence confrontation between Germany and the Soviet Union over Finland was one of a number of disputes and developments in German-Soviet relations between the summer of 1940 and the spring of 1941. Economic relations between the two countries were suffering, there was increasing tension and disagreement about spheres of influence in the Balkans, and the buildup of German forces in the east had led to rumors

55. *DGFP, 1918–1945*, ser. D, vol. 12, no. 16, 24–26; no. 42, 75–76.

56. *Blue-White Book*, nos. 63–67, 92–94, and Krosby, *Finland, Germany, and the Soviet Union*, 142.

57. U.S. Department of State, *DGFP, 1918–1945*, ser. D, vol. 13 (Washington, D.C.: Government Printing Office, 1964), no. 109, 196–97; no. 139, 248–50; no. 204, 352–53.

of a German plan to attack the Soviets.[58] Stalin was trying to prevent a complete breakdown in German-Soviet relations while attempting to improve his country's strategic position and preparedness for war. Stalin was prepared to assert Soviet dominance where there was no risk of German opposition (eastern Poland, the Baltic states, Bessarabia). The buildup of German forces in the east and Germany's increasingly hard line in negotiations with the Soviets on other issues reinforced the credibility of Germany's position in the Petsamo dispute, but direct and active German intervention in support of Finland was necessary to convince Stalin that the risks of pressing Finland were too high. Although the overall state of German-Soviet relations cannot be ignored in an analysis of the Petsamo outcome, Germany's firm support for Finland was critical.

The firm-but-flexible bargaining strategy of Germany convinced the Soviet Union that Germany was determined to support Finland fully in the Petsamo dispute. The military aspects of Germany's deterrent posture were implicit and ambiguous. Although German reinforcements in the Kirkenes were, for example, intended to deter the Soviets, Germany did not explicitly acknowledge this. The only verbal deterrent action taken by Germany was the warning Hitler issued in the 13 November meeting with Molotov. The most direct and sustained indicator of Germany's support for Finland was the firm position it adopted in the negotiations with the Soviet Union on the Petsamo question. Germany's bargaining strategy consisted of an opening move of limited accommodation followed by a strict policy of tit for tat. The Germans pursued a very conservative firm-but-flexible strategy by indicating their willingness to make a concession on one important issue (ownership of the Petsamo concession) while standing firm on all other points. They then maintained that bargaining position for the remainder of the negotiations, offering no additional concessions. As a result, the Soviet negative responses in the negotiations were reciprocated by Germany in an equally firm bargaining position. In comparison, the British bargaining strategy in the dispute with Russia over the Afghan frontier was more cooperative: the British proposed a

58. F. H. Hinsley et. al., *British Intelligence in the Second World War: Its Influence on Strategy and Operations,* vol. 1 (New York: Cambridge University Press, 1979), chap. 14, and John Erickson, *The Road to Stalingrad: Stalin's War with Germany,* vol. 1 (London: Weidenfeld and Nicolson, 1975), chaps. 1–2.

number of initiatives in the early stages of the negotiations to break deadlocks.

The firm-but-flexible bargaining strategy of Germany not only established Germany's interest in the Petsamo question, it also enhanced the deterrent impact of German military actions and the warning by Hitler. Against the background of firm support for Finland in diplomatic negotiations, both the reinforcement of German troops in northern Norway opposite Petsamo and Hitler's statement of opposition to another Russo-Finnish war assumed greater significance as indicators of an intention to use force if necessary to protect German interests in the Petsamo area. Through the bargaining process Germany also effectively communicated to the Soviets the vital economic interests at stake for Germany in Finland. German representatives stressed to the Soviets on numerous occasions the importance of nickel ore deliveries from Finland for German armaments production. The dogged insistence by the Germans that the Soviets guarantee their rights to 60 percent of the nickel ore provided further evidence of just how vital the Germans considered the imports. In a number of direct and indirect ways the firm-but-flexible diplomatic strategy of Germany seems to have deterred Stalin from incorporating the Petsamo region and Finland into the Soviet sphere of influence. The dispute over the Petsamo region between Germany and the Soviet Union also illustrates the general point that in many deterrence cases the protégé is of economic and/or strategic value to both defender and potential attacker. In such cases it is difficult to determine which side the balance of interests favors and thus whether deterrence is likely to succeed.[59] In this particular case, German economic interests were substantial, but the Soviets had clear strategic interests at stake in occupying the Petsamo region as they sought to extend a territorial buffer against a growing German military presence in northern Norway.

Cases of Deterrence Failure

The outbreak of the Russo-Japanese War, 1903–1904. The foreign policy interests of Russia and Japan came increasingly into conflict in

---

59. Richard K. Betts argues the same point in his analysis of U.S.-Soviet and U.S.-PRC confrontations in the postwar period. See *Nuclear Blackmail and Nuclear Balance* (Washington, D.C.: Brookings Institution, 1987), 132–43.

the Far East by the end of the nineteenth century. In July 1894 Japan went to war with China to end China's claim to suzerainty over Korea. Japanese armed forces inflicted a series of decisive defeats on China, and by December China was prepared to conclude a peace settlement. A cease-fire was established by March 1895 and a peace treaty was signed in April.[60]

A number of Great Powers opposed the terms of the peace treaty. Russia in particular objected to the cession of the peninsular part of Liaotung to Japan. Russia actively sought and secured the support of France and Germany to pressure Japan to revise this article of the peace treaty. A collective note was delivered to the Japanese ''advising'' the government to modify its territorial demands on China. On 1 May the Japanese government officially responded to the collective note by agreeing to yield the Liaotung Peninsula with the exclusion of Port Arthur. The Russian government, however, considered the Japanese response unacceptable and pressed France and Germany to participate in a joint naval demonstration in Korean waters. Isolated and confronted with a superior show of force, Japan reluctantly agreed to retrocede the Liaotung Peninsula, including Port Arthur, to China in return for an indemnity. Japan deeply resented this diplomatic defeat at the hands of Russia.[61]

In November 1897 German naval and land forces occupied Kiaochow Bay along the Chinese coastline. The Russian government initially considered contesting the German occupation but decided instead to offset the German territorial gains by dispatching naval forces to Port Arthur in December and pressing the Chinese government to grant a lease to the territory. Great Britain and Japan protested the Russian action and consulted on the possibility of joint action to oppose the Russian occupation. Both countries decided against forceful measures, and in March 1898 the Chinese government agreed to the Russian

60. Morinosuka Kajima, *The Diplomacy of Japan, 1894–1922*, vol. 1 (Tokyo: Kajima Institute of International Peace, 1978), 31–75, and Ian Nish, *Japanese Foreign Policy, 1869–1942: Kasumigaseki to Miyakezaka* (London: Routledge and Kegan Paul, 1977), 39–41.

61. William J. Langer, *The Diplomacy of Imperialism, 1890–1902*, 2d ed. (New York: Alfred A. Knopf, 1956), 167–91, and Ian Nish, *The Origins of the Russo-Japanese War* (London: Longman, 1985), 21–35.

demands for the lease of Port Arthur.[62] The Russian acquisition of Port Arthur was another bitter setback for the Japanese. When in 1895 Russia had forced Japan with the support of France and Germany to relinquish claims to Port Arthur, it had argued that control of Port Arthur by a foreign power would constitute a serious threat to the security of China and the independence of Korea.

During the Boxer Rebellion in the summer of 1900 troops were dispatched by the Great Powers to China. The Russian government responded by occupying Manchuria. After the rebellion was quashed, the Great Powers withdrew their forces from China. The Russian government refused to withdraw its forces unless China signed an agreement giving Russia a preponderant position in Manchuria. China, with the support of the Great Powers and Japan, refused to sign such an agreement, and Russian troops remained in Manchuria. By April 1902 an agreement was reached in which Russia pledged to withdraw all of its troops from Manchuria (except for those permitted by previous agreements to be stationed at Port Arthur and at points along the Russian railroad system in Manchuria) within eighteen months. The evacuation would be carried out in three stages beginning on 8 October 1902 and finishing by 8 October 1903.[63]

The Japanese leadership regarded a Russian military presence and position of exclusive rights in Manchuria as a threat to Japanese interests in Korea. Korea was considered to be of vital strategic, as well as economic, importance to Japan. Japanese policy toward Korea was based on the assumption that Korea was incapable of maintaining its independence in the face of pressure from foreign powers. Protection of these vital interests required that Korea be under the protection, if not complete control, of Japan.[64] Japanese foreign policy sought to ensure that Russia withdraw its military forces from Manchuria and not be permitted a privileged position in the region.

The Russian attempts to secure a privileged position in Manchuria escalated Russo-Japanese competition for influence in the Far East to a

62. Langer, *Diplomacy of Imperialism* 445–80, and Nish, *Origins of the Russo-Japanese War,* 36–49.

63. John Albert White, *The Diplomacy of the Russo-Japanese War* (Princeton: Princeton University Press, 1964), 76–94.

64. Ibid., 99.

direct conflict of interests. Prolonged negotiations had transpired between the two countries from January 1901 to early 1903 in an effort to reach an agreement on each country's sphere of influence in the region. The negotiations had been unsuccessful. Japan called on Russia to accept Japan's predominant position in Korean affairs and to respect China's sovereignty over Manchuria and the rights of other states in the area. The Russian government, in turn, called on Japan to recognize Russia's predominant position in Manchuria and the need to neutralize Korea.[65]

The second stage of Russian withdrawal from Manchuria should have been completed by 8 April 1903, but the Russians did not withdraw any further forces from Manchuria during April. Shortly thereafter the Japanese government received reports that reinforcements of Russian troops would be sent to Port Arthur. On 21 April an informal high-level meeting of Japanese government leadership and influential elder statesmen, the Genro, was convened. The Japanese leaders agreed on the following points: (1) Japan should protest Russia's failure to honor the Manchurian Evacuation Agreement; (2) negotiations with Russia should be initiated to resolve the Korean question; (3) Japan should obtain recognition of its predominant rights in Korea; (4) Japan should recognize Russia's predominant rights in Manchuria.[66]

Within the Japanese military discussions on the course of Japanese policy were being held. At a General Staff meeting on 8 June army and navy leaders concluded that Japan should be prepared to demand from Russia both the withdrawal of its troops from Manchuria and a guarantee concerning Japan's security in the Far East. If Russia failed to accept Japan's demands in negotiations, Japan should resort to the use of armed force to achieve its objectives.[67]

There was a growing consensus within the Japanese leadership that the time to resolve the Korean-Manchurian question had arrived. On 23 June an imperial conference, attended by leading elder statesmen and cabinet ministers of Japan, was held. The conferees were to decide on the course of policy to adopt with Russia. It was concluded that continuation of the Russian military presence in Manchuria would eventually threaten Korea and hence Japan. Direct negotiations would

65. Ibid., 84–89.
66. Nish, *Origins of the Russo-Japanese War,* 153.
67. Ibid., 157.

be resumed in a final attempt to place strict limits on the rights and activities of Russia in both Manchuria and Korea. The Japanese leadership recognized that such a policy would encounter Russian opposition and that force might be required to achieve such goals. As Foreign Minister Jutarō Komura stated in a memorandum that formed the basis for Japanese policy toward Russia, "It is expected, however, that it will be extremely difficult to obtain Russia's concurrence in such an agreement. Consequently, I believe it to be essential that, in commencing negotiations, Japan be firmly resolved to achieve its objectives whatever the costs."[68] The Japanese prime minister and foreign minister believed that Russia would view the decision to reopen negotiations as an open challenge either to accommodate the demands of Japan or to accept the costs of a military confrontation. Other members of the leadership, the Genro in particular, were less pessimistic about the chances of a negotiated settlement and were willing to adopt a more flexible bargaining position in the negotiations. The Japanese political leadership was thus split between a hard-line faction determined to use force to protect its country's interests in Korea if Russia did not agree to significant concessions and a more moderate faction, led by the Genro, which was willing to consider mutual compromise in the interests of a diplomatic settlement and the avoidance of war with Russia.[69]

A critical factor, then, would be how the bargaining position of Russia influenced the struggle for control of policy between these two factions within the Japanese leadership. As Okamoto argues, "Within the Japanese decision-making circles, only the Genro had the power to press for, and willingness to maintain, a conciliatory attitude. A conciliatory posture on the part of Russia, however, was a prerequisite to enabling them to maintain their stand on the negotiations."[70]

Within the Russian government a series of high-level meetings had been convened as well to formulate policy toward Manchuria and Korea. At a conference on 24 January 1903 the leadership decided unanimously to terminate the military occupation of Manchuria. Evacuation of Manchuria was to be conditioned on adequate guarantees by China on the safety of Russian interests in the region (the Russian-

---

68. As quoted in Shumpei Okamoto, *The Japanese Oligarchy and the Russo-Japanese War* (New York: Columbia University Press, 1970), 77.

69. Ibid., and Nish, *Origins of the Russo-Japanese War*, 160–62.

70. Okamoto, *Japanese Oligarchy*, 80.

financed railway system connecting Harbin and the military base at Port Arthur). A subsequent conference held on 7 February reaffirmed the decision to evacuate Manchuria and formulated in greater detail the guarantees to be required of China, while discussions on Korea concluded that an agreement with Japan would be desirable.[71] At a meeting on 8 April a decision was reached to limit the Yalu concession along the Korean border to a purely commercial venture, thereby limiting government support, but to extend the concession to both banks of the Yalu in order to deny a position to other states.[72]

The Russian leadership reconvened on 20 May to discuss two principle issues. First they considered the security of Russian interests in Manchuria. They decided that the exposed position of the railway zone in Manchuria and the base at Port Arthur, once forces were evacuated from all other areas of Manchuria, would require defenses in those two areas to be increased. The second issue was policy toward northern Korea. Russian policymakers concluded that the Yalu region was of critical strategic importance as a defensive shield against potential Japanese threats to Port Arthur and the railway system in Manchuria. They approved a policy of defending the Yalu region and preventing its control by Japan.[73] Russia's Far Eastern policy in the spring of 1903 was essentially defensive in its objectives—withdrawal of forces from Manchuria and prevention of a foreign presence along the Yalu and in northern Manchuria. To achieve these objectives the Russian leadership believed that a tough diplomatic stance backed up by military force was necessary to protect its interests in a negotiated settlement with other countries. But the new course in Russian policy was on a collision course with the policies of the hard-line faction within the Japanese leadership.

Japan informed the Russian government on 28 July 1903 of its desire to reopen negotiations on Korea and Manchuria. A few days later Russia informed Japan that it was willing to enter into negotiations. Japan submitted its initial proposal on 12 August. The principal

71. White, *Diplomacy of the Russo-Japanese War,* 52, and Andrew Malozemoff, *Russian Far Eastern Policy, 1881–1904* (Berkeley: University of California Press, 1958), 202–6.
72. Nish, *Origins of the Russo-Japanese War,* 169–70.
73. Ibid., 171–72, and White, *Diplomacy of the Russo-Japanese War,* 60–61.

points of the Japanese bargaining position were outlined in Articles I, II, and V of the proposal:

I. Mutual engagement to respect the independence and territorial integrity of China and Korea and to maintain the principle of equal economic opportunity for all nations in those countries.

II. Reciprocal recognition of Japan's preponderant interests in Korea and Russia's special interests in railway enterprises in Manchuria. The right of Japan to take in Korea and Russia in Manchuria such measures as may be necessary to protect their respective interests.

V. Recognition on the part of Russia of the exclusive right of Japan to give advice and assistance in the interest of reform and good government in Korea including military assistance.[74]

The Japanese proposals called for an exchange of Manchuria for Korea, though on terms favorable to Japan. The Russian counterproposals were not presented until 3 October. In the intervening period reinforcements from European Russia began to arrive at Port Arthur, and troops were dispatched to the Far East by the Trans-Siberian Railway. The Russian counterproposals recognized Japan's right to advise Korea on civil administration, and Russia pledged not to impede Japan's economic activities in Korea. But on the critical issues the Russians were uncompromising. They proposed that Japan could dispatch troops to Korea only with Russia's knowledge, that Korean territory could not be used for strategic purposes, and that a neutral zone would be established north of the thirty-ninth parallel. Russia also refused to make any engagement regarding China's independence or territorial integrity and proposed that Japan recognize Manchuria as outside its sphere of interest. In effect, the Russian proposals sought to exclude Manchuria from the discussions and secure complete freedom of action in that region, while focusing the negotiations strictly on the limitations on Japan's position in Korea.[75]

Despite the stiff Russian counterproposals, the Genro pushed for compromises in the Japanese bargaining position. On 30 October the Japanese government presented its second set of proposals to Russia.

74. Okamoto, *Japanese Oligarchy,* 79–80.
75. Ibid., 97, and Nish, *Origins of the Russo-Japanese War,* 185–86.

The new proposals contained a number of concessions and points for reciprocal compromise. For example, although Japan continued to insist that Russia respect the independence and territorial integrity of China, Japan proposed that it would recognize Manchuria as outside its sphere of influence if Russia likewise recognized that Korea was outside its sphere of influence. Japan also proposed to recognize Russia's special interests in Manchuria and its right to take measures to protect those interests. Japanese leaders did not reject the idea of a neutral zone in northern Korea but proposed that any such zone extend fifty kilometers on each side of the Korean-Manchurian frontier. Finally, although Japan reserved the right to use Korean territory for strategic purposes, the Japanese pledged not to establish on the coasts of Korea any military bases that would threaten freedom of navigation in the Korean Straits.[76]

The second set of Russian counterproposals, presented on 11 December, did not respond to the Japanese initiatives for compromise. The Russians instead maintained a firm bargaining position, avoiding compromise on the critical issues. The Russian proposals continued to insist that Korean territory not be used for strategic purposes and that a neutral zone be established north of the thirty-ninth parallel. Russia again refused to commit itself to respect the independence and territorial integrity of China and avoided any mention of Manchuria. Thus the Russian bargaining position continued to exclude any explicit limits on Russian freedom of action in Manchuria while seeking to impose its preferred restraints on Japanese influence in Korea.[77]

The lengthy delays and uncompromising position of Russia in the negotiations effectively undercut the moderating influence of the Genro within the Japanese leadership. Within the Japanese military command the army had been preparing plans for war with Russia since mid-October.[78] At a high-level conference on 16 December the efforts of the moderate elder statesman Hirobumi Itō to maintain a flexible bargaining position were defeated as the arguments of the hard-liners led by the prime minister and foreign minister prevailed. The Japanese leadership concluded that Russia should be asked to reconsider its position, Manchuria should be reinjected into the negotiations, Japan

76. White, *Diplomacy of the Russo-Japanese War,* 353–54.
77. Okamoto, *Japanese Oligarchy,* 98, and ibid., 196.
78. White, *Diplomacy of the Russo-Japanese War,* 193.

should maintain the right to use Korean territory for strategic purposes, and the Russian proposal for a neutral zone should be dropped.[79] These terms, which were the basis of Japan's third set of proposals submitted to Russia on 21 December, represented a return to the more inflexible and one-sided position that Japan had presented in its original proposal on 12 August.

Within the Japanese leadership almost all hope of concluding a satisfactory negotiated settlement with Russia had dissipated. The Japanese army command on 21 December submitted to the government for approval plans to send an expeditionary force to Korea at the outbreak of war. Within the military the army pressed for immediate action, whereas the navy adopted a more cautious policy, insisting that the navy required more time to prepare for war.[80] On 24 December the two senior Genro, Itō and Aritomo Yamagata, gave their unqualified support for plans to prepare for war, and on 28 and 30 December conferences were held to discuss the final military preparations for the possibility of war.[81]

By this time the only way war could have been avoided required that the Russian leadership reverse its bargaining strategy and offer concessions in the negotiations to demonstrate its willingness to compromise and interest in a diplomatic solution. At a 28 December meeting of the Czar and his top-level foreign policy advisers, a number of policymakers expressed serious doubts concerning the inflexible bargaining position of their country in the negotiations with Japan. All of the advisers present agreed that war should be avoided if possible, but they expressed confidence that time was on Russia's side, since large numbers of troops were on their way to the Far East via the Trans-Siberian Railway.[82] In fact, the Russian leadership completely failed to appreciate the mounting pressures for war developing within Japan. The third set of Russian counterproposals, presented on 6 January 1904, contained no offers designed to break the diplomatic deadlock. The Russian proposals continued to insist on a neutral zone north of the thirty-ninth parallel, required that Japan agree not to use Korea for

79. Okamoto, *Japanese Oligarchy*, 99, and ibid., 354–55.

80. Nish, *Origins of the Russo-Japanese War*, 198–201.

81. Okamoto, *Japanese Oligarchy*, 99, and White, *Diplomacy of the Russo-Japanese War*, 114–115.

82. Nish, *Origins of the Russo-Japanese War*, 203.

strategic purposes, and contained a narrowly defined statement on Manchuria that was far short of what Japan was likely to consider acceptable.[83]

The Russian proposals confirmed the views of those in the Japanese leadership who argued that negotiations with Russia were futile. An imperial conference was held on 12 January to evaluate the latest Russian proposal. The conference reached the unanimous conclusion that "Russia had made no adequate concession over Korea and even refused to enter into negotiations over Manchuria, while at the same time trying to build up her military strength there."[84] Japan submitted a fourth set of counterproposals to the Russian government on 13 January since the navy required additional time to prepare for an attack.[85] The Japanese proposals reflected the rigid stance adopted by the leadership in response to the intransigence of Russia: elimination of restrictions on the use of Korean territory for strategic purposes, exclusion of the issue of a neutral zone entirely, insistence on a Russian pledge to respect the independence and integrity of China, and insistence on recognition by Russia that Korea lay outside its sphere of influence in return for Japanese adoption of a similar position toward Manchuria. The Japanese proposals concluded with the warning that "the Imperial Government further hope for an early reply from the Imperial Russian Government, since further delay in the solution of the question will be extremely disadvantageous to the two countries."[86]

Foreign Minister Shinichirō Kurino repeatedly requested a prompt reply from the Russian government. On 24 January the Japanese prime minister met with the emperor and presented the options available to Japan. War was judged as very likely but not inevitable. Katsura proposed that if Russia were to accept some of Japan's demands and make concessions then Japan would have to consider its policy further.[87] But because Japanese naval and land forces were fully prepared for war, any further delay would only benefit Russia, which lagged behind Japan in military preparations. When by the end of January there was no reply from the Russian government, the Japanese leader-

83. White, *Diplomacy of the Russo-Japanese War*, 355.
84. Nish, *Origins of the Russo-Japanese War*, 206.
85. Ibid., 207–8, and Okamoto, *Japanese Oligarchy*, 100.
86. White, *Diplomacy of the Russo-Japanese War*, 356–58.
87. Nish, *Origins of the Russo-Japanese War*, 208.

ship decided to break off diplomatic relations with Russia and commence hostilities at once.[88] On 6 February Japan formally severed diplomatic relations with Russia, and two days later Japanese naval forces destroyed a large portion of the Russian Far Eastern fleet at Port Arthur in a surprise attack. On the following day Japanese troops disembarked on Korean territory at Chemulpo, and on 10 February Japan declared war on Russia.

The military leadership of Japan was not highly confident of victory in a war with Russia. The army estimated the chances of victory at fifty-fifty, whereas the navy calculated that it would lose half its naval forces in defeating the Russian navy.[89] Based on strict military calculations Russia's prospects for successful deterrence would have seemed favorable since the costs of victory for the Japanese were estimated as high. Military calculations, however, became critical only after it was apparent that negotiations would not succeed. Although Russia had steadily reinforced its defensive capabilities in Manchuria and the Far East since autumn 1903, Russian land and naval forces in the region were not prepared for immediate action. Japanese land and naval forces, in contrast, had been mobilized and were well-prepared for immediate action. The logical military strategy for Japan was to strike before Russia had the opportunity to strengthen its military position in the Far East to a state of full readiness for war.[90] This was a risky strategy because the sheer size of the Russian military ensured that even early defeats would not deprive it of the capability to continue the war and eventually reinforce with superior forces in a war of attrition.

The intransigent and uncompromising bargaining strategy of Russia convinced the Japanese leadership that a satisfactory diplomatic solution was not possible. As hypothesized in chapter 3 the critical weakness of a bullying strategy is that it fails to provide a way for the potential attacker to back down from its threats and demands without a loss of face, thus significantly raising the political costs of not using force. The leading proponent of compromise with Russia within the Japanese leadership, Itō, summarized the negotiations with Russia following the outbreak of war: ''There is no question but that Russia's

88. Ibid., 211–12.

89. Okamoto, *Japanese Oligarchy,* 101.

90. White, *Diplomacy of the Russo-Japanese War,* 135–49, and Nish, *Origins of the Russo-Japanese War,* 240–41.

aim was from the start to increase her military and naval forces and then reject Japan's demands. . . . This being so, if Japan does not now go to war and defend her threatened interests, she will eventually have to kowtow to the Russian governor of one of her frontier provinces.''[91]

Russia's failure to respond positively to the second set of Japanese proposals presented on 30 October represented a critical turning point in the negotiations. The 30 October Japanese proposal, unlike the initial proposals submitted to Russia, contained a number of offers providing the basis for mutual compromise and a satisfactory diplomatic settlement. Russia rebuffed the offer of compromise and continued to push for an agreement that would have forced Japan to make concessions on all of the critical issues in dispute. This behavior discredited the moderate position of the Genro within the Japanese leadership, which had pressed for the compromises in the 20 October proposals, and increased the influence of the hard-liners. The bullying strategy of Russia had been counterproductive: instead of forcing Japan to back down, it provoked deep opposition within the Japanese leadership and strengthened the position of the pro-war faction in the policymaking process.

The negative impact of Russia's bullying strategy was reinforced by Russia's behavior in past confrontations with Japan. Both the Russian intervention in 1895 that compelled Japan to relinquish the territorial gains of military victory over China and the Russian occupation of Port Arthur in 1897–98 were major diplomatic setbacks for Japan. The results of the probit analysis in chapter 4 suggest that if the potential attacker was forced to accept a diplomatic setback in a previous confrontation with the defender then the probability of deterrence success would decrease because the attacker would be determined to avoid another blow to its bargaining reputation.

The diplomatic setbacks caused by Russia had embittered the leadership of Japan and prompted the determination to reverse the setbacks in a future confrontation. The Japanese leadership was unwilling to submit to another show of Russian strength and firmness in the negotiations on Korea. The hard-liners were opposed to any compromise, whereas the Genro were willing to accept reciprocal compromise. But Russia's bullying strategy led the Japanese leadership to conclude that

91. Nish, *Origins of the Russo-Japanese War*, 207.

the only alternative to another diplomatic humiliation was to stand firm and to go to war if necessary. The stubborn refusal of Russia to consider compromising reflected an underlying disdain for the Japanese and an underestimation of Japan's military capabilities. As the Japanese ambassador in St. Petersburg stated, ''I do not think Russia desires war in the Far East, on the contrary, she wishes for a peaceful solution but seems to be laboring under a tremendous conceit which leads to the opinion that an agreement regarding Manchuria would be looked upon as a great humiliation.''[92] Russian policymakers were confronted with growing domestic economic and political problems throughout the negotiations with Japan over Korea and Manchuria. There is no compelling evidence, however, that the Czar and his closest advisers sought to provoke an armed conflict with Japan in order to divert attention from internal discontent.[93]

The diplomatic setback for Japan in the confrontation with Russia in 1895 contributed to the failure of deterrence in another way. Following the setback, the leadership of Japan embarked on a systematic, large-scale program of military expansion to ensure that their country would not have to capitulate again from a position of military weakness to Russian demands. In 1897–98 the Japanese program of expansion was in its early stages, and Japan was not prepared militarily to confront Russia over the occupation of Port Arthur. But by 1903–04 the program of military expansion was completed, and Japanese military leaders were in a position to argue to the political leadership that although victory in war could not be assured there was a reasonable chance of success if Japan seized the initiative. The Japanese alliance with Great Britain ensured that Japan did not have to worry about the intervention of Russia's ally, France. Given the certain costs of not standing firm, the Japanese leadership considered a reasonable chance of success sufficient to justify the risks of war with Russia.

The outbreak of World War I. In the decade preceding the outbreak of World War I the conflict between Austria-Hungary and Serbia in the Balkans contributed to increasing tensions between Germany and Russia. In October 1908 Austria-Hungary announced the annexation of the

92. As quoted in White, *Diplomacy of the Russo-Japanese War,* 127.

93. Dietrich Geyer, *Russian Imperialism: The Interaction of Domestic and Foreign Policy, 1860–1914,* trans. Bruce Little (New York: Berg Publishers, 1987), 218–19.

Turkish province of Bosnia-Herzegovina. Serbia, with its own ambitions to control the territory, immediately protested Austria-Hungary's unilateral action, demanded territorial compensation, and began to mobilize its armed forces to support its demands. Austria-Hungary refused to compensate Serbia and responded with reciprocal mobilization of its army. The Russian government came reluctantly to the defense of Serbia and called for a European conference. Germany fully supported Austria's position of no compensation. The crisis persisted for months as Austria-Hungary and Serbia maintained their armed forces in a state of partial mobilization and as each side refused to back down. The deadlock ended in March 1909 when Germany presented Russia with a virtual ultimatum. Confronted with this German demarche, the Russian government backed down and forced Serbia to recognize the annexation without compensation. The Russian leadership felt deeply humiliated and embittered by Germany's intransigence in support of its ally Austria-Hungary.[94]

The Austro-Serbian conflict again escalated to the point of war in autumn 1912. After defeating Turkish forces in the initial stages of the first Balkan war Serbian troops moved into the Turkish province of Albania, and the Serbian government demanded both a port on the Adriatic Sea and the incorporation of Albania. Austria-Hungary adamantly opposed the Serbian demands and proposed that Albania be given its independence. Austria-Hungary mobilized forces along the Serbian border, and the two countries were on the verge of war. The Russian government was about to mobilize its own forces along the Austrian border, but the decision was reversed when it became clear that Germany would fully support Austria-Hungary. Russia adopted an accommodative diplomatic posture, and Albania gained its independence.[95] The firm posture of Germany in both of these Austro-Serbian confrontations had forced Russia to back down in its support for its protégé Serbia and to accede to the demands of Austria-Hungary. The

94. Bernadotte Schmitt, *The Annexation of Bosnia* (Cambridge, England: University Press, 1937), and Luigi Albertini, *The Origins of the War of 1914,* vol. 1, Isabella Massey, trans. and ed. (London: Oxford University Press, 1952), 190–300.

95. Ernest Christian Helmreich, *The Diplomacy of the Balkan Wars, 1912–1913* (Cambridge: Harvard University Press, 1938), 193–230, and L. C. F. Turner, ''The Edge of the Precipice: A Comparison Between November 1912 and July 1914,'' *Royal Military Historical Journal* 3 (1974):10–12.

outcomes of these past confrontations would have a critical impact on the policy adopted by the Russian government in July 1914.

The assassination of Archduke Franz Ferdinand—the heir apparent to the Austro-Hungarian throne—and his wife on 28 June 1914 at Sarajevo precipitated another crisis in Austro-Serbian relations. Austro-Hungarian leaders immediately concluded that the assassins, Serb nationalists, had been supported and aided by the Serbian government in carrying out their plot and decided to take strong action against Serbia. Hungarian Prime Minister Stephan Tisza thought it sufficient to inflict a severe diplomatic defeat on Serbia, whereas the foreign minister and chief of the general staff favored military action.[96]

On 5 July the Austrian ambassador met with Kaiser Wilhelm II to discuss Austrian policy toward Serbia. The ambassador presented a memorandum to the kaiser that called for strong actions against Serbia. The kaiser replied that he could not give a definite answer before consulting with the chancellor but that he did not anticipate opposition from the chancellor in pledging Germany's full support. The kaiser proceeded to advise Austria-Hungary to use military force against Serbia without delay while international conditions were favorable.[97] Later that day the kaiser met with Bethmann Hollweg and the German military leadership to discuss Germany's policy toward Austria-Hungary. The chancellor supported the kaiser's position in extending Germany's full support. The consensus within the German leadership was that Austria-Hungary should move forcefully against Serbia as soon as possible and that Russia was unlikely to intervene. Bethmann Hollweg informed the Austrian ambassador on 6 July that Germany would fully support Austria in whatever action it decided to take.[98] Tisza yielded to the arguments of his colleagues and sanctioned the use of force against Serbia. To justify the use of force against Serbia, the Austrian leadership decided to draw up a list of unacceptable demands that would be presented to Serbia in the form of an ultimatum. Serbia's refusal to

96. Luigi Albertini, *The Origins of the War of 1914*, vol. 2, trans. and ed. Isabella Massey (London: Oxford University Press, 1953), 120–33; Eugenia V. Nomikos and Robert C. North, *International Crisis: The Outbreak of World War I* (Montreal: McGill-Quenn's University Press, 1976), 32–33.

97. Albertini, *Origins of the War*, vol. 2, 138–39.

98. Konrad H. Jarausch, "The Illusion of Limited War: Chancellor Bethmann Hollweg's Calculated Risk, July 1914," *Central European History*, 2: 1 (1969):55–56.

accede to the demands would then be used as a pretext to declare war on Serbia.[99]

Germany's leaders, Bethmann Hollweg in particular, recognized that the decision to fully support Austria-Hungary carried with it the risk of a European war. Germany believed, however, that preservation of Austria-Hungary as a Great Power and ally required that Germany support Austria's desire to take forceful measures against Serbia. German leadership believed that an Austro-Serbian conflict could be localized because Russia would back down, as it had in the past, if Germany exerted heavy pressure on the Russian government. Gottlieb von Jagow, the secretary of state to the Ministry for Foreign Affairs argued, "The more boldness Austria displays, the more strongly we support her, the more likely is Russia to keep quiet. There is certain to be some blustering in St. Petersburg, but at bottom Russia is not now ready to strike."[100] Similarly, Alfred Zimmerman, the under secretary of state for foreign affairs stated, "Bluffing constitutes one of the favorite weapons of Russian policy, and while the Russian likes to threaten with the sword, yet he does not willingly draw it for the sake of others at the critical moment."[101] The chancellor was not certain that Russia could be deterred from intervention but nevertheless believed it would be to Germany's advantage to go to war against Russia and its ally France if the conflict could not be localized. Bethmann Hollweg and the military leadership were deeply concerned about trends in the relative balance of military power between Russia and Germany. Russia's current program of military modernization was to be completed by 1917, and German leaders believed that when Russia had completed its military buildup Germany would be militarily vulnerable. The German General Staff had argued to the chancellor that Germany could win a continental war at present but not in the future given Russia's modernization program. There was thus a widespread belief that if Germany was to go to war against Russia it would be advantageous to fight while Germany retained a margin of military superiority over Russia. Beth-

99. Albertini, *Origins of the War,* vol. 2, 164–78, 254–58, and Bernadotte E. Schmitt, *The Coming of the War, 1914,* vol. 1 (New York: Howard Fertig, 1966), 352–57.

100. As quoted in Albertini, *Origins of the War,* vol. 2, 158. See also 149–50, 157–64.

101. As quoted in Schmitt, *Coming of the War, 1914,* vol. 1, 320.

mann Hollweg sanctioned Germany's full support for Austria based on the calculated risk that an Austro-Serbian conflict could be localized but that even if Russia and its ally France intervened, Germany could still win a decisive military victory. The one possibility that the German chancellor was not willing to risk was a general European war in which Great Britain intervened against Germany and Austria. The chancellor and the German leadership believed that Britain would remain neutral.[102]

Austria presented the ultimatum to Serbia on 23 July and informed Serbia that unconditional compliance was required within forty-eight hours. On the morning of 24 July Austrian Ambassador Friedrich von Szápáry met with Russian Foreign Minister Sergei Sazonov and read the terms of the ultimatum delivered to Serbia. Sazonov angrily charged that Austria was seeking a war and that the demands were unacceptable. He warned that Austria had created a grave situation. The Russian chargé in Vienna was instructed to warn Austrian Foreign Minister Leopold von Berchtold that "any Austrian action of a character unacceptable to the dignity of Serbia would have serious consequences."[103] The critical questions were whether Germany could deter Russia from intervening militarily in support of Serbia and whether British actions would convince Germany that British intervention was likely.

Following his meeting with the Austrian ambassador, Sazonov telephoned the emperor and stated without a doubt that Germany fully supported the course of action being taken by Austria-Hungary. Nicholas II ordered a meeting of the Council of Ministers to determine Russia's response to the Austrian ultimatum. The decisions reached at this meeting of 24 July served as the basis of Russian policy for the duration of the 1914 crisis. Germany's past behavior toward Russia had a decisive impact in shaping the Russian leadership's perception of both the issues at stake and the type of response necessary.

Sazonov began the meeting by stating that Russia had shown a great deal of moderation in its relations with Germany in the past decade.

102. Jarausch, "Illusion of Limited War," 57–59, 75. For a broader theoretical analysis of the relationship between the concept of the preventive motive and the outbreak of war, see Jack Levy, "Declining Power and the Preventive Motivation for War," *World Politics* 40: 1 (1987):82–107.

103. As quoted in Albertini, *Origins of the War*, vol. 2, 293–94, and Nomikos and North, *International Crisis*, 94.

Nevertheless, "Germany had looked upon our concessions as so many proofs of our weakness and far from having prevented our neighbors from using aggressive methods, we had encouraged them." In Sazonov's view the time had come for Russia to take a firm stand and to obstruct Austria's German-backed plans to turn Serbia into a de facto protectorate of the Central Powers. Sazonov concluded by arguing that Russia's bargaining reputation and international position were at risk. If Serbia were abandoned "she [Russia] would be considered a decadent state and would henceforth have to take second place among the powers," losing "all her authority," and permitting Russian prestige in the Balkans "to collapse utterly."[104]

The next leader to speak was Minister of Agriculture Alexander Krivoshein, one of the most powerful and respected members of the government. Krivoshein noted that Russia's military position had improved in recent years but cautioned that Germany still maintained a clear technological advantage. He argued that Russia must adopt a firm position because the past policy of concessions had proven ineffective: "Our exaggeratedly prudent attitudes had unfortunately not succeeded in placating the Central Powers. . . . All factors tended to prove that the most judicious policy Russia could adopt was a return to a firmer and more energetic attitude towards the unreasonable claims of the Central European Powers."[105]

The Russian ministers of war and the navy followed Krivoshein and stressed that although Russia had made great strides in improving its military strength since 1905 the program of rearmament was not completed. They nevertheless stated that "hesitation was no longer appropriate," and that they supported "a display of greater firmness in our diplomatic negotiations." The minister of finance, Peter Back, warned that "the financial and economic stability of the country would be endangered" by high levels of wartime expenditures. Despite these risks Back supported the cabinet's final decision because "the honor, dignity, and authority of Russia were at stake."[106] The remaining ministers supported the policies of Sazonov and Krivoshein. The council recommended the adoption of the following policy, which was approved by Nicholas II: (1) Austria-Hungary should be asked to

104. As quoted in D. C. B. Lieven, *Russia and the Origins of the First World War* (New York: St. Martin's, 1983), 141–42.
105. As quoted in ibid., 142–43.
106. As quoted in ibid., 143–44.

extend the time limit of the ultimatum; (2) Serbia should adopt a conciliatory position and meet the demands of Austria-Hungary as long as they do not violate its independence; and (3) Russia should be prepared to mobilize the Odessa, Kiev, Kazan, and Moscow military districts.

The leadership of the Russian government had decided that the reputation and prestige of the country required that it not retreat under German pressure as in the past. Russia was prepared to pressure Serbia to adopt an accommodative stance, but if Austria-Hungary, with the support of Germany, refused to enter into negotiations on the more extreme demands of the ultimatum and declared war, Russia would use force to defend its protégé. The Russian leadership recognized that war with the Central Powers was a risky policy. As the arguments of the ministers at the council meetings indicated, another diplomatic setback against Germany was unacceptable. The flexibility and willingness of Germany to consider compromise would determine Russia's final decision for war or peace in July 1914.

At a meeting between Sazonov and the German ambassador soon after, Friedrich von Pourtalès informed Sazonov that the present conflict should be localized and treated as a strictly Austro-Serbian matter. The German ambassador also stressed the propriety of Austria's demands. Sazonov strongly disagreed and argued that the obligations that Serbia had assumed after the Bosnia crisis of 1908–09 were to Europe and that it was therefore up to Europe to investigate whether Serbia had lived up to those obligations. Sazonov then warned Pourtalès that Russia would go to war to defend Serbia.[107] Russian proposals were subsequently rejected in Vienna, and the Austrians refused to extend the forty-eight hour time limit on the ultimatum. In Berlin, Foreign Secretary Jagow rejected a Russian proposal that Germany advise Austria-Hungary to extend the time limit.[108] Confronted with the intransigent position of the Central Powers in the initial round of diplomatic exchanges, Russia began preparations to mobilize its forces on 25 July.[109]

The British cabinet on 24 July considered the growing crisis in the

107. Albertini, *Origins of the War*, vol. 2, 298–301.

108. Nomikos and North, *International Crisis*, 94–96, 98–99.

109. Lieven, *Russia and the Origins*, 144, and L. C. F. Turner, "The Russian Mobilization in 1914," in *The War Plans of the Great Powers, 1880–1914*, ed. Paul Kennedy (London: Allen and Unwin, 1979), 261–62.

Balkans for the first time. At the meeting Foreign Secretary Sir Edward Grey stressed the need for negotiations between Russia and Austria and proposed mediation by the remaining Great Powers to facilitate an agreement.[110] Grey met with the German ambassador that afternoon and urged Germany to restrain Austria from initiating immediate military action so that mediation could be attempted. Grey also expressed doubts that the conflict could be localized and predicted a European war involving the four powers of Germany, Austria, Russia, and France (no mention of the potential British intervention, which was quickly picked up by the German chancellor).[111] Grey urged Germany to participate in mediation efforts.[112]

The initial British actions did not change the German perception that Britain would remain neutral. Germany continued to support the intransigent position of Austria and urged its ally to act quickly against Serbia to achieve a fait accompli. The Serbian government officially responded to the ultimatum on 25 July with a conciliatory note in which it agreed to almost all of the demands put forth by Austria-Hungary. Austria-Hungary rejected the Serbian reply immediately and severed diplomatic relations with Serbia that day.[113] In a meeting with the German ambassador on 26 July Sazonov argued that a solution that satisfied most of the demands of Austria-Hungary could be negotiated. In another meeting that same day Sazonov pressed the Austrian ambassador to have his government enter into negotiations.[114]

The Russian proposals continued to meet with evasive, if not negative, replies from Germany and Austria-Hungary. On 27 July the Austrian ambassador would only state that, as long as a war between Austria and Serbia remained localized, the Dual Monarchy would refrain from territorial acquisitions (which was a false representation of Austrian policy). On 28 July Sazonov met again with the German ambassador and urged Germany to advise its ally to enter into negotiations. Pourtalès maintained that the Austro-Serbian conflict was a

110. Michael G. Ekstein and Zara Steiner, ''The Sarajevo Crisis,'' in *British Foreign Policy Under Sir Edward Grey,* ed. F. H. Hinsley (Cambridge: Cambridge University Press, 1977), 400.

111. Albertini, *Origins of the War,* vol. 2, 425.

112. Ibid., 334, 340.

113. Ibid., 361–73, 425–26, 453–59.

114. Ibid., 403–7.

purely local affair. He assured Sazonov of Austria's territorial disinterestedness and warned that military preparations by Russia aimed at Germany would lead to mobilization and war against Russia. Pourtalès concluded by advising the Russian government to "take an expectant attitude toward the affair."[115]

Such top-level Foreign Office officials within the British government as Sir Eyre Crowe and Sir Arthur Nicolson were urging Grey to adopt a firmer stand in support of Russia and to warn Germany of Britain's intention to support its entente allies. The foreign secretary was unwilling to accept such recommendations because of a lack of support in the cabinet for such a policy and because he feared that a pledge of support for Russia and France would lead the allies to stiffen their bargaining positions and to provoke Germany. The British cabinet preferred to maintain an equivocal position because "if both sides do not know what we shall do, both will be less willing to run risks."[116] Grey continued to propose negotiations and issued no warnings to Germany. On 26 July a proposal was dispatched to the major European capitals for an ambassadors' conference in London during which all active military operations would be suspended in order to settle the Austro-Serbian conflict. In a statement before the Commons Grey summarized the diplomatic initiatives supported by the British government and stated that if any conflict spread beyond Austria and Serbia it would end in the greatest disaster for Europe. Grey did not issue a warning to Germany despite recommendations to do so from some of his advisers. The German government rejected the British proposal for an ambassadors' conference on 27 July, stating that it would not interfere in the dispute between Austria and Serbia.[117]

By adopting an uncompromising diplomatic posture coupled with a threat of war Germany believed it could deter Russian intervention and enable its ally, Austria-Hungary, to crush Serbia in a military confrontation. But German intransigence and threats only reinforced Russian perceptions of the costs of inaction and the futility of a diplomatic solution to the conflict.[118] On 28 July Sazonov was informed that

---

115. Nomikos and North, *International Crisis,* 95, 130–31.

116. Ekstein and Steiner, "Sarajevo Crisis," 401.

117. Albertini, *Origins of the War,* vol. 2, 390–95, 415.

118. Lieven, *Russia and the Origins,* 146, and Nomikos and North, *International Crisis,* 131.

Austria-Hungary had declared war on Serbia. Sazonov met with the Czar that evening and secured Nicholas' agreement on partial mobilization against Austria-Hungary beginning on 29 July.[119]

Further talks between the German ambassador and the Russian foreign minister on 29 July remained deadlocked. Sazonov charged that Austria-Hungary had not responded to his proposal for direct conversations and called for a four-power conference to resolve the conflict. Pourtalès skirted a direct answer by referring to Austria's pledge of territorial disinterestedness and the need to consult with his government before replying. Later that day the Austrian ambassador informed Sazonov that his government refused to negotiate any of the specific demands presented in the ultimatum to Serbia. The final blow came that evening during the third meeting between the German ambassador and the Russian foreign minister. Pourtalès warned Sazonov that further Russian mobilization would force Germany to mobilize, in which case a European war would be very difficult to prevent.[120] Sazonov concluded that it was hopeless to pursue further attempts at a satisfactory diplomatic solution and that the primary task was to prepare for war. As D. C. B. Lieven states, "The events of 29 July convinced him [Sazonov] that war with the Central Powers was inevitable and that the vital point was to prepare to wage it with the greatest possible chance of success."[121] On 30 July Sazonov convinced a reluctant Nicholas II that general mobilization was necessary.[122]

The Austrian declaration of war against Serbia convinced the British foreign secretary that a warning should be delivered to the German government. In the afternoon of 29 July Grey met with the German ambassador and proposed that Austria halt its military advance in Belgrade while mediation by the Great Powers resolved the outstanding issues between Austria and Serbia. Grey warned that if negotiations failed and the conflict escalated into a European war then Britain might be forced to intervene.[123] This was the first warning issued by the British government, and it had an immediate impact on the German chancellor. Grey's warning was received in Berlin around 9:00 P.M.

119. Lieven, *Russia and the Origins*, 146.
120. Nomikos and North, *International Crisis*, 146–48.
121. Lieven, *Russia and the Origins*, 146.
122. Ibid., and Albertini, *Origins of the War*, vol. 2, 570–82.
123. Albertini, *Origins of the War*, vol. 2, 513–14, 521–22.

and after reading the dispatch Bethmann Hollweg recognized for the first time that British neutrality was not likely. The chancellor decided to reverse German policy and attempt to convince Austria to stop its military operations and pursue a negotiated settlement. In the early morning hours of 30 July the German ambassador in Vienna received instruction to press the Austrians to stop military operations with the occupation of Belgrade and to agree to mediation by the Great Powers. Shortly thereafter another telegram was sent to Vienna instructing the German ambassador to propose to Austria that direct negotiations with Russia be initiated.[124] But the Austrian leadership was now unwilling to back down from its intransigent position. Austrian policymakers believed that mediation and negotiations would require Austria to soften its demands on Serbia. Furthermore, Russian mobilization along the Austrian border had to be countered. Encouraged initially by Germany to adopt an unyielding position and to attack Serbia, Austria's leaders resented the German pressures for moderation and believed that a retreat would weaken Austria's prestige.[125]

On 29 July the German chancellor proposed British neutrality in return for which Germany would not annex French continental territory, would respect Dutch neutrality, and would restore Belgium's territorial integrity after the war. On the following day the British ambassador, acting on instructions from Grey, flatly rejected the German proposal. Grey issued the clearest warning of Britain's position to the German ambassador on 31 July:

> I said to the German Ambassador this morning if Germany could get any reasonable proposal put forward which made it clear that Germany and Austria were still striving to preserve European peace, and that Russia and France would be unreasonable if they rejected it, I would support it at St. Petersburg and Paris and go the length of saying that if Russia and France would not accept it His Majesty's Government would have nothing more to do with the consequences; but otherwise, I told the German Ambassador that if France became involved we should be drawn in.[126]

But the British warning was too late. The pace of military prepara-

124. Ibid., 522–24.
125. Ibid., 655–71.
126. As quoted in ibid., 632–33, 642.

tions undercut further diplomatic efforts as the German military pressed for immediate action based on the Schlieffen Plan.[127] On 30 July Helmuth Von Moltke, the chief of the German General Staff, pressed Bethmann Hollweg to order mobilization measures in response to news of Russian partial mobilization against Austria. Late in the morning on 31 July news was received in Berlin of Russia's order for general mobilization. The chancellor immediately authorized a proclamation of a "state of imminent danger of war," and early that afternoon the German ambassador in St. Petersburg was instructed to announce that unless Russia stopped all military preparations within twelve hours Germany would mobilize. Instructions for an ultimatum were also sent to the German ambassador in France that afternoon.[128] The Russian government did not respond to the German ultimatum, and on the evening of 1 August Germany declared war on Russia. France, in support of its ally Russia, rejected the German ultimatum, and on 3 August Germany declared war on France. On the morning of 4 August German troops began the invasion of Belgium despite British warnings that the violation of Belgian neutrality by Germany would lead to British intervention. On 5 August Great Britain declared war on Germany.

Germany's failure to deter Russia's intervention in support of Serbia in 1914 is consistent with the results of the probit analysis. A bullying strategy by a defender is not an effective bargaining strategy for promoting successful deterrence, and a record of diplomatic defeat for the potential attacker in a previous confrontation with the defender reduces the chances of successful deterrence.

The past behavior of Germany had a critical impact on the crisis decisions of Russian policymakers. As the statements of one Russian minister after another at the Council of Ministers meeting on 24 July indicated, Russia's leaders believed that their country's reputation and

127. For a detailed analysis of the impact of the European powers' war plans on the outbreak of WWI see Stephen Van Evera, "The Cult of the Offensive and the Origins of the First World," *International Security* 9:1 (1984):58–107; Jack Snyder, "Civil-Military Relations and the Cult of the Offensive, 1914 and 1984," *International Security* 9:1 (1984):108–46; and Scott D. Sagan, "1914 Revisited: Allies, Offensive, and Instability," *International Security* 11:2 (1986):151–76.

128. Luigi Albertini, *The Origins of the War of 1914,* vol. 3, trans. and ed. Isabella Massey (London: Oxford University Press, 1957), 34, 38–40.

standing as a European power was at stake. After Russia's defeat in the war with Japan in 1904–05, which left the country in a weak military position, Russian leaders felt compelled to adopt accommodative policies when confronted with firm German opposition. In the Bosnian crisis the Russian minister of war warned the political leadership that Russia was not even capable of fighting a defensive war against the Central Powers, whereas in November 1912 Russian leaders warned the Czar that Russia was far from prepared to confront Germany.[129] A large-scale program of military expansion and modernization was initiated in 1913, and by July 1914 the military position of Russia was greatly improved: European depots and magazines were fully restocked; the field artillery was rearmed with modern weapons; the railway system was extended into western Russia; and plans for a more efficient system of mobilization had been developed.[130] The Russian leadership—mirroring Japan's decision in 1904—concluded that although victory in war was not certain Russia was sufficiently strong that capitulation to German demands and intransigence were no longer justifiable. Having backed down in two previous confrontations with Germany, the Russian leadership was determined to stand firm and fully support its ally Serbia. A bullying strategy may prevail in the short term against a weaker adversary, but if that adversary improves its military position further attempts at bullying are likely to fail. Although a policy of bullying and intransigence may produce immediate diplomatic victories, in the long run it is likely to be self-defeating.

German policymakers failed to appreciate how serious Russia perceived the stakes to be and attempted to bully Russia as they had in the past. Although policymakers are sensitive to threats and challenges to their own country's bargaining reputation and prestige, they all too easily convince themselves that their opponent is not as heavily constrained by such considerations and can therefore be forced to back down without serious domestic or international costs. The determination of the Russian leadership to avoid another diplomatic setback did not rule out the possibility of a peaceful resolution of the 1914 crisis. From 24–29 July Sazonov presented a number of proposals to Germany to reach a negotiated settlement, but Germany adopted an un-

129. Lieven, *Russia and the Origins,* 108, and Turner, ''Edge of the Precipice,'' 10–12.
130. Lieven, *Russia and the Origins,* 111.

compromising negotiation position that offered no viable diplomatic solution to the conflict for Russia. Modest concessions by Germany might have been sufficient to satisfy Russia because the leadership of Russia was not confident of victory in a military confrontation. But the unyielding position of Germany provided no grounds for the Russian leadership to claim that even its minimal demands had been satisfied. Faced with the alternative of capitulation or the use of force, Russian leaders chose to accept the risks of war rather than sacrifice their country's future position of international influence. As with Japan's decision to wage war against Russia in 1904, the perceived political and long-term strategic costs of inaction, rather than short-term military calculations, were decisive in shaping the final decision of the Russian leadership.

The failure of Britain to deter Germany is useful for deviant case analysis. The initial German calculation that Britain would remain neutral was influenced by the recent history and state of British-German relations. The German belief that Britain would remain neutral, however, was not based on British irresolution in previous confrontations with Germany, as the generalizations of the probit analysis would suggest. In fact, in the Moroccan crises of 1905–06 and 1911 Britain had strongly supported France and had forced Germany to accept diplomatic defeats. British behavior in the Moroccan crises provided no basis for Germany to expect British noninvolvement in a crisis in which France was threatened by Germany. Instead, the improvement and development of a detente in relations between Britain and Germany from 1912 to 1914 contributed to the German miscalculation of British intentions. The detente in Anglo-German relations was based on cooperation during the Balkan War crises of 1912–13, the agreement over the Portuguese colonies in August 1913, the Baghdad Railway agreement concluded in June 1914, and the absence of direct clashes over naval armaments following the failure of the Haldane Mission in 1912.[131]

The German chancellor believed that Britain would remain neutral if Russia and Serbia were portrayed as the aggressor in a Balkan dispute. When he was confident that Britain would remain neutral,

131. Sean M. Lynn-Jones, "Detente and Deterrence: Anglo-German Relations, 1911–1914," *International Security* 11: 2 (1986):129–35.

Bethmann Hollweg adopted an unyielding diplomatic posture in support of Austria. Only on 29 July and thereafter, when Bethmann Hollweg lost confidence in British neutrality, did the chancellor attempt to reverse the course of German policy. But German intransigence in support of Austria had already convinced Russian leaders that war could not be avoided, and Russia had begun mobilization.

The Anglo-German detente shaped not only Germany's initial approach to the July crisis but also that of Britain. Based on Anglo-German cooperation at the London Conference during the Balkan Wars of 1912–13 Foreign Secretary Grey believed that Germany would cooperate in managing crises centered in the Balkans. Grey assumed that the most effective way to deal with Germany in managing a crisis in the Balkans was not to threaten Germany but to try and cooperate with Germany to identify the terms of a diplomatic settlement.[132] Grey's assumptions concerning crisis management were badly misplaced when applied to German intentions in July 1914. Bethmann Hollweg was not interested in a diplomatic settlement as long as a European war did not provoke British intervention. If Germany was to have been deterred in July 1914 British actions and behavior would had to have increased Germany's perceived risk of British intervention in the early stages of the July crisis. Instead, Grey emphasized at the outset of the crisis Britain's desire for a diplomatic solution and avoided such coercive measures as verbal warnings designed to enhance the credibility of the threat of British intervention if diplomacy failed.

By the time Grey issued warnings on 29 and 31 July, German intransigence had already provoked Russian mobilization measures, which in turn led the German military to press for countermobilization. Britain's firm-but-flexible diplomatic strategy developed too slowly in relation to the pace of military preparations. The evolution of the British diplomatic position from an early emphasis on mediation and attempted cooperation in negotiations to a firmer diplomatic position backed up by deterrent warnings was just the reverse of the policy required to deter Germany. Initial firmness and demonstration of British resolve might have convinced the German chancellor that British neutrality was unlikely, and then British proposals for mediation and

132. Ibid., 138–41.

compromise could have been used by Germany to secure a favorable diplomatic settlement for Austria.[133] A lack of support within the British cabinet for intervention until 2 August certainly constrained Grey's diplomatic position, but the foreign secretary issued warnings, on 29 and 31 July even though the cabinet was divided. Grey did not adopt a firm stand from the very beginning of the crisis because he miscalculated German intentions and because he believed that a policy of mediation and cooperation with Germany, which had proved successful at the London Conference in 1912–13, could be repeated.

133. The German military leadership would have been more difficult to deter since the intervention, if delayed, of the British Expeditionary Force at the outset of war was not viewed as likely to prevent a quick and decisive German victory over France. The German political leadership and the chancellor and the kaiser in particular, however, did not want Germany involved in a war against Britain, and it was the chancellor who determined the initial course of German policy in the July crisis. Not until 29 July did the military exert heavy pressure to begin mobilization in response to Russian military preparations. See Albertini, *Origins of the War*, vol. 3, 505; Scott Sagan, "1914 Revisited," 170–71; and Stephen Van Evera, "Cult of the Offensive," 91–92. For an alternative argument that German motivated misperception rather than British policy led to the failure of deterrence in 1914, see Richard Ned Lebow, *Between Peace and War: The Nature of International Crisis* (Baltimore: Johns Hopkins University Press, 1981), 119–47.

7

Implications for Crisis Management and Future Research

> Above all, while defending our own vital interests, nuclear powers must avert those confrontations which bring an adversary to the choice of either a humiliating defeat or a nuclear war.
>
> —PRESIDENT JOHN F. KENNEDY

In the contemporary international system, challenges to extended deterrence in regional conflicts threaten to involve the United States and the Soviet Union in a direct armed confrontation. The Middle East remains an unstable region in which the superpowers have important economic and political-military interests at stake. The Arab-Israeli conflict remains unresolved, and another war would risk a superpower confrontation, as in 1973. A decisive victory for Iran in the protracted war with Iraq could have far-reaching security implications for the entire Persian Gulf region, which would be of great concern to both superpowers. Great Power confrontations have been the most war-prone of all international militarized disputes over the past 160 years.[1] The potential for future U.S.-Soviet confrontations and the risk of escalation to nuclear war require careful attention to crisis management in order to reduce the danger of misguided policies producing deterrence failure.

1. Charles S. Gochman and Zeev Maoz, "Militarized Disputes, 1816–1976: Procedures, Patterns, and Insights," *Journal of Conflict Resolution* 28: 4 (1984):600–2.

I argued in chapter 1 that a successful policy of extended deterrence requires a fine balance between the preparations to use military force and demonstrations of resolve and the provocation of the potential attacker. A trade-off often exists between policies designed to enhance the credibility and stability of deterrence. Crisis management is similarly concerned with the difficult problem of how to combine elements of conflictual and cooperative behavior in an overall policy to protect the national interests of a state while avoiding armed conflict. Phil Williams provides an excellent description of the essential tasks of crisis management:

> Crisis management is concerned on the one hand with procedures for controlling and regulating a crisis so that it does not get out of hand and lead to war, and on the other hand with ensuring that the crisis is resolved on a satisfactory basis in which the vital interests of the state are secured and protected. The second aspect will almost invariably necessitate vigorous actions carrying substantial risks. One task of crisis management, therefore, is to temper these risks . . . while the other is to ensure that the coercive diplomacy and risk-taking tactics are as effective as possible in gaining concessions from the adversary and maintaining one's own position relatively intact.[2]

A number of analysts, however, have questioned whether the bargaining and signaling that are central in theories of coercive diplomacy and deterrence are actually effective in the resolution of international crises. The failure of the United States, for example, to prevent North Vietnam from escalating its support for the Viet Cong in the Vietnam War seemed to indicate serious constraints on the ability of governments to coordinate diplomacy and military actions in order to signal intentions and resolve to an adversary.[3] Research on problems of misperception, cognitive rigidity, and the effects of stress on decision-making also cast doubt on the effectiveness of crisis bargaining. In his study of international crises, Richard Ned Lebow argues that because

2. Phil Williams, *Crisis Management: Confrontation and Diplomacy in the Nuclear Age* (New York: Wiley, 1972), 30.

3. Wallace J. Thies, *When Governments Collide: Coercion and Diplomacy in the Vietnam Conflict, 1964–1968* (Berkeley: University of California Press, 1980), 284–348.

policymakers are often strongly committed to particular policies from the outset of a crisis, they ignore or interpret new information to make it consistent with their own expectations. By implication, the efforts by a state (a defender of the status quo) to correct the misperceptions of its adversary or to clarify its intentions are likely to fail in a crisis. As Lebow argues, "If policy makers rationalize the conditions for the success of a foreign policy to the extent they feel compelled to pursue it, efforts to impart credibility to commitments may have only a marginal impact on the adversary's behavior. Even the most elaborate efforts to demonstrate prowess and resolve may prove insufficient to discourage a challenge."[4]

One important conclusion of this book, however, is that short-term military and diplomatic actions do have a strong impact on crisis outcomes.[5] As the results of probit analysis indicated and the case studies illustrated, the adoption by the defender of both a firm-but-flexible position in negotiations and a policy of tit for tat in military escalation contributed substantially to the success of deterrence, whereas alternative diplomatic and military strategies were less effective, if not counterproductive.

One reason that my findings do not support Lebow's argument is that in a majority of my cases of attempted deterrence the potential attacker was not fully committed to the use force from the outset of the confrontation. Instead, the potential attacker initiated threats and pressed demands on the protégé of the defender, more often than not in an attempt to test the resolve and if possible to erode any commitment of the defender regarding the defense of its protégé. This is contrary to Lebow's argument that a potential attacker's threat to use force is often based not'on the opportunity to challenge an ambiguous commitment

---

4. Robert Jervis, Richard Ned Lebow, and Janice Gross Stein, *Psychology and Deterrence* (Baltimore: Johns Hopkins University Press, 1985), 183.

5. The results of a number of empirical studies indicate that bargaining behavior has an important impact on crisis outcomes: Glenn H. Snyder and Paul Diesing, *Conflict among Nations* (Princeton: Princeton University Press, 1977), 183–281; Russell J. Leng and Hugh G. Wheeler, "Influence Strategies, Success, and War," *Journal of Conflict Resolution* 23: 4 (1979):655–84; Russell J. Leng and Charles S. Gochman, "Dangerous Disputes: A Study of Conflict Behavior and War," *American Journal of Political Science* 26: 4 (1982):654–87; and Charles S. Gochman and Russell J. Leng, "Realpolitik and the Road to War: An Analysis of Attributes and Behavior," *International Studies Quarterly* 27: 1 (1983):97–120.

but on the need to respond to perceived threats to its power and influence domestically and/or internationally. A potential attacker, Lebow argues, is likely to feel justified in taking what it regards to be defensive actions to protect its own interests.[6]

The recognition that defensive concerns can contribute to a potential attacker's decision to challenge deterrence is not incompatible with the potential attacker also being motivated by offensive goals. In many cases offensive aims represent the maximum objectives of the potential attacker, whereas defensive aims are likely to define the minimal goals of the attacker. The decision by the Syrian leadership to intervene in the Jordanian civil war was probably motivated by both a desire to defend the guerrilla forces against the Jordanian army and the possible opportunity to overthrow a moderate Arab frontline state and replace it with a much more radical government. The Russian advance along the Afghan border in 1885 was similarly based on the desire to end raids and disputes along the border as well as the desire to secure a frontier that rendered Afghanistan a weak buffer state and would have enabled Russia to pose a credible military threat to India in the event of a future Anglo-Russian confrontation over Turkey.

The critical implication is that a potential attacker's uncertainty about the intentions of the defender and the potential consequences of inaction do not necessarily lead to wishful thinking and rigid policies. In many cases the potential attacker relies on the bargaining behavior of the defender for critical information that can be used to determine the risks and potential gains of using force or seeking a diplomatic settlement to the conflict. A potential attacker often copes with uncertainty not by imposing preexisting beliefs and expectations on the interpretation of new information but by comparing initial beliefs and expectations with the immediate bargaining behavior of the defender to test the validity of those ideas and expectations. In a study of U.S. decision-making in three Middle East crises, Alan Dowty reaches a similar conclusion regarding the receptivity of policymakers to new information:

> Policy-makers proved willing to accept evidence that challenged prevailing perceptions on many issues, such as the nature of opposition goals in Lebanon, the likely costs of U.S. action in 1970, and

6. Jervis, Lebow, and Stein, *Psychology and Deterrence*, 180–232.

the military balance in 1973. . . . There was also sensitivity to negative feedback from policies carried out, as shown by the way policy-makers weighed the costs of negative reactions in decisions on aiding Lebanon, Jordan, or Israel. On the whole, then, there was no cognitive rigidity, but rather considerable adaptability in analyzing situational factors and preferred strategies.[7]

Often the initial calculations of the potential attacker are based on misperceptions and overly optimistic assessments of the defender's response. The critical question is whether the diplomatic and military actions of the defender help to correct those initial misperceptions and miscalculations or whether they fail to clarify or even reinforce those initial errors. The importance of bargaining strategies is related, then, to the defender's ability to address both the defensive and offensive motivations of the potential attacker. On one hand, the defender must clarify its resolve and capability to respond with force if necessary in order to reduce the potential attacker's uncertainty about the likely costs of using force. On the other hand, the defender must reassure the potential attacker that it is not determined to impose a one-sided solution to the conflict or preparing to strike first in anticipation of failed deterrence.

Reciprocity and Crisis Management

The underlying principle of a firm-but-flexible diplomatic strategy and a policy of tit for tat in military escalation is reciprocity. Reciprocity at both the diplomatic and military levels seems to be the most effective strategy for dealing with the opposing offensive and defensive motives of the potential attacker and strikes the necessary balance between credibility and stability.

In military actions, analysts often stress the dangers of how the interactive process of move and countermove by adversaries in a crisis can quickly lead to an escalating spiral of mutual suspicion and insecurity that can undermine the chances of a peaceful solution to a conflict.[8]

---

7. Alan Dowty, *Middle East Crisis: U.S. Decision-Making in 1958, 1970, and 1973* (Berkeley: University of California Press, 1984), 340.

8. Robert Jervis, *Perception and Misperception in International Politics* (Princeton: Princeton University Press, 1976), 62–82.

The positive deterrent impact of a tit-for-tat policy in military escalation illustrates that the dangers of a spiral of reciprocal military escalation in a crisis can often be effectively managed. A spiral of reciprocal escalation is more likely to occur if the defender, not the potential attacker, initiates rapid escalation of military preparedness in the early stages of a crisis. The unilateral escalation of the defender is likely to trigger an equally forceful response by the attacker, with the result that the pace of military events will outstrip the time required for diplomacy. Russia's decision to order general mobilization in support of Serbia in July 1914 triggered German general mobilization against Russia and France and an ultimatum that Russia refused to accept, before firm-but-flexible diplomacy by Great Britain had clarified the British intention to support France. Similarly, Egypt's decision in 1967 to mobilize its armed forces in an attempt to deter a possible Israeli attack on Syria quickly led to Israeli mobilization and a tense crisis that escalated to war when Israel launched what it believed to be a preemptive first strike.

The potential attacker's perception of vulnerability to attack and strategic disadvantage will create pressures to act quickly. The potential attacker may, furthermore, perceive the defender's unilateral escalation as a bald attempt to force concessions under the threat of armed conflict. The response of the potential attacker is likely to be defiant and forceful because the actions of the defender pose not only a military threat but also a challenge to the attacker's bargaining reputation. Not to respond in an equally forceful manner would be politically and militarily dangerous for the potential attacker.

A policy of tit for tat in military escalation reduces the risks of provoking the potential attacker. It demonstrates the defender's resolve and capability to intervene if necessary, contributing to the credibility of deterrence. At the same time, it mitigates the counterproductive impact of the potential attacker's fear that its military forces are vulnerable to attack or that it is at a strategic disadvantage if armed conflict should suddenly break out, thus enhancing deterrence stability. A tit-for-tat policy tends to avoid military actions that contribute to severe stress and pressures to make quick decisions in a crisis. A number of studies on decision-making have presented evidence that high levels of stress and perceptions of limited time to make decisions reduce the quality of decision-making and hence, are more likely to contribute to poor policy choices. A moderate level of stress, however, is believed to improve the quality of decision-making.[9] Dowty, in his study of U.S. decision-making in crises, found that in periods of high stress policy-makers tended to narrow their focus to the consideration of military options, paying less attention to diplomatic alternatives.[10] A tit-for-tat policy may induce that intermediate level of stress that presses decision-makers to reconsider alternatives but also enables them to be confident that there is sufficient time to change or adopt existing policies. An important objective of crisis management is to avoid military preparations that are likely to place intense stress on decision-makers and to reduce the time allowed for adversaries to reconsider their alternatives and the type of response to be adopted. A policy of tit for tat contributes effectively to this objective.

It is also important to recognize that the adverse effects of pressure to act quickly in a crisis can result not only from a sense of vulnerability and insecurity but also from a perception of opportunity and short-term advantage. A defender's failure to match the military escalation of the potential attacker can encourage the potential attacker to believe that a fait accompli can be achieved with the use of force, thereby deterring the defender from actually intervening in defense of its ally. Hitler's military plans for an attack on Czechoslovakia in 1938 and Poland in 1939 were based on such assumptions, and the U.S. decision to cross the thirty-eighth parallel in 1950 was influenced by the belief that PRC intervention could be preempted by the rapid defeat of the North Korean army. Windows of vulnerability as well as windows of opportunity perceived by the potential attacker can threaten the success of deterrence in a crisis.

Decisions concerning the level and timing of military escalation in a crisis invariably involve difficult questions about what trade-offs need to be made between military and political considerations. Military officers, although often cautious in advocating the use of force, are likely to argue that the armed forces should be fully prepared for

9. Alexander L. George, ''The Impact of Crisis-Induced Stress on Decision Making,'' in *The Medical Implications of Nuclear War* (Washington, D.C.: National Academy Press, 1986), 529–52, and Irving L. Janis and Leo Mann, *Decision Making: A Psychological Analysis of Conflict, Choice, and Commitment* (New York: Free Press, 1977), 45–80.

10. Dowty, *Middle East Crisis,* 343.

combat if deterrence fails and that steps should be taken to position and build up forces to full strength. Political leaders are likely to be more concerned with the limited movement of military forces to signal resolve and buttress deterrence as well as with the impact of military actions on the prospects for a diplomatic solution.[11] There is no completely satisfactory solution to this dilemma, but the results of this study suggest that a policy of reciprocal escalation by the defender can effectively enhance the credibility of deterrence without compromising the efforts of policymakers to resolve the conflict through diplomacy and negotiations.

In a confrontation between the two superpowers conventional military escalation may still be an important deterrent despite the impact of nuclear weapons. In this study the deterrent impact of a tit-for-tat policy of conventional escalation was based on both the defender signaling the intention and resolve to use force and the defender effectively denying the potential attacker a decisive advantage in the immediate balance of forces. The threat of nuclear use, even if quite small, is likely to act as a strong deterrent—a superpower would not consider the use of force unless a quick and decisive conventional military operation could be completed so as to minimize the risks of escalation from the conventional to the nuclear level. Robert Jervis is probably correct in arguing that U.S. and Soviet policymakers would in any crisis think beyond the immediate local balance of conventional forces to the dangers of nuclear escalation,[12] but I believe that the only reason policymakers might discount the threat of nuclear escalation would be the calculation that a fait accompli could be achieved locally by conventional military forces. The threat of nuclear escalation would weigh heavily, but the risks might be accepted if the local balance of conventional forces were favorable enough. Conventional military escalation would remain crucial to the success of extended deterrence in regional confrontations with initial imbalances in conventional forces. The mutual vulnerability of the superpowers to a nuclear retaliatory strike is a powerful deterrent, but the conventional balance of forces remains important because the scenario most likely to lead to a challenge of

11. Alexander L. George, "Crisis Management: The Interaction of Political and Military Considerations," *Survival* 26: 5 (1984):223–34.

12. Robert Jervis, *The Illogic of American Nuclear Strategy* (Ithaca: Cornell University Press, 1984), 126–46.

nuclear deterrence is the failure of local conventional deterrence. I believe that NATO's nuclear threat in Western Europe is credible because nuclear forces are closely integrated into the conventional force structures. Soviet political and military leaders are likely to perceive the risk that a conventional war will escalate to the nuclear level as substantial. The dangers associated with NATO's strategy of flexible response include the risk of inadvertent escalation and the potential for Soviet conventional or nuclear preemptive strikes against NATO nuclear forces in a crisis.[13] In a U.S. confrontation with the Soviet Union—where U.S. ground forces and nuclear weapons are not linked—the threat of nuclear escalation may be less important than whether there is an imbalance in local conventional forces.

The importance of conventional military escalation to superpower crisis management relates to the dangers associated with nuclear alerts in a crisis. The trend toward increased nuclear counterforce capabilities and the vulnerability of command and control centers[14] amplify the provocative nature of using nuclear alerts to signal resolve in a crisis between the superpowers. The increasing danger to crisis stability strongly suggests that nuclear threats should be eschewed as instruments of coercive diplomacy in confrontations between the superpowers. Unless one superpower increases the alert status and preparedness of its strategic nuclear forces, the other superpower should refrain from alerting its nuclear forces. The United States has increased the alert status of its strategic forces in such past confrontations with the Soviet Union as the Cuban Missile Crisis and the 1973 Arab-Israeli War. The Soviets did not reciprocate U.S. alert measures, and as a result the two superpowers do not have experience in managing a mutual escalation in nuclear alerts.[15]

13. Paul Bracken, *The Command and Control of Nuclear Forces* (New Haven: Yale University Press, 1983), chap. 5; Daniel Charles, *Nuclear Planning in NATO: Pitfalls of First Use* (Cambridge: Ballinger, 1987); Steven S. Meyer, "Soviet Theatre Nuclear Forces, Part I: Development of Doctrine and Objectives," Adelphi Paper 187 (London: International Institute for Strategic Studies, 1983); and Michael MccGwire, *Military Objectives in Soviet Foreign Policy* (Washington, D.C.: Brookings Institution, 1987), chaps. 3–4.

14. Bruce Blair, *Strategic Command and Control: Redefining the Nuclear Threat* (Washington, D.C.: Brookings Institution, 1985).

15. See Richard Ned Lebow, *Nuclear Crisis Management: A Dangerous Illusion* (Ithaca: Cornell University Press, 1987), chaps. 2–3 for an analysis of the potential problems.

The strong positive contribution of a firm-but-flexible diplomatic strategy to the success of deterrence indicates that a potential attacker's calculus of loss and gain entails more than estimates of the military balance and attention to the positioning of the defender's military forces. As the case studies of deterrence failure in chapter 6 illustrated, a potential attacker's desire to protect the credibility of its bargaining reputation can weigh heavily in decisions involving war or peace. The important implication is that the potential attacker's perception of the costs of not using force can play a critical role in the success or failure of deterrence. The emphasis in deterrence theory has been on the need for the defender to possess sufficient military strength to inflict substantial costs on the attacker in an armed conflict and on ways to make a military response by the defender seem as credible as possible. But it is important to recognize that military considerations often provide a partial, if not insufficient, explanation of deterrence outcomes.[16] For successful crisis management, the defender needs to appreciate the political costs of not pressing ahead with force for the potential attacker—potential damage to bargaining reputation and domestic political support.

A defender may find it difficult to offer some form of compromise or limited concessions, in the belief that its position is fully justified and the demands of the potential attacker unwarranted. The fear of political leaders that domestic political opponents will use a compromise settlement as evidence of weakness creates pressure to adopt hard-line diplomatic and military policies in a confrontation. These pressures may be strong in democracies, where political leaders are held accountable by the public in periodic elections, in particular in the United States, where the Soviet Union has been perceived as the principal adversary throughout the postwar period. Short-term popular support for presidents, for example, has increased following strong action in international crises regardless of whether the actions taken (in a major-

---

16. A number of scholars of deterrence theory have emphasized this point: Bruce Russett, "Pearl Harbor: Deterrence Theory and Decision Theory," *Journal of Peace Research* 4: 2 (1967):89–106; Alexander L. George and Richard Smoke, *Deterrence in American Foreign Policy: Theory and Practice* (New York: Columbia University Press, 1974), 588–615; and Jervis, Lebow, and Stein, *Psychology and Deterrence*, chaps. 3, 5, 9.

ity of cases verbal warnings and threats and/or military actions) were effective in resolving the crisis.[17]

Some analysts argue that domestic political pressures and vulnerabilities shaped President Kennedy's decision to respond with a naval quarantine, without first exploring the possibility of a diplomatic initiative, to the Soviet attempt to place nuclear missiles in Cuba.[18] Some type of compromise solution is essential if the fears of the potential attacker concerning its domestic and international reputation are to be alleviated. In the Cuban Missile Crisis the Soviet withdrawal of missiles was accompanied by a U.S. pledge not to invade Cuba and a private assurance that U.S. missiles in Turkey would be withdrawn soon after the crisis.[19] In a study of U.S.-Soviet crisis behavior Russell Leng found that the Soviets responded defiantly to United States threats 75 percent of the time, whereas they responded defiantly to positive inducements only about 13 percent of the time.[20] Unless the military position of the potential attacker is too weak to oppose the defender, the potential attacker is unlikely to back down in a crisis without some symbolic if not tangible gains. Of the fourteen cases in this study where the defender adopted a bullying strategy, deterrence succeeded in all six cases when the defender was a Great Power and the potential attacker a regional power. Deterrence succeeded in only three of the eight cases when the defender and potential attacker were both either Great Powers or regional powers.[21]

17. John Mueller, *War, Presidents, and Public Opinion* (New York: Wiley, 1973), 196–241, and Samuel Kernell, "Explaining Presidential Popularity," *American Political Science Review* 78: 2 (1978):506–22. Charles Ostrom and Dennis Simon report that presidential popularity in surveys transiently increased 4–5 percent following conflictual behavior toward the Soviet Union. See "Promise and Performance: A Dynamic Model of Presidential Popularity," *American Political Science Review* 79: 2 (1985):334–58.

18. Graham T. Allison, *Essence of Decision: Explaining the Cuban Missile Crisis* (Boston: Little, Brown, 1971), and Fen Osler Hampson, "The Divided Decision-Maker: American Domestic Politics and the Cuban Crisis," *International Security* 9: 3 (1984–85):130–65.

19. Allison, *Essence of Decision*, 218–30.

20. Russell J. Leng, "Reagan and the Russians: Crisis Bargaining Beliefs and the Historical Record," *American Political Science Review* 78: 2 (1984):344–45.

21. Charles S. Gochman and Russell J. Leng, "Realpolitik and the Road to War," found that bullying strategies were generally only effective in confrontations between states that were unequal in military capabilities.

An intransigent bargaining position by the defender can discredit the moderate policymakers of the potential attacker who advocate mutual compromise and enhance the position of hard-liners who reject compromise. The loss of influence of the moderate Genro within the Japanese oligarchy in the negotiations preceding the outbreak of the Russo-Japanese War illustrates this point. Although the defender must demonstrate its determination not to back down under pressure to temper the aggressive objectives of the potential attacker, a firm bargaining position needs to be mixed with a willingness to consider compromise. An unyielding position often does not respond to the more limited yet crucial defensive concerns of the potential attacker. Russian policymakers in July 1914 concluded that Serbia should adopt a conciliatory position in the dispute with Austria-Hungary, but the Russian leadership also agreed that any demands that violated Serbia's sovereignty would have to be opposed. Germany's failure to exercise a moderating influence on its Austrian ally and to adopt a compromising position in diplomatic exchanges with Russia pushed the Russian leadership into a corner from which it perceived no other alternatives than capitulation to the Central Powers or the use of force to defend its international reputation.

Diplomatic and military actions should be closely coordinated so that the signals communicated by the defender are not contradictory or ambiguous but consistent and mutually reinforcing. In most cases of firm-but-flexible bargaining strategy the defender adopted an unyielding position in the early stages of negotiations and subsequently offered or accepted a compromise settlement to break the deadlock.[22] In a few cases (British negotiations with Russia on the Afghan border or British diplomacy in July 1914) the defender proposed reciprocal compromise or fully supported negotiations at the outset of the crisis and subsequently adopted a more resolute position on the terms of the proposed settlement.

In the second pattern of firm-but-flexible strategy it is important for the defender to back up the initially accommodative approach with military actions and verbal warnings that demonstrate credibility. Otherwise the potential attacker may miscalculate that the defender can be

22. Snyder and Diesing, *Conflict among Nations,* 489, find this to be the typical pattern of bargaining in crises that are resolved short of war.

coerced into further concessions and may even back down, encouraging further intransigence and military escalation. A tit-for-tat policy of escalation in such a situation can compensate for the possibility of the potential attacker misinterpreting the defender's intentions based solely on its negotiating behavior. In the Afghan border dispute initial concessions by the British were backed up by military preparations and warnings that signaled to the Russian government that the British were determined not to concede further. Conversely, the failure of Britain's policy of deterrence in July 1914 was due to Grey's failure to couple support for negotiations with preparations early in the crisis for a possible British military intervention and a verbal warning to Germany that if it failed to cooperate Britain might be forced to intervene in support of its entente allies. The defender's subsequent shift to a firm negotiating position following the initial attempts at accommodation will reinforce the potential attacker's perception of the defender's resolve based on its reciprocation of military escalation.

When the defender adopts the first pattern of a firm-but-flexible strategy the danger is that the defender's negotiating behavior risks being interpreted in the early stages of a crisis as too belligerent. The defender's initially firm stand can result in deadlocked negotiations, and the potential attacker may perceive the defender as unlikely to compromise on its position. In such a situation the military actions and preparedness of the defender can risk escalation in two ways. First, unilateral escalation may convince the potential attacker that the defender is bent on forcing a diplomatic defeat on the attacker or that it is not seriously interested in a diplomatic settlement, seeking the advantage in the opening stages of a war. The potential attacker might then react with vigorous military countermeasures. Second, if the defender's truculent diplomatic posture is coupled with a relatively low level of military preparedness the potential attacker might be tempted to strike first while the military advantage persisted. In either case the military posture of the defender increases the risks of armed conflict. A tit-for-tat policy of military escalation at this stage of the crisis would reduce the potential attacker's fears of strategic disadvantage or the temptation to strike first and provide further time to break the stalemate in the negotiations through proposals for compromise and limited concessions.

A tit-for-tat policy of escalation by the defender can play a crucial supportive role to the diplomatic efforts of the defender. A firm-but-flexible bargaining strategy is the most effective strategy for eliciting cooperation from a potential attacker, but the timing and sequence of accommodation and intransigence in a firm-but-flexible strategy can create the potential for miscalculation. A tit-for-tat policy of military escalation in a crisis can buy the time necessary to use a firm-but-flexible strategy to form a coherent bargaining position in negotiations with the adversary.

The empirical evidence from past cases of deterrence supports the argument that a tit-for-tat policy of military escalation contributes to the effectiveness of diplomacy and that guidelines for sound policy require the close coordination of military actions and diplomacy in a crisis. But such coordination is not always possible, and a tit-for-tat policy may not be as effective in the future. The problems of coordinating military actions with diplomacy are particularly acute in a large, complex military establishment like the United States. The worldwide deployment of U.S. naval, air, and ground forces necessitates some measure of delegation of authority and the reliance on preplanned rules for the alerting and engagement of forces. Political leaders thus lack detailed knowledge and understanding of the military operations that they are considering. As Scott Sagan states, ''The alert procedures and rules of engagement of the American Unified and Specified Commands are exceedingly complex, and no Secretary of Defense or Ex Comm can be expected to absorb the details, or even to learn all the essential elements, in highly pressured moments of crisis.''[23]

Despite intensive efforts by President John F. Kennedy and Secretary of Defense Robert McNamara in the Cuban Missile Crisis to closely monitor and control United States military actions blockading Cuba, they remained unaware of vigorous antisubmarine warfare operations that included the dropping of depth charges to force Soviet submarines to surface.[24] Ensuring that political leaders adequately understand and control military actions will be essential to the success of crisis management in another superpower confrontation.

Problems of command and control are compounded by the integration of increasingly accurate extended-range conventional weapon sys-

23. Scott D. Sagan, ''Nuclear Alerts and Crisis Management,'' *International Security* 9: 4 (1985):138.
24. Ibid., 112–18.

tems into the force structure of the United States. The blurry distinction between defensive and offensive military preparations will become even more difficult to discern, and perceptions of limited time to make decisions for an adversary like the Soviet Union will increase in a crisis. Even a tit-for-tat policy of conventional military escalation by the United States in a confrontation with the Soviet Union could be perceived as more provocative than in the past. In general, advances in military technology are rendering a tit-for-tat policy of escalation more and more dangerous and reducing the time available for diplomacy to de-escalate a future superpower confrontation. But political leaders are not likely to forgo the movement and/or alerting of military forces in a crisis to signal resolve. United States policymakers should not be overly confident of the deterrent value of a tit-for-tat policy of escalation in a confrontation with the Soviet Union based on its effectiveness in past deterrence crises.

Military actions can support but not replace diplomacy. Sole reliance on threats and military shows of force is insufficient to resolve the underlying political conflict in a crisis. Leng found that U.S. threats used alone elicited a defiant Soviet response in three U.S.-Soviet crises. A mixed strategy of threats coupled with positive inducements consistently elicited Soviet compliance.[25] Sole reliance on either military or diplomatic approaches to crisis management and deterrence stability is likely to be inadequate. The combination of the two approaches can promote conflict resolution by simultaneously increasing the costs to the attacker of using force and reducing the costs of maintaining peace. Given the increasing risks of a tit-for-tat policy in a future superpower confrontation, vigorous diplomatic initiatives at the outset of a crisis, including a willingness to compromise are essential to prevent the pace of military events from dictating overall policy.

Implications for Future Research

The fundamental objective in the study of deterrence is to explain the political and military conditions that typically lead policymakers to threaten the use of force and initiate confrontations with other states. I will now assess the relevance of the conditions that contribute to

---

25. Leng, "Reagan and the Russians," 344–45, 352.

successful extended-immediate deterrence to understanding why a potential attacker threatened to use force against the protégé, linking this to the broader issues of extended-general deterrence and crisis prevention.

The discussion to follow is speculative and not a set of conclusions based on systematic analysis of cases of extended-general deterrence. A preliminary analysis of the balance of forces at the outset of each case of immediate deterrence indicated that the potential attacker was invariably in a strong military position relative to the protégé. In many cases the intervention of the defender and the buildup of military forces erased this initial advantage, but the consistent advantage of the potential attacker at the outset supports the conclusion that policymakers are unlikely to initiate a confrontation with another state unless the prospects of military success if the adversary refuses to concede are favorable. In a strictly bilateral conflict between the potential attacker and protégé the former was generally in a position of escalation dominance, and in a majority of cases there were no military forces of the defender on the protégé's territory when the potential attacker initiated the confrontation. Thus as the trip-wire role for defender forces in immediate deterrence cases suggests, a favorable immediate or local balance of forces seems to be important in the decision of policymakers to challenge extended-general deterrence and threaten the use of force. In many cases the critical question for the potential attacker in initiating the confrontation with the protégé was what impact the threatened intervention of the defender would have on the local balance of forces. As George and Smoke argue, an important factor contributing to the failure of extended-general deterrence is the belief by the potential attacker that the risks of escalation can be controlled and further escalation avoided if changes in the military situation require a reassessment of potential risks.[26]

If the local balance of forces is important in determining whether general deterrence is challenged then alliance ties between defender and protégé should not have much general deterrent impact. In the analysis of immediate deterrence cases alliance ties did not significantly affect outcomes because the potential attacker seemed to assess the credibility of defender's threat of retaliation based on the defender's

26. George and Smoke, *Deterrence in American Foreign Policy*, 529.

capability to prevent a rapid defeat of the protégé. When the defender possessed such a capability and demonstrated the resolve to use that capability through diplomatic actions and military preparations, then deterrence success was more likely. When the defender lacked such a capability the threat of intervention lacked credibility, and an alliance commitment could not overcome this weakness in the defender's deterrent posture. The German high command in 1914 hoped to exploit this perceived weakness in the Russian and British alliance commitment to France to achieve a decisive victory at the outset of war with the entente powers. Hitler discounted the British and French commitment to Poland in 1939 in part because the Western powers were not prepared to intervene before Poland was defeated. If this characterization of the potential attacker's calculus in situations of immediate deterrence is correct, then alliance ties might also have little deterrent value when the potential attacker is considering initiating a confrontation with the protégé. The political commitment represented by an alliance may be discounted by an adversary unless the defender also has a credible military option for protecting its protégé. Alliance ties are not likely to enhance the credibility of extended-general deterrence unless peace-time military cooperation between the allies includes the deployment of forces from the stronger power on the territory of the weaker power. The deterrent value of an alliance commitment cannot be separated from the analysis of the immediate balance of forces and the importance of a trip-wire force in position for the defender.

In immediate deterrence cases a firm-but-flexible diplomatic strategy contributed to successful deterrence. The importance of reciprocal compromise and of providing some way for the potential attacker to back down in crisis diplomacy suggests that intransigence by the protégé or defender in previous negotiations contributed to the potential attacker's initial decision to threaten force. The threat to use force may have represented an attempt to break the stalemate in negotiations by applying coercive pressure that would lead the protégé and defender to compromise. A preliminary analysis of the cases indicates that an uncompromising diplomatic posture by the protégé and defender prompted the decision by the potential attacker to threaten the use of force in approximately twelve cases. Examples include France's dispatch of a small force to Fashoda in 1898 in an attempt to compel Britain to negotiate on territorial rights in Africa and Serbia's mobilization of forces in 1908 following the refusal of Austria-Hungary to compensate Serbia for the annexation of Bosnia-Herzegovina. In most cases, however, the potential attacker was not provoked to threaten to use force by the intransigence of the other party in negotiations but because the protégé would not capitulate to the potential attacker's demands. The failure of the protégé and defender to be flexible in negotiations and to consider seriously compromise was generally not a major factor in the potential attacker's initial decision to threaten the use of force. More often than not, the potential attacker, in a strong military position relative to the protégé, was not seriously interested in compromise agreements in bilateral negotiations with the protégé. The intervention of the defender in support of the protégé in many cases of successful immediate deterrence forced the potential attacker to reconsider its bullying strategy and to settle for far more limited gains or a stalemate.

If the defender had been forced to back down in a previous confrontation with the potential attacker, the defender's subsequent attempt at immediate deterrence was less likely to succeed. The defender's record of weakness might also have contributed to the initial decision by the potential attacker to threaten the use of force and risk a wider confrontation. An analysis of the origins of the immediate deterrence cases indicates that such calculations probably played an important role in about eight cases. The weak response of the British government to the Russian occupation of Merv in spring 1884 may have contributed to the belief within the Russian leadership that the Liberal government of Gladstone would not react strongly to further advances along the Afghan border. British and French paralysis during the Rhineland crisis of 1936 and the Austrian annexation of 1938 reinforced Hitler's belief that Czechoslovakia could be crushed without provoking Western opposition. The lack of a more forceful Egyptian response to Israeli air strikes against Jordan and Syria in 1966 and 1967 may have contributed to Israeli perceptions that a strict policy of reprisal strikes against Syria for guerrilla attacks would not provoke a larger conflict with Egypt.[27] The defender's past behavior was not a consistently critical factor in decisions by the potential attacker to

27. Daniel Dishon, ed., *Middle East Record, 1967,* vol. 3 (Jerusalem: Israel Universities Press, 1971), 165, 179.

challenge extended-general deterrence and to threaten the use of force.

Although the strength of economic and military ties between defender and protégé did not contribute to the success of immediate deterrence in the probit analysis, the defender had both strong economic and military ties to the protégé in only a few cases. This suggests that high levels of economic and military cooperation in combination between defender and protégé may contribute to the credibility of extended-general deterrence. Small states with multiple and strong ties to larger powers may be less likely to be the targets of threats and coercive pressure by other states.

In his study of the origins of international crises Lebow argues that domestic political pressures often push policymakers to adopt more aggressive foreign policies.[28] Preliminary analysis indicated that domestic political pressures were important in between twelve and fifteen cases. A firm conclusion would require a much more extensive reading of secondary and primary sources. This line of analysis, which could be broadened to include domestic economic conditions, is a promising avenue for further research because it provides potentially useful indicators of the potential attacker's evaluation of the status quo—an aspect that is not fully incorporated in the model specified for empirical testing in this study. A closer look at political conditions for the protégé indicated deep splits and divisions within the political leadership of weak central governments in more than fifteen cases. Japan's determination to dominate Korea at the turn of the century was based partly on the perception that Korea's government was too weak to withstand pressure from outside powers, in particular Russia, which would eventually jeopardize Japan's vital economic and security interests in the country. In other cases the instability of the protégé's political system may lead the potential attacker to calculate that the protégé is weak militarily and that an armed attack will lead to the collapse of the government and a quick military victory. The deep divisions and instability of the South Vietnamese government in 1965 probably encouraged the North Vietnamese to increase their military pressure based on the calculation that the country was on the verge of both political and military collapse. Iraq's decision to attack Iran in 1980

28. Richard Ned Lebow, *Between Peace and War: The Nature of International Crisis* (Baltimore: Johns Hopkins University Press, 1981), 66–80.

was based on the expectation that a quick and decisive military victory would be possible because of political upheaval in Iran.[29]

Both similarities and differences in the political and military conditions determine the outcome of extended-general and extended-immediate deterrence. An important task for future research is the systematic examination of the origins of extended deterrence confrontations so that a careful comparison of the conditions that influence crisis initiation and crisis outcome could be undertaken.

Are the theoretical approach and empirical results in this study on extended deterrence relevant to the analysis of direct deterrence—bilateral confrontations between a potential attacker and defender? An important conceptual difference between the two types of deterrence cases is the degree of uncertainty associated with the resolve of the defender to carry through its threat of retaliation if attacked. Uncertainty about the defender's intention to protect its protégé is a fundamental characteristic of most extended deterrence cases and serves as the analytical foundation from which to formulate and test hypotheses. But in situations of direct deterrence the potential attacker is not likely to question the defender's resolve to retaliate with military force for an attack on its own territory. The potential attacker's military calculations are simplified and reduced to a question of relative capabilities.

In situations of extended deterrence the bargaining behavior and military actions of the defender are important to analyze for the signals they communicate about the resolve to use force. But in situations of direct deterrence the defender's military actions are critical to analyze largely for assessing the balance of military forces at the outset of an armed confrontation between potential attacker and defender. The importance of the security dilemma and the problems of balancing deterrence stability and credibility remain. The risk of provocation in direct deterrence might be even more acute because many direct deterrence cases involve confrontations between contiguous states. The lack of military actions by the defender would not, however, signal a lack of resolve to use force but rather the lack of capability to respond quickly to an attack.

29. Thies, *When Governments Collide,* 253–83, and William O. Staudenmaier, "Iran-Iraq, 1980– ," in *The Lessons of Recent Wars in the Third World,* vol. 1: *Approaches and Cases,* ed. Robert E. Harkavy and Stephanie G. Neuman (Lexington: D. C. Heath, 1985), 211–12.

In extended deterrence the impact of the defender's military actions on the immediate or local balance of military forces was an important explanatory variable because of the theoretical emphasis on the potential attacker's desire to achieve quick and decisive results with the use of force. Whether such a theoretical focus is appropriate to cases of direct deterrence is questionable. I doubt that a potential attacker in a situation of direct deterrence would pursue a limited arms strategy based on the expectation that a fait accompli in the seizure of territory would deter the defender from counterattacking. Immediate military setbacks short of massive defeat would be unlikely to discourage the defender from committing additional armed forces to its territorial defense. A potential attacker's military calculations should thus be more heavily influenced in cases of direct deterrence by the costs and probability of victory in a war against the fully mobilized armed strength of the defender. The immediate balance of forces then is far less powerful in explaining the outcome of direct deterrence than was true of cases of extended deterrence. But I argue as with cases of extended deterrence that the long-term balance of forces would carry little explanatory weight in the analysis of direct deterrence. The potential attacker's decision to use force is based on expectations of victory, not in a protracted war, but in a relatively short, large-scale armed conflict with the defender.

As with the military actions of the defender, the role of diplomacy in signaling the resolve and clarifying intentions is secondary in cases of direct deterrence. The extent to which the diplomatic actions of the defender indicated a willingness to compromise remains essential. As with cases of extended deterrence, the political costs for the potential attacker of continued peace and acceptance of the status quo are important to analyze. In situations of direct deterrence the defender would probably find it more difficult to propose or accept compromise because concessions would be more likely to affect its own security and national interests. Although a firm-but-flexible diplomatic strategy by the defender in situations of extended deterrence often entailed some sacrifice of interests, these were largely at the expense of the protégé. I hypothesize then that diplomacy, in particular a firm-but-flexible strategy, increases the likelihood of direct deterrence success but that the defender is far less likely to adopt such a policy.

I expect past behavior of the defender to play a role similar to that hypothesized in cases of extended deterrence. The past behavior of the defender in confrontations with states other than the potential attacker would not, for example, have a significant impact on direct deterrence outcomes, whereas the behavior and outcome of past confrontations between defender and potential attacker would be far more important. An important caveat is that the past behavior of the defender would be relevant only if the previous confrontation centered on issues that directly affected the security and interests of the defender. I would not expect the behavior of the defender in support of another country to be a guide to the defender's behavior in support of its own interests and security.

The theoretical and empirical analysis of extended-immediate deterrence presented in this study can provide a useful basis for the further study of deterrence in various situations and stages of conflict escalation. Potentially important and interesting differences between extended and direct deterrence or general and immediate deterrence do exist. Further theoretical and empirical work on deterrence is essential to achieve a more comprehensive and satisfactory understanding of the causes of international conflict and war.

Index

Abéché, 100, 102
Acheson, Dean, 9, 140
Afghan border dispute, 66, 202, 210–11, 216; and Russian military threat, 150–52, 157; and British deterrent actions, 151–52; and Anglo-Russian negotiations on border, 152–54, 156–60; and bargaining reputation of Russia, 158; and firm-but-flexible strategy, 158–60
Afghanistan, 24. *See also* Afghan border dispute
Albania, 24, 184
Alliance. *See* Value of protégé to defender
Allison, John, 139
Allon, Yigal, 90, 92
Amman, 88, 92–93
Anglo-German Naval Agreement of *1935*, 131
Aouzou Strip, 97, 99
Arab-Israeli wars: *1967* War, 10, 31*n*, 86–87, 204, 216; *1970* War of Attrition, 45, 95; *1973* War, 12, 19, 36, 50, 199, 207
Arafat, Yassir, 89, 93
Argentina. *See* Falklands Islands War
Arms Transfers. *See* Value of protégé to defender
Asad, Hafiz al-, 95–96
Atasi, Nureddin al-, 89, 95–97
Attrition strategy, 35–36, 118, 137, 181; definition of, 37; and balance of forces, 38–39, 57, 60–61. *See also* Deterrence by punishment

Austin, Warren, 140–41, 146
Austria, 115–16, 216
Austria-Hungary, 24, 216. *See also* World War I
Axelrod, Robert, 51, 53, 159*n*

Baath Party, 95, 96*n*
Back, Peter, 188
Bandung Conference, 112, 114
Bargaining behavior. *See* Conciliatory, Firm-but-flexible, and Bullying strategies
Bargaining reputation, 1–2, 8, 10, 35, 204, 208; definition of, 6; and deterrence outcome, 11, 31, 33; and economic sanctions, 53*n;* and firm-but-flexible strategy, 48, 53, 78; and past behavior, 54–55, 80–81. *See also* Afghan border dispute, Russo-Japanese War, and World War I
Belgium, 24, 194
Belize, 25
Berchtold, Leopold von, 187
Berlin crisis of *1961,* 9, 25; of *1948,* 24, 42
Betts, Richard, 2, 12, 40, 50
Blitzkrieg attack, 40, 79–80
Bosnia-Herzegovina, 184, 216
Boxer Rebellion, 173
British Expeditionary Force, 4, 4*n,* 198*n*
Bueno de Mesquita, Bruce, 43–44
Bulgaria, 24
Bullying strategy, 209–10, 216; definition of, 51–52; and past behavior, 55;

Bullying strategy (*continued*)
  measurement of, 65–67, 69, 71; and
  probit results, 78, 81. *See also* Russo-
  Japanese War and World War I
Burckhardt, M., 133

Cairo Agreement, 93
Cameroon, 98
Case Green, 117–18, 121, 124–25
Case-study method, 13–14, 85–86
Central African Republic, 98, 102
Chad, 25. *See also* Chadian civil war
Chadian civil war, 86; and French deter-
  rent actions, 99–103; and balance of
  forces, 100, 103; and Libyan military
  intervention, 100, 103–04; and tit-
  for-tat policy, 103
Chamberlain, Neville, 30; and Czecho-
  slovakian crisis, 116–17, 119, 124–
  27; and Polish crisis, 129–30, 132–
  33, 135
Changkufeng dispute, 58–59
Cheysson, Claude, 99
China, 24, 172–80 passim. *See also*
  People's Republic of China
Ciano, Count Galeazzo, 133
Colombia, 24
Conciliatory strategy, definition of, 52;
  measurement of, 65–67, 71; probit
  results, 78, 81
Cooper, Duff, 124–25
Correlates of War Project, 61
Costa Rica, 24
Costs of Inaction. *See* Bargaining repu-
  tation
Crete, 24
Crisis management, 199–200, 205–06,
  208, 212
Crowe, Sir Eyre, 8, 191
Cuban Missile Crisis, 207, 209, 212
Cyprus crisis, 25, 71
Czechoslovakia, 24. *See also* Czecho-
  slovakian crisis
Czechoslovakian crisis, 5, 30, 36, 58–
  59, 66, 68, 205; and British deterrent
  actions, 116–17, 120–21, 124–27;
  and Hitler's plan of attack, 117–18,
  121, 124–25; and Hitler's view of
  British, 118, 121, 125; and French-
  British consultations, 118–19, 126;

and policy of caution, 125, 128; and
  balance of forces, 125–26, 128; and
  lack of tit-for-tat policy, 128

Danzig, 129–33
Dayan, Moshe, 10, 89
Detente in Anglo-German relations,
  196–97
Deterrence. *See* Direct-general and Di-
  rect-immediate deterrence and Ex-
  tended-immediate and Extended-
  general deterrence
Deterrence by denial, 15, 74, 113, 137
Deterrence by punishment, 15, 74, 137
Diesing, Paul. *See* Snyder, Glenn
Direct foreign investment, 46*n*
Direct-general deterrence, 17–18
Direct-immediate deterrence, 18, 218–
  20
Domestic incentives to use force, 147–
  48, 183, 217–18
Dowty, Alan, 202–03, 205
Dulles, John Foster, 54, 106–07, 109,
  111–12

Economic ties. *See* Value of protégé to
  defender and potential attacker
Egypt, 24–25, 95–96. *See also* Arab-Israeli wars
Eisenhower, Dwight D., 108–09, 111–
  12, 114
En-lai, Chou, 114, 142–43
Ethiopia, 24
Extended-general deterrence, 16–17,
  21–22, 214–18. *See also* Extended-
  immediate deterrence
Extended-immediate deterrence: credibility of, 1–6, 33–34, 48–52, 54–
  56, 200, 203–04; stability of, 11,
  33–34, 48–52, 200, 203–04; definition of, 15–17, 21; reasons for study-
  ing, 18–20; criteria for selecting
  cases, 23–25; definition of success
  and failure, 26–27. *See also* Extended-general and Direct-immediate
  deterrence

Fait accompli, 86, 103, 118, 130, 132,
  190, 205–06, 219
Falklands Islands War, 5, 12, 22, 50

Fashoda crisis, 10–11, 57, 59, 65–66, 70–71, 215
Faya-Largeau, 99–100
Fedayeen, 87–89, 93, 95
Ferdinand, Archduke Franz, 185
Finland, 24. *See also* Petsamo dispute and Soviet-Finnish War
Firm-but-flexible strategy, 149; definition of, 51; hypotheses on, 52–53, 55; measurement of, 65–67, 69–71; and probit results, 73, 75–78, 81; and crisis management, 201, 203–04, 208–13 passim; and extended-general deterrence, 215; and direct deterrence, 219. *See also* Afghan border dispute, Petsamo dispute, and World War I
Forces Armées Nationales Tchadiennes (FANT), 99–100, 103
Formosa Resolution, 108
France, 24–25, 36–37, 172, 183, 186–87, 193–94, 204. *See also* Chadian civil war and Czechoslovakian and Fashoda crises

Galtieri, Gen. Leopoldo, 5
Genro, 210. *See also* Russo-Japanese War
George, Alexander, 43, 214
German-Polish Nonaggression Pact, 129, 131
German-Soviet Nonaggression Pact, 162, 167
Germany, 24, 172. *See also* Czechoslovakian and Polish crises, Petsamo dispute, and World War I
Giers, N. K. (foreign minister), 152–54, 158
Gladstone, W. E., 150–51, 159, 216
Goa, 24
Golan Heights, 86, 90, 93
Göring, Hermann, 132
Goukouni, Weddeye, 98–99, 104
Granville, Lord, 152–54, 156
Great Britain, 24–25, 109, 172, 183. *See also* Afghan border dispute, Czechoslovakian crisis, Falklands Islands War, Fashoda and Polish crises, and World War I
Greece, 24–25. *See also* Cyprus crisis

Grey, Sir Edward, 8, 43. *See also* World War I
Guatemala, 25
Guerrilla forces. *See* Fedayeen

Habash, Georges, 89
Habré, Hissene, 98–101, 104
Halder, Franz, 121, 124
Halifax, Viscount, 119, 132
Henderson, Sir Nevile (British ambassador), 119–21, 124, 131–36 passim
Henlein, Konrad, 116, 124
Hitler, Adolph, 2, 5, 30, 36, 41, 205, 215–16. *See also* Czechoslovakian and Polish crises and Petsamo dispute
Hollweg, Bethmann. *See* World War I
Howard, Michael, 6, 15, 41–42
Hussein, King, 20–21, 87–89, 92–93

Immediate balance of forces, 4, 206; hypothesis on, 39–41; measurement of, 57–59; and probit results, 73–77, and NATO, 79–80; and extended-general deterrence, 214; and direct deterrence, 219. *See also* Chadian civil war, Czechoslovakian crisis, Deterrence by denial, Jordanian civil war, Korean War, Polish crisis, Quemoy-Matsu crisis, and Russo-Japanese War
Inchon landing, 142–43
India, 24–25, 150–51, 158–59
Indonesia, 24–25, 77
Intelligence information, 2–3
International crisis, 16, 19, 21, 54, 200
Iran, 24, 29–30
Iran-Iraq war, 41, 45, 199, 217–18
Iraq, $93n$
Irbid, 89, 91–92
Israel, 25. *See also* Arab-Israeli wars and Jordanian civil war
Issues at stake. *See* Bargaining reputation, Domestic incentives to use force, and Value of protégé
Italy, 24
Itō, Hirobumi, 178, 181–82

Jagow, Gottlieb von, 186, 189
Japan, 4, 24, 37, 61. *See also* Russo-Japanese War

Jervis, Robert, 11*n*, 53*n*, 55
Jordan, 25. *See also* Jordanian civil war
Jordanian civil war, 20–22, 27, 33, 202; and Syrian military intervention, 89–91, 93–97; and Israeli deterrent actions, 89–94; and U.S. position, 92, 96*n;* and tit-for-tat policy, 94, 96–97; and balance of military forces, 94, 97; and Soviet position, 95–96
Jung-chen, Gen. Neih, 143

Kai-shek, Chiang, 22, 104
Keitel, Wilhelm, 117
Kennedy, John F., 9, 199
Khartoum, 151
Kiaochow Bay, 172
Kiderlen, Alfred von, 6, 10
Kimberley, Lord, 152, 154
Kissinger, Henry, 49, 92
Komura, Jutarō, 175, 178
Korea, 24, 217. *See also* Russo-Japanese War
Korean War, 9, 18–19, 22–23, 40, 58–59, 85–86, 205; and Soviet position, 138, 141–48 passim; and U.S. decision to cross thirty-eighth parallel, 139–41, 144–48; and PRC deterrent actions, 140–43, 146–47; and balance of forces, 144–48; and domestic pressures on Truman, 147–48
Krivoshein, Alexander, 188
Kurino, Shinichirō, 180
Kuwait, 24

Lagos Accord, 98
Laos, 24
Lebow, Richard Ned, 1, 32–33, 200–02, 217
Leng, Russell, 51, 209, 213
Liaotung Peninsula, 172
Libya, 25, 45. *See also* Chadian civil war
Lieven, D. C. B., 192
Limited aims strategy, 90, 94, 113, 219; definition of, 35–36; and balance of forces, 38–39, 57, 59
Lithuania, 164
Local balance of forces. *See* Immediate balance of forces

London Conference, 197–98
Long-term balance of forces 4; hypothesis on, 39–41; measurement of, 57, 60–62; and probit results, 73*n*, 74; and direct deterrence, 219. *See also* Deterrence by punishment

MacArthur, Gen. Douglas, 139–40, 144–46
Malaysia, 25
Manchukuo, 24
Manchuria, 33, 58, 139–41, 143–44, 173–78, 180, 183
McNamara, Robert, 212
Mearsheimer, John, 36, 38–40
Merv, 150, 216
Military balance. *See* Immediate, long-term, and short-term balance of forces
Military escalation. *See* Policies of caution and strength and Tit-for-Tat policy
Military organizations, 39–40
Mitterand, Francois, 99–102, 104. *See also* Chadian civil war
Molotov, Vyacheslav, 161–69 passim
Moltke, Helmuth Von, 194
Moroccan Crisis of *1905-06,* 43, 196; of *1911,* 8, 10, 196
Morocco, 24–25
Motivated misperception, 3, 198*n*, 201
Munich agreement, 127
Mussolini, Benito, 115, 121

Nasser, Gamel, 95
Ndjamena, 98–99, 102
Netherlands, 24, 77
Nicholas II, 187–88, 192
Nicolson, Sir Arthur, 8, 191
Nigeria, 98–99
North Atlantic Treaty Organization (NATO), 10, 40, 42*n*, 79–80, 207
North Korea, 24. *See also* Korean War
North Vietnam, 24–25. *See also* Vietnam War
Norway, 161–62, 164–66, 170–71
Nuclear weapons: hypothesis on deterrent value, 41–42; measurement of, 62; and probit results, 81–82; and crisis management, 206–07. *See also* North Atlantic Treaty Organization

Operation Manta, 102
Operation Reindeer, 164
Operation Shark, 36
Operation White, 130, 132, 134–36
Organization of African Unity (OAU),
    98–99
Outer Mongolia, 24

Paasikivi, Juho Kusti, 164–66, 168
Pakistan, 25
Palestine Liberation Army, 89
Palestinian Liberation Organization
    (PLO), 20–21, 33, 93
Panama, 24
Panikkar, K. M., 143, 146
Panjdeh, 66, 151–54, 156–60. *See also*
    Afghan border dispute
Past behavior, 13, 34–35, 56; hypoth-
    eses on, 54–55; measurement of, 68–
    71; and probit results, 73, 75, 80–81;
    and extended-general deterrence, 216;
    and direct deterrence, 219–20. *See
    also* Polish crisis, Russo-Japanese
    War, and World War I
People's Liberation Army (PLA). *See*
    Korean War and Quemoy-Matsu cri-
    sis
People's Republic of China (PRC), 25,
    42. *See* Korean War and Quemoy-
    Matsu crisis
Petsamo dispute, 70–71; and Soviet
    threats against Finland, 162, 164,
    166–69; and German-Soviet negotia-
    tions, 162, 165, 167–69; and German
    deterrent actions, 164–67, 170–71;
    and firm-but-flexible strategy, 170–71
Philippines, 109
Poland, 24
Policy of caution, hypothesis on, 49–
    50; measurement of, 67–68; and pro-
    bit results, 79. *See also* Czechoslo-
    vakian crisis
Policy of strength, 204; hypothesis on,
    49–50; measurement of, 67–68; and
    probit results, 79
Polish corridor, 129–31
Polish crisis, 4–5, 18, 40, 85–86; and
    Hitler's plan of attack, 130, 132,
    134–36; and British deterrent actions,
    130–35; and Hitler's view of British

threat, 133–37; and balance of forces,
    134–35, 137–38; and past behavior,
    133, 137; and tit-for-tat policy, 138
Port Arthur, 29, 172–73, 176–77, 181–
    83
Port Hamilton, 152
Portugal, 24
Pourtalès, Friedrich von, 189–92
Preemptive strike, 9–10, 12, 31*n*, 33,
    48, 50, 80, 204

Qaddafi, Col. Moamer, 97–98, 100,
    103–04
Quemoy-Matsu crisis, 24, 42, 86; and
    PRC military buildup, 106–13; and
    U.S. deterrent actions, 108–09; and
    threat of nuclear weapons, 111, 113–
    14; and balance of forces, 112–13;
    and tit-for-tat policy, 113

Rabin, Yitzhak, 92
Radford, Arthur, 112
Ramtha, 88–95 passim
Rapid offensive attack, 125, 130, 147;
    definition of, 35–38, 41; and balance
    of forces, 57–60; and extended-gen-
    eral deterrence, 215. *See also*
    Blitzkrieg attack, Case Green, and
    Operation White
Reciprocity: and hypotheses on bargain-
    ing, 48, 50–53; and probit results,
    75–76; and crisis management, 203–
    04, 206; and extended-general deter-
    rence, 215
Red Line, 102–03
Rhee, Syngman, 138
Rhineland crisis, 216
Ribbentrop, Joachim von, 119, 120,
    124, 129, 136–37
Romania, 24, 164
Rusk, Dean, 139
Russell, Sen. Richard, 45
Russett, Bruce, 44
Russia, 24. *See also* Afghan border dis-
    pute, Russo-Japanese War, and
    World War I
Russo-Japanese War, 18, 29, 33, 40,
    210; and position of Genro on nego-
    tiations, 174–79 passim, 182; and
    position of Russia on negotiations,

Russo-Japanese War (*continued*)
175–80; and military balance, 181; and bullying strategy, 181–82; and bargaining reputation of Japan, 182; and past behavior, 182–83; and domestic pressures within Russia, 183

Sagan, Scott, 212
Salisbury, Lord, 157–59
Sazonov, Sergei, 187–92, 195
Schelling, Thomas, 3–4, 53–54
Schlesinger, Arthur, 9
Schlieffen Plan, 37, 194
Schulenburg, Friedrich W. Von, 165, 169
Sensitivity to threats, 1–2, 6–11. *See also* Bargaining reputation, Bullying strategy, and Policy of strength
Serbia, 24, 215–16, *See also* World War I
Short-term balance of forces: hypothesis on, 39, 41; measurement of, 57, 60; and probit results, 73–77; and direct deterrence, 219. *See also* Czechoslovakian crisis and Jordanian civil war
Simon, Sir John, 120
Sino-Indian war, 18
Sino-Japanese war, 172
Sino-Soviet border, 17–18
Smoke, Richard. *See* George, Alexander
Snyder, Glenn, 6, 30, 32, 33*n*
South Korea, 17, 109. *See also* Korean War
South Vietnam, 25. *See also* Vietnam War
Soviet-Finnish war, 17–18, 161–62
Soviet Union, 2, 7–8, 17, 19, 24–25, 29–30, 42, 45. *See also* Cuban Missile Crisis, Jordanian civil war, Korean War, North Atlantic Treaty Organization, and Petsamo dispute
Spain, 25
Staal, M. De, 151–58
Stalin, Joseph, 3, 61, 164, 170
Stein, Arthur, 40
Stein, Janice Gross, 10
Strategic importance. *See* Value of protégé to potential attacker
Strategic triad, 7

Sudan, 24, 151, 153
Sudetenland, 116, 120, 127–28
Surprise attack, 7, 12, 35*n*, 50, 181
Syria, 24–25. *See also* Arab-Israeli wars and Jordanian civil war
Szápáry, Friedrich von, 187–88, 192

Tachen Islands, 107
Taiwan, 22–24, 23*n*, 141, 144. *See also* Quemoy-Matsu crisis
Taylor, Telford, 125
Tisza, Stephan, 185
Tit-for-tat policy: hypothesis on, 49–51; measurement of, 67–68; and probit results, 73, 75–77, 79–80; and crisis management, 203–07 passim, 211–13. *See also* Chadian civil war, Czechoslovakian crisis, Jordanian civil war, Polish crisis, and Quemoy-Matsu crisis
Transitional National Union Government (GUNT), 99–100, 103
Treaty of Moscow, 161, 165
Tripoli, 24
Trip-wire, 79, 103, 128, 144, 147, 214–15
Truman, Harry S., 105–06, 138–41, 144, 148
Tunisia, 24
Turkey, 184, 202, 209. *See also* Cyprus crisis

United Nations, 139–46 passim
United States, 2, 7–8, 17, 19, 24–25, 30, 37, 39–40. *See also* Cuban Missile Crisis, Jordanian civil war, Korean War, North Atlantic Treaty Organization, Quemoy-Matsu crisis, and Vietnam War

Value of protégé to defender, 56, 171; hypotheses on, 43–46; measurement of, 62–64; and probit results, 73*n*, 82–84, 160–61; and relevance to extended-general deterrence, 214–15, 217
Value of protégé to potential attacker, 34; hypotheses on, 46–47; measurement of, 64–65; and probit results, 73*n*, 83–84

Venezuela, 24
Vietnam, 25, 42
Vietnam War, 3, 19, 40, 42, 45, 76, 200, 217

Weizsäcker, Ernst von, 120, 134
West Bank, 86–87, 93
Western Sahara, 25
West Irian, 24, 77
Wilhelm II, Kaiser, 185, 198*n*
Williams, Phil, 200
Window of opportunity, 205
Window of vulnerability, 8, 205
World War I: and balance of forces, 4, 59; and rapid offensive attack, 37, 41, 215; and policy of strength, 68, 204; and past behavior, 184, 187, 189, 194–96; and decisions of Bethmann Hollweg, 185–87, 193–94, 196–97; and bargaining reputation of Russia, 188–89, 194–95; and actions of Sir Edward Grey, 190–93, 197–98; and bullying strategy, 191, 194–96, 210; and firm-but-flexible strategy, 197, 211
World War II. *See* Polish crisis
Worst-case analysis, 6–9

Yamagata, Aritoma, 179

Zimmerman, Alfred, 186
Zulfiqar Pass. *See* Afghan border dispute